Nature Smart

Nature Smart

AWESOME PROJECTS TO MAKE WITH MOTHER NATURE'S HELP

**Discover the world around you
with these hands-on crafts**

wind vanes · beach baskets · bird feeders · scented soap
· barometers · paper bag books · light bulb puppets
· snow candles · herb dolls · eggshell mosaics
and much more . . .

GWEN DIEHN, TERRY KRAUTWURST & BOBBIE NEEDHAM

A Main Street Book
New York

10 9 8 7 6 5 4 3 2 1

Published by Main Street, a division of Sterling Publishing Co., Inc.
387 Park Avenue South, New York, NY 10016
This book is comprised of the following titles published by Lark Books,
a division of Sterling Publishing Co., Inc.:
Nature Crafts for Kids © 1992 by Gwen Diehn and Terry Krautwurst
Kid Style Nature Crafts © 1995 by Gwen Diehn and Terry Krautwurst
Ecology Crafts for Kids © 1998 by Lark Books
© 2003 by Sterling Publishing Co., Inc.
Distributed in Canada by Sterling Publishing
C/o Canadian Manda Group, One Atlantic Avenue, Suite 105
Toronto, Ontario, Canada M6K 3E7
Distributed in Great Britain and Europe by Chris Lloyd at Orca Book
Services, Stanley House, Fleets Lane, Poole BH15 3AJ, England
Distributed in Australia by Capricorn Link (Australia) Pty. Ltd.
P.O. Box 704, Windsor, NSW 2756, Australia

ISBN: 1-4027-0515-8

Table of Contents

Introduction 12

Seasonal Nature Projects 14

Sweet Smelling Grass Mat 16
Earth's Never-Ending
Water-Go-Round 19
Rustic Wren House 20
Bird Drinking Fountain 22
Recycled Kite 24
The Wings of a Bird;
Kissing and Spishing for Birds 26-27
Pressed Flower Lamp Shade 28
Butterfly & Moth Hatchery 29
Mix a Mess of Midnight
Moth Goop; What Makes
a Moth . . . a Moth? 31-32
Accordion-Fold Nature Journal 33
Seashell Wind Chime 35
What Are Seashells and Where
Do They Come From? 36
Fern Picture Frame 37
Willow Whistles 38
Hey, Bud! 41
Garden Edge Bricks 42
Stepping Stones 45
Watching Bugs and Other
Small Critters 47
Mint Leaf Candies 48

Herbal Vinegars 49
Rose Petal Jam &
Decorated Lid 50
Incredible (But True!)
Hummingbird Facts 52
Garden Trellis 53
Hooray for Flying Fur! 56
Garden Markers 57

Wild Vegetables 58
Potpourri 59
Fancy Covers for
Potpourri Jar Lids 61
Why Do Flowers Have Colors
and Different Shapes? 62
Fish Print T-Shirts 63
Fins, Gills, and . . .Yipe!
What's That Stripe? 65
Twig Wreath 66
Blackberry & Onion Skin Dyes 68
Daylily Leaf Hat 70

Pressed Flower Note Cards 73
   Nature's Papermakers 75
Lotus Book
   (Origami-style Journal) 76
Tree Branch Hideaway 79
   How Big Is Your Favorite Tree?;
   Some National Champion Big Trees 81-82
Gathering Basketry Materials 83
Wild Basket 86
   Nature's Icing 89
Gourd Dipper 90
Gourd Drum 92
Shakeree 94
   Great Gobs O' Gourds! 97
Seed Necklace 98
Rutabaga Lantern 99
   Roots and Vegetables;
   Root Power 100
Chili Pepper Garland 102
   What's So Hot About

   Chili Peppers? 103
Seed Drying Frame 104
   The Mighty Acorn 106
Seed Packets 107

Save Those Seeds! 108
Apple Crisp 109
Gathering Wood 110
Rustic Twig Shelf 112
Evergreen Wrapping Paper 116
Seashell Candles 117
   Fantastic Floating Water;
   Make Your Own Icicles! 118-119
Potato Paper 120
   Warm, Snuggly Snow 124
Winter Berry Garland 125
Terrarium & Terrarium Stand 126
   Winter's Invisible Wildflowers 128
Prehistoric Paints 129
   Earth's Amazing Caves 131
Nature Sketching 132
   What Big Eyes and
   Ears You Have! 135
Pocket Sketchbook 136
Bird Feeder 138
   Bir-r-r-rd, It's Cold Outside! 141

Rain
Cement Birdbath 142
   Rain Facts 145
   Rain and Clouds 147
Barometer 148

Wind
Wind Vane 150
   Wind Names Around the World;
   Wind Power; Wind; What Makes
   the Wind Blow? 151-155
Fish Kites 154

Birds
Nesting Shelf   156
Eggs with Pressed Flowers
   and Leaves   158
   Egg Shapes and Colors;
   Egg Records   159
Eggs Dyed with Onion Skins   160

Flowers
Wildflower Candles   162
Gift Tags, Bookmarks,

   Note Cards   163
   Candied Violets   165

Critters
Wormery   167
   Eat Dirt, You Worm!   167

Sun
Sun Prints   169
Sun Clock   171
Pocket Sundial   173

Leaves and Stems
Leaf Print   175
   Which Leaf Is Which?   176
Nature Kaleidoscope   177
   What Do Leaves Do?   180
Mushroom Spore Prints:
   Mysterious Mushrooms   181
Pan Pipes   183

Herbs
Herb Dolls   185
Bath Bags   186
Plant Perfumes   186
Pet Collars   187

Critters
Ant House   189
Pooter   190
Bug Box   191

Seashore
Sand Candles   192
   The Amazing Ocean   194

Fish Print 195
Banner 196
Sand Painting; What Is Sand? 197
Beach Basket 199

Leaves
Leaf Stained Glass 203
   Why Do Leaves Turn Colors
   in Autumn? 204
Leaf Collection Box 205
   Why Do Trees Drop Their Leaves? 206
Needle Knowledge;Evergreen Garland
   207-208
Paper with Inlaid Leaves 209

Nuts and Seeds
Seed Mosaic; Traveling Seeds 213
Twig-and-Cone Wreath 215
Nut-Stenciled Bandanna 217

Harvest
Apple Monsters 219

Corn Husk Flowers 221
Turnip Lanterns 223

Critters
Casts of Animal Tracks 225
   Animal Tracks;
   The Tracker; Walk Like a Bear;
   Bigfoot Tracks? 227-230

Snow
Snow Candles; Snow 231-232
Snow Sculpture 233
   Snow Facts, Snow Folklore;
   The Snowflake Man 234-236

Birds
Birds' Midwinter Tree 238
Bird Feeder 239

Who Eats What? 241

The Night Sky

Nocturne Night Dial — 243

   How to Find the North Star
   and Cassiopeia — 244

Constellation Viewers — 248

Bark and Twigs

Bark Rubbing;
   Identifying Bark — 249

Twig Weaving — 252

Gee-Haw Whimmy Diddle — 253

Flowers and Herbs

Pomander — 255

Scented Soap — 256

Ecology Crafts — 259

Introduction to Ecology Crafts — 261

Talking Trash — 263

1   Excellent Eco-Extravaganzas — 265

Clay Pinch Pots and Animals — 266

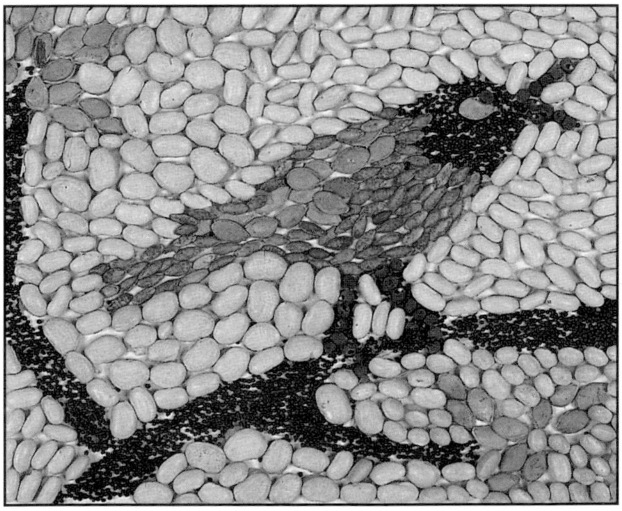

Find and Clean Your Own Clay — 268

Make Your Own Sawdust Kiln — 269

Twig Frame — 271

Collecting Bag — 272

Birch Bark Basket — 273

You Can Do It — 275

Tree-Saver Chair — 277

   We'd Be up a Tree
   without Trees — 279

Special Prints Gift Wrap — 280

   Oh, Christmas Tree! — 282

Bag Bonnets — 283

Fly-Away-Home Gourd Birdhouse — 285

   What's a Bald Eagle?;
   What's a Grizzly Bear? — 288

2   Awesome Eco-Adventures — 291

Backyard Wetland — 292

   The Wet, Wet World of Water — 294

Collections Box — 295

Birch Bark Canoe — 297

Happy Earth Day! April 22   300

Log Cabin Planter   301

Bat House   303

Up with Bats!   306

Achy Breaky Pots   307

Potato Print Shirts   309

Make Your Own Compost   311

Save the Manatee   312

Sketch-and-Press

     Nature Journal   313

Cool Tool: Keep a Tree Diary   316

3   Rockin' Eco-Recycling   **317**

Calendar Boxes   332

Hurray for the

Tree Muskateers!   335

That Can't Be Paper! Beads   336

Easy Recycle Bin   337

Is That a Soda Bottle

You're Wearing?   338

Picture-Perfect Postcards   339

Cool Cut-and-Paste

     Bottles and Jars   340

Light Bulb Puppets   318

Make Your Own Papier Mâché Mix   321

Paper Bag Bouquets   322

Paper Bag Books   324

Eco-envelopes   326

Nature's Gardens: Bottles and Jars   327

Paper or Plastic?   328

Recycling Kids, Inc.   329

Totally Recycled Albums   330

4   Terrific Eco-Trash   343

Fantastic Flower Pots   344

Dog Biscuit Photo Frame   346

Eggshell Mosaic   347

Mosaic-An Earth-Friendly Art   348

License Plate Bird Feeder   349

You're Invited!   351

Corny Sunflowers

Dry Your Own Corn Husks 354
Cornhusk Angels 355
Beach Glass Jewelry 367
You Don't Need a Garage
for a Garage Sale 358
Kissy Fish Piñata 359
Trees, Please 361
Gourd Witch 363
Eco-Party 366

5 Happenin' Eco-Hits 367

Rock Houses 368
Papier Mâché Bird 369
A Wonderful Wild Man:
John Muir 371
The Sierra Club Today 373
Bottle Gardens: Simple
Bottle Garden 374
Green Bottle Garden 376
Desert in a Jar 376
How is a Rainforest Like
Your Bathroom? 377

Paper Quilts 378
Beautiful Earth:
Natural Cosmetics 382
Ocean Waves Bath Salts 383
Lavender and Roses Powder 384
Lemonade Lip Gloss 385
Make an Earth-Friendly
Art Box 386
Tin Can Marionette 387
Adopt a Piece of the Planet 390
Bean and Pasta Mosaic 391
It is Always Sunrise Somewhere 392

Metric Conversion Chart 394

Index 396

iNTRODUCTiON

When you look at a pinecone, what do you see? You might notice its shape, size, and color, and that's about all. But when you gather a bunch of pinecones from the outdoors and make something with them--a wreath, for example--you learn a lot more: how sticky pinecones can be, how prickly some kinds are, how they're put together, how they smell and feel, and where you can find the best ones. You become a pinecone expert. (And you get a nice wreath, too!)

That's the basic idea behind this book. *Nature Smart* is for people who like to learn by doing as well as by reading and looking. This book is for anyone who likes to make things, and who's interested in the outdoors and preserving our environment.

There are dozens of terrific projects in these pages. Some are simple; others are more challenging and will take a little more time. Part I, "Seasonal Crafts," contains projects that show you how to make something that's useful, attractive, or just plain interesting. At the same time, each one helps you see and feel and understand the natural world you live in a little better. Part II, "Ecology Crafts" contains projects and interesting facts that help you interact in positive and helpful ways with all the living things in your world.

Nature Smart is jam-packed with rewarding things to make and do. Through the making and doing, you're going to discover some exciting things about nature and ecology, and about how everything in it (including you!) is important and special.

Come on, let's get going!

Ten Tips to Making Crafts

1. Read the instructions all the way through once or even twice before you start. This will give you a chance to really understand what you're about to do.

2. Try to imagine yourself going through each step. This is a well-known approach followed by the best chefs, carpenters, basket makers, and other people who make crafts.

3. Even though you want to dive right into a project, collect or buy all the materials you need before you begin. It can be so frustrating to find yourself in the middle of a project only to realize you are missing the one thing you need to finish!

4. For a few projects, you may need tools or hardware that you've never used before or with which you may not be familiar. No problem. Salespeople who work in stores that sell these things are used to people of all ages asking "What's this?" or "How do I use that?" So don't be shy. March right up to the person with the name tag and ask for help in finding a plastic, number 4, hand-held, 2-inch-long watcha-ma-jig. It really is true that the right tool (or material) for a job can make what seemed impossible pretty easy.

5. If you absolutely can't find a certain material or tool, try to substitute something that you think will work just as well. Adults can give you some help in this area by suggesting other materials you can use.

6. On the subject of adults: in a few cases we tell you to ask an adult to help you with a step that might be dangerous, such as using a hacksaw. We only mention this when we think it's important. Please practice good safety skills when making any of the projects.

7. We've tried our best to give you clear and detailed instructions. But if there's a step that doesn't make sense, try it out with a scrap of material or even with a piece of paper. Often, written instructions come to life when you act them out this way.

8. Don't let where you live get in your way. Whether you live in the city, country, or suburbs, you can enjoy making the projects in this book. City birds will appreciate a bird feeder; a garden trellis works great in a tiny backyard; you can find a fish for making a fish-print t-shirt even in desert country.

9. Use this book as a jumping-off point. Make up your own projects. Be in charge of your own exploring. The more things you make with natural materials, the more you'll find out about the natural world around you.

10. Keep digging! If you get excited about one of the topics, look for other books that deal with these same subjects.

A Metric Conversion Table appears on page 394

Seasonal Nature Projects

Sweet Smelling Grass Mat

The Navahos invented a kind of loom that made weaving mats an easy job. You can build your own Navaho loom any size you want depending on what you want to make. Directions given here are for a small mat or sit-upon. To make a sleeping mat, just make your loom slightly longer than you want the finished mat to be. The length of the grasses you use will determine how wide the mat can be.

What You'll Need

9 straight sticks, 1 or 1-1/2 inches
    in diameter and about
    2 feet long
A hammer
A ball of jute or other lightweight
    rope or heavy twine
Scissors
Dry grasses *

In early spring you may be able to find, still standing in fields and along roadways, grasses that have dried over the winter. These are the perfect material for making a mat. Cut or break off the grasses, keeping the stems as long as possible. Carry and store the grasses with all the stems going the same direction to save time later. If you can't find dried grasses, you'll have to wait until later in the spring when cattail leaves, daylilies, and grasses have grown long. Cut them as long as possible and let them dry in a cool, airy place before using green materials.

What to Do

1. Pound two of the sticks into the ground about 18 inches apart.
2. Use rope to lash a stick across the top of these sticks.
3. Pound five sticks into the ground in a line with about 3 inches between each stick. This line needs to be about 3

feet away from the first two sticks if you are going to make a small mat. For a larger mat, they must be a little farther away than the length you want the finished mat to be.

4. Cut five pieces of rope at least 1 foot longer than the distance between the two rows of sticks. Tie one piece to each of the sticks in the five-stick row.

5. Tie the other ends of these five pieces of rope to the crosspiece of the two-stick row. Tie each piece so that the rope is taut between the posts. The ties on the crosspiece should be about 3 inches apart. **1**

6. Cut five pieces of rope at least 2 feet longer than the distance between the two rows of sticks. Tie these to the crosspiece right next to the other pieces of rope.

7. Lay the final stick on the ground alongside the row of five sticks on the outside of this row. Tie the other end of each of the longer pieces of rope to this stick. The ties

should be about 3 inches apart. **2** You should be able to raise and lower the stick that is resting on the ground. This stick is called a *heddle*.

8. Begin to weave by lifting the heddle and placing a bundle of grass in between the ropes that are tied to the crosspiece

and the ropes of the heddle. Put this bundle as close to the crosspiece as possible. Now lower the heddle, and you will see that the grass is held in place by the ropes. **3**

9. Hold the heddle down, and place another bundle of grass between the two sets of rope.

ropes of each pair from the heddle, and tie the two ropes together in a knot around the last bundle of grass. **7** Trim the ends of rope to about 1 inch. Then untie each set of ropes from the crosspiece, and tie those pairs of ropes together around the first bundle of grass. Trim the ends to about 1 inch. **8**

12. Shake out your mat gently to get rid of any loose pieces of grass. You can roll the mat up to carry it and store it. Unroll it when you want to sit for a while or when you need a pillow under your head while you watch the clouds sail by.

Push this bundle as close as possible to the first bundle. Now raise the heddle and lock the bundle in place. **4**

10. Continue weaving this way until your mat is as big as you want it to be. **5** and **6**

11. To finish the mat, untie both

Earth's Never-Ending Water-Go-Round

It's a hot, dry day, and the thirsty stegosaurus lumbers to the river for a drink. Slowly, it lowers its head to the cool liquid and—GULP—swallows a mouthful of water. Billions of water molecules gurgle down the dinosaur's long throat (a water molecule is the tiniest bit of water possible). Ahhhh.

It's another hot, dry day, 150 million years later. You walk to the kitchen sink, fill your glass with water, raise it to your lips, and—GULP—take a drink. Surprise! You may have just swallowed some of the same water molecules that thirsty stegosaurus drank!

All of the water on earth today has been here since our planet's beginning, over three billion years ago. Nature doesn't make new water. It just constantly recycles and renews what's always been here, in a never-ending process called the *water cycle*.

The "pump" that keeps the water cycle going is the sun. It heats water on the planet's surface. When the water is warm enough, the molecules evaporate (turn into a gas, or vapor) and rise into the air. High in the sky, the invisible vapor becomes cooler and condenses: it changes into tiny water droplets. When millions of water droplets cluster together, they make a cloud.

As more and more water vapor condenses, the cloud gets more and more crowded. The droplets bump into each other and stick together, forming larger, heavier droplets. Eventually, they become so heavy they fall as rain. Or sometimes they freeze in cold air and come down as snow or hail.

Most of the water falls right back where most of it comes from: the oceans. The oceans contain 97% of all the water on earth! Only a tiny bit falls to land, where it soaks into the ground or runs into creeks and streams, rivers and lakes.

That's why it's so important not to waste water. People and plants can't drink salty ocean water. At any one time, only a small amount of earth's water is fresh and drinkable. And we humans use a lot of fresh water for a lot of things besides just drinking!

Over and over, the water cycle keeps going. Pure water vapor rises from the oceans, leaving its salt behind. Some of the clouds drift toward land, carrying fresh rainwater with them. Meanwhile, water already on land moves constantly toward a place where it can evaporate easily. Streams run into lakes, lakes drain into rivers, rivers flow into oceans. Water in the soil is drawn up by plants and trees and given off through their leaves. Even water deep underground, soaked into rock and sand, moves slowly toward the sea.

Animals are a part of the cycle too. Your body is over 50% water. Every time you eat or drink, you take more water in. And every time you perspire or breathe out, you give some back to the air.

Next time you fill a glass with water, think about the amazing stuff you hold in your hand. Without water, nothing on earth can live. And maybe some of those molecules really were gulped down by a roving dinosaur. Or were carried in battle inside a Roman soldier's canteen. Or came down with a plunk in a drop of rain on Abraham Lincoln's stovepipe hat. Or . . . ?

Rustic Wren House

This nesting box will help you attract birds to live near your home. Birds are fussy about their nesting places, and different kinds of birds have different requirements for their houses. A wren is one of the least choosy and is therefore one of the easiest birds to attract. It needs an entrance hole about 1-⅛ inch in diameter in a 4-by-6-by-8-inch box that is set on a 6-foot-high post. The entrance hole must be large enough for the wren to get through, yet small enough to keep out larger birds and predators. When placing the house, remember that wrens prefer to build their nests near a bushy feeding area.

What You'll Need

3 feet by 9 inches of
     ¼-inch plywood
A ruler
A pencil
A saw
A hand drill
A ¼-inch drill bit
A 1-⅛-inch expansion drill bit
A few small nails
A hammer
Carpenter's glue
Twigs
Pruning shears
A 2-by-4-inch post 8 feet long
Wood stain (optional)
A rag
A shovel

What to Do

1. Saw the plywood into the following pieces: two sides, 6 inches by 9 inches each; one top, 5 inches by 8 inches; one bottom, 4 inches by 6 inches; one front, 4-½ inches by 8 inches; one back, 4-½ inches by 9 inches.
2. Draw a line 1 inch in from one short edge on the two side pieces and the back. **1**
3. Drill four ¼-inch holes in the bottom piece for drainage.

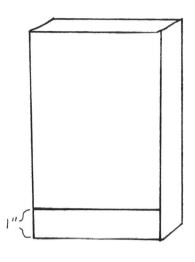

1

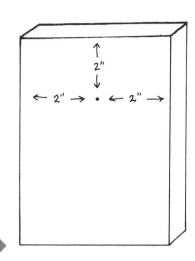

2

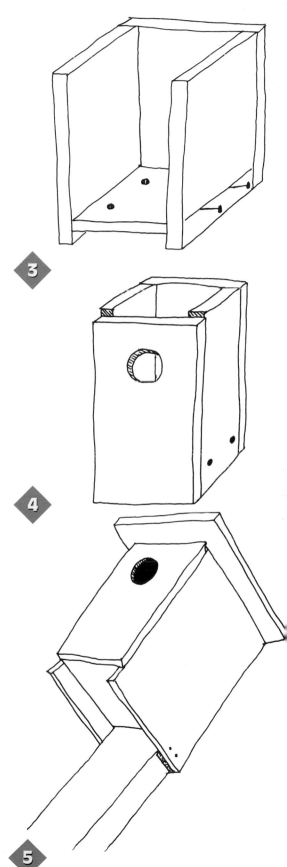

3

4

5

4. Using the expansion drill bit set at 1-⅛ inch, drill the front hole with its center 2 inches down from the top and in the middle of the front. **2**

5. Hammer two nails into the back and side pieces along the lines you have drawn. Hammer until the points come through. Then put glue all along the two side edges of the bottom and the back edge of the bottom. Nail the sides and back to the bottom. The nails are to help hold the pieces in place while the glue dries and to give extra strength. You will probably need someone to help hold these pieces in place while you nail. Note the 1-inch overhang at the bottom. **3**

6. After the glue has dried on the bottom, lay the nesting box on its back and glue the front on. Push the front piece down about ⅛ of an inch so that there will be a thin space at the top for ventilation under the roof. **4**

7. Glue the top on. Let the roof overhang in the front. Let all glue dry overnight.

8. Place the nesting box over one end of the post. Nail the side overhangs of the box to the sides of the post. Use scraps of plywood to push in beside the post for a snug fit before you nail. **5**

9. Cut twigs with the pruning shears to 3-inch and 6-inch lengths as well as some shorter pieces and some forked pieces. Glue the twigs over the entire surface of the box in a design that you like.

10. Stain the post with wood stain if you want to. Just rub the stain on with the rag and let it dry.

11. Dig a hole about 18 inches deep and set the post in it. Turn the box so that its entrance faces away from the direction from which the wind usually blows. Pile the soil back in the hole, and tamp it down firmly with your foot.

Bird Drinking Fountain

Birds will enjoy perching on the branches of this bird drinking fountain while they have a cool drink.

What You'll Need

A 6-inch clear plastic flowerpot saucer

A 10-inch clear plastic flowerpot saucer

A hole puncher

16 thin, straight branches, about 12 inches long and $\frac{1}{8}$ inch in diameter at the fat end

An awl or a large nail

6 feet of jute or other lightweight rope or heavy twine

Scissors

What to Do

1. Punch 16 holes around the rim of the 10-inch saucer. Begin by punching two holes directly across from one another; then punch two others midway between the first two holes. **1** Punch four holes midway between each of these holes. Then punch eight holes midway between each of these holes.

2. Now you will weave the thin branches around the saucer. From the outside, poke one end of a branch into any hole. Pull the tip of the branch across the inside of the saucer and out the fourth hole in either direction across the rim. Adjust the branch so that the same amount sticks out from each end. **2**

3. Continue placing branches in one hole and out the fourth hole away. After a few branches are in place, it will be necessary to put two branches in the same hole. **3** If the holes seem too small, use the awl to slightly enlarge them.

4. When you have used up all the branches, adjust them so they are evenly placed, with the tips crossing one another.

5. Cut three 2-foot-long pieces of light rope. Tie them with double knots to three holes spaced evenly around the rim. **4**

6. Gather the three ends of the ropes together and tie them in one knot. Be sure that the drinking fountain hangs straight.

7. Fill the 6-inch flowerpot saucer with water and place it in the center of the 10-inch saucer. Hang the fountain from a sturdy tree branch in your yard, one that gives you a good view of the birds gathering to refresh themselves.

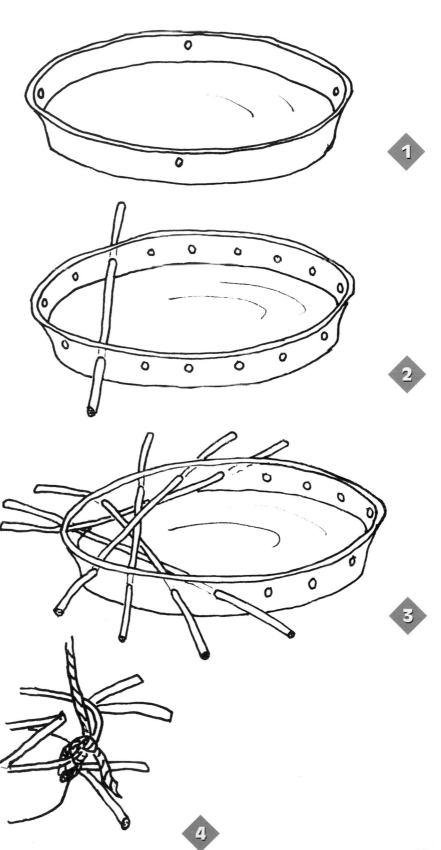

23

Recycled Kite

What is spring without a kite? And if you like to make things, the perfect kite should be one you've made yourself. But kites must be carefully balanced, and unless you're an experienced kite maker, chances are slim that your homemade kite will get off the ground, much less glide around overhead with grace and elegance. So here's a compromise: recycle an old, store-bought kite. You can replace the covering and add your own design, while still getting the benefit of a kite that flies easily and well.

What You'll Need

An old kite *
Old newspaper
Masking tape
A colored marker
Covering material that you can
    decorate before or after mak-
    ing the kite **
Scissors
Glue ***
An awl or a sharp nail
Kite string
Cellophane tape or strapping tape
Materials to decorate the cover-
    ing: fabric paints, glitter, mark-
    ers, watercolors, etc.

It's okay if the paper or plastic covering is torn as long as the sticks, or spars, are in good condition.

**Gift-wrap colored cellophane, tissue paper, or other lightweight paper work well; ripstop nylon or a large plastic trash bag also make fine kites.*

***Use airplane glue, white craft glue, or fabric cement, depending on the kind of covering material.*

What to Do

1. Spread out a double-wide sheet of newspaper on the floor or a tabletop, and lay the old kite on it so that you can make an outline of it. If necessary, tape extra sheets of newspaper together to make a large enough sheet. Trace around the entire kite with the marker. Make notes about how it is put together. For example, tell where the spars are glued to the covering, where the strings are attached, and where any holes need to be made. It's impor- tant to make clear, complete notes to refer to when you put the kite back together.

2. Put the drawing aside for now, and clear a big space on the floor or tabletop. Carefully peel the covering from the spars of the old kite. If it tears in places, that's okay, but keep ALL the pieces (use some tape to hold them together if you need to).

3. Spread out the new covering material, and lay the old cov- ering on top of it. Use short pieces of masking tape to tape the old pieces to the new material. **1**

4. Cut out the new material, carefully following the edges of the old pieces. When you come to a piece of tape, cut right through it and keep on going. When you have cut out the new piece or pieces, gently pull the new ones from the old where they are still held together by edges of tape. Save the old pieces in case you need them for information later.

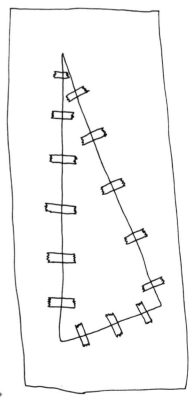

5. Get out your drawing to see where the spars should be glued to the covering, and then glue the spars to the new pieces of covering material, following the directions on your drawing. Let the glue dry overnight.

6. When the glue is completely dry, put in any cross spars that are used to stiffen the kite. Tie kite strings to your recycled kite in exactly the same places that your drawing tells you they were tied on the old kite. If you need to make a hole in the new covering material in order to tie on some string, first put a 1-inch-square of cellophane tape or strapping tape over the area. Then punch the hole through the strengthened material with an awl. **2**

7. If you haven't decorated the covering material before making the kite, do so now.

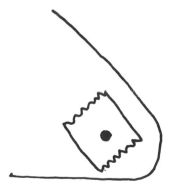

The Wings of a Bird

Next time you see a bird flying or perched on a branch, take a close look at its wings. You can tell a lot about how and where a bird lives by the size and shape of its wings.

Short, rounded wings tell you that the bird is an escape artist. It probably lives in woods, bushes, or on the ground, where a bird has to be able to take off quickly to avoid enemies. Stubby wings are great for fast getaways and for turning and twisting through small openings in brush and other tight places. (That explains why stunt airplanes made especially for doing fancy up-in-the-air tricks have short, rounded wings too!) Quail, grouse, doves, and songbirds such as cardinals, chickadees, and sparrows all are short-winged, quick-getaway birds.

Wide wings with feathers that spread out like fingers at the ends are a clue that the bird is a hunter and a sky rider. Eagles, hawks, and vultures don't flap their broad, feathery wings often, except to take off or to change direction. Instead, they spread their wings wide and ride upward on swirling currents of warm air called thermals or on breezes blowing over hills and mountains. Then, when the bird gets to the top of the current, it glides slowly down in big circles, looking for a meal—or for another "air elevator" to take it back up again.

Long, skinny wings with sharp-looking tips are a sure sign that the bird is a wind-surfing sailor. Gulls and albatrosses don't sail on the water, though. They glide over it by keeping their wings open and riding the strong breezes that blow across the ocean's surface. Thin-winged sea birds can surf along on air waves for hundreds of miles.

Narrow, pointed wings that angle back, like the wings on a jet, tell you that the bird is a speedster.

Instead of soaring or gliding, this type of bird sweeps through the sky by flapping its wings very rapidly, then suddenly dives or climbs to snatch a meal out of the air. Their streamlined wings make falcons, swallows, swifts, and shorebirds such as sandpipers the fastest-flying birds in the world. A peregrine falcon can travel 100 miles an hour while flying level—and, when it dives, can zoom to nearly 200 miles an hour!

Kissing and Spishing for Birds

Watching birds and trying to figure out what kinds you're seeing can be a lot of fun. But have you ever tried to sneak up on a bird to get a really close look? Lotsa luck! Birds can hear even the slightest noise or rustle. And their eyesight is about eight times sharper than human eyesight.

Your chances of creeping up near a bird before it sees or hears you and flies away are really slim. A better idea is to learn how to call birds to come to you. And no, you don't need a special bird call. Just use your body!

First, find a place where there are some trees and bushes. Sit or squat down, so that the leaves or branches partially hide you. Get comfortable, so that you won't have to shift position or move around once you start calling.

Now you're ready to try "kissing." Make a loose fist, and hold it up to your mouth so that your thumb and curled-up index finger are facing you. Now put your lips together, press them to the fleshy part of your hand between your thumb and index finger (just below and behind the small opening between your index finger and palm), and make a long, loud, squeaky kiss noise. Wait a few seconds, then do it again, and again. Experiment a little. Try a few short, high-pitched kisses, one right after the other. Or try a combination of long and short squeaks. Do the birds around you react differently to different "kisses"? With a little practice, you'll learn which kinds of squeaks attract the most birds.

Another body bird call is even easier, and often brings in even more birds. Just make a long, drawn-out *spish-h-h-h* sound three or four times in a row. You've got it right if the call makes a hissing, shushing noise (as though you were saying shhhhhhh, but with an extra *sp* in front). Or try just *pish-h-h-h*. Do it over and over, in a steady rhythm. And don't be shy about it. Good, loud spishing or pishing often attracts all sorts of woodland birds, including chickadees, nuthatches, jays, sparrows, wrens, and even woodpeckers.

No one is exactly sure why kissing and spishing work. It's possible that the sounds resemble the birds' alarm calls. Have you ever noticed a flock of small birds chasing a crow or hawk in the sky? Or perhaps some sparrows dive-bombing a cat? Ornithologists (scientists who study birds) call that behavior *mobbing*. You might think that a small bird would quickly fly far away when it sees a dangerous enemy. But instead, many birds send out an alarm call—loud squeaks or chirps. When other birds hear it, they come running (well, flying) to help chase the troublemaker away.

So birds might come to kissing or spishing because they think it's a call for help. Or maybe they're just curious to see what's causing the strange sound. For that matter, maybe they just want to get a closer look at that funny human sitting in the bushes making kissing noises!

Pressed Flower Lamp Shade

This lamp shade looks as though it were made of expensive handmade paper inlaid with pressed flowers. It's actually very easy to make, and it will remind you of a field of spring flowers all year long.

What You'll Need

A smooth-surfaced paper
    lamp shade *
A collection of pressed flowers
A pack of white tissue
    wrapping paper
Scissors
White craft glue
A 1-inch flat paintbrush

Any color is fine, although a white one was used for the shade pictured here. An old one will do as long as it isn't damaged or very dirty. Many lamp shades are made of plasticized paper covered with gathered cloth. It's usually easy to remove the cloth covering by making a starter cut through one of the gathers of cloth and then gently peeling the glued cloth off the shade.

What to Do

1. Cut the tissue paper into pieces that are about 2 inches by 3 inches.
2. Hold the lamp shade on its side. Starting anywhere you want, place a pressed flower on the surface of the shade and lay a piece of tissue paper over it.
3. Paint over the entire piece of tissue with glue. Smooth out all bubbles and wrinkles. Be sure the edges are glued down. The paper over the flowers may not stick perfectly flat, but brush over it several times to smooth it as much as possible. As the glue dries, the paper will become much more transparent and the flowers will show up better.
4. Continue to glue flowers and tissue until the entire shade is covered in an arrangement that you like.
5. Examine the shade carefully to see if there are any places without tissue paper glued to them. Cover these gaps with plain pieces of tissue so that the surface of the shade is completely covered by tissue.
6. Let the glue dry; then place the shade on a lamp.

Butterfly & Moth Hatchery

Sometimes in early spring you may be lucky enough to find a butterfly chrysalis or moth cocoon. The chrysalis or cocoon is actually a case inside of which a caterpillar is changing into a butterfly or moth. The insect in this stage of its life is called a "pupa." Although pupae are very delicate, you can build a special hatchery for them that closely matches the natural conditions they need. Then, you can watch them emerge with their new wings.

When you find a cocoon or chrysalis, break off the whole section of the branch to which it is attached (they often hang down from leaves). If you find it in soil, scoop out a cup or so of the soil so that you can bury the pupa in a pot of the same soil. Once your butterfly or moth comes out of its casing, it will need to rest for a few hours while its wings dry and finish developing. When it begins to fly around inside the hatchery, release the moth or butterfly into a garden or field so it can enjoy its life the way nature intended.

What You'll Need

A 10-by-12-by-12-inch corrugated cardboard box, with either a lid or top flaps that close

A 12-by-36-inch piece of vinyl screen cloth, available in hardware stores

Scissors

A razor knife

A roll of self-adhesive plastic shelf paper

12 inches of cotton rope

An awl or a large nail

6 brass paper fasteners

3 rubber bands

Cutout pictures of butterflies and moths or drawings of butterflies and moths

A glue stick

Masking tape

A container for plants and soil

What to Do

1. Stand the box so that the side that opens faces the back. If the open side has four flaps, cut off the two side flaps.
2. Tape the sides of the bottom flap on the back of the box with masking tape so that only the top flap opens. **1**

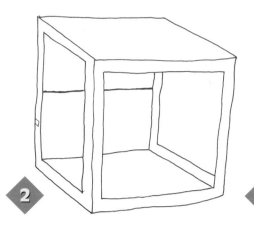

3. Use the razor knife to cut out squares from the front and two sides of the box. Leave a strip about 1-inch wide all around each opening. **2**
4. Use masking tape to stretch the screen cloth over the three openings.
5. Cover the entire box, inside and out, with self-adhesive plastic shelf paper.
6. Use an awl or large nail to poke two holes, 3 inches apart, in the top of the cage.
7. Push the ends of the cotton

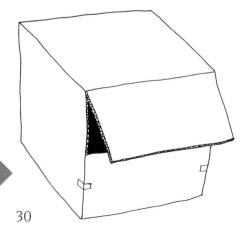

rope in through the holes. Tie a knot on each end of the rope to hold it to the cage top and to make a handle for the cage. **3**
8. Use the awl to make holes on the back flap of the box and on the bottom flap and both sides. **4**

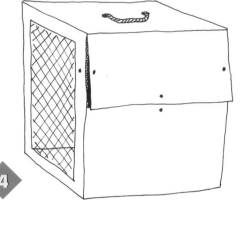

9. Push a paper fastener into each hole and spread its feet to hold it in place. **5**
10. Wrap rubber bands around the pairs of paper fasteners to close the flaps.
11. Decorate the front and sides of the cage with cutout paper butterflies and moths if you wish.
12. When you find a chrysalis or cocoon, make an environment in the cage like the environment in which you found it. Include some of the plant on which you found the pupa or some of the soil in which it was buried. Add some branches from nearby plants. When the moth or butterfly comes out of its casing, put a cotton ball soaked in honey water in the cage for food.
13. Hang the cage in a cool, shady place where you can watch the exciting developments take place.

Mix A Mess Of Midnight Moth Goop

Did you know there are five times as many kinds of moths in the world as there are butterflies? Scientists think there are about 20,000 types, or species, of butterflies—and at least 105,000 different kinds of moths!

People usually see more butterflies than moths, though. That's because most moths fly at night, when we humans are sleeping. Besides, moths can be hard to spot in the dark.

Here's a fun way to make studying these interesting creatures easier. Just mix a batch of Midnight Moth Goop, and invite the moths to spend an evening with you!

First, you'll need the special ingredients:

> 2 cups of orange juice that you've kept out of the refrigerator for two days
>
> 3 or 4 soft, squishy, too-ripe bananas
>
> 1/2 cup molasses, corn syrup, or honey

You'll also need a food processor or blender for mixing your Goop, a 1-inch (or wider) paintbrush, a bucket or other container, and a small flashlight.

Ready? Put the bananas in the food processor or blender and mash them on high speed until they're a smooth, gooey paste. Then pour in the molasses, syrup, or honey, plus one cup of the orange juice. Whirl it all together until it's completely mixed. Then add more orange juice, a little at a time, until your Midnight Moth Goop is about as thick as house paint. If it gets too runny, mash another banana or two into the Goop.

Pour the mixture into your container, cover it with foil, and let it sit in the sun for a couple of hours. Now you're ready to go "sugaring" for moths. Find a place where there are several trees at the edge of a clearing of some sort. A meadow next to woods is a good choice. So is your yard, if your neighborhood has lots of trees and bushes. A park is a good place, too, but be sure to get permission first from park officials.

The best nights for attracting moths are cloudy, warm, and still. Just before sunset, go out and "paint" two to six trees. Using the brush, slather a coating of Midnight Moth Goop on the bark of each tree over an area about half as big as this page.

A few hours later, when it's really dark, go back outside with your flashlight to meet your late-night dinner guests. (If your flashlight's very bright, put some red cellophane or tissue paper over the lens to make the light dimmer; that way, you won't disturb the moths as they feed.) With luck, you should see several moths on most of the trees. Many of the types that are attracted to Midnight Moth Goop are especially big and beautiful. If you bring along a field guide, you can try to figure out what kinds they are.

You'll probably see other insects such as ants and beetles slurping up the Goop too. Be sure to take time to study them closely, as well. And look around you. Listen to the sounds. Maybe you'll hear an owl or see a bat flying overhead. Isn't this world after dark, the world of moths and other nighttime creatures, an interesting place? Nature never sleeps!

What Makes a Moth...a Moth?

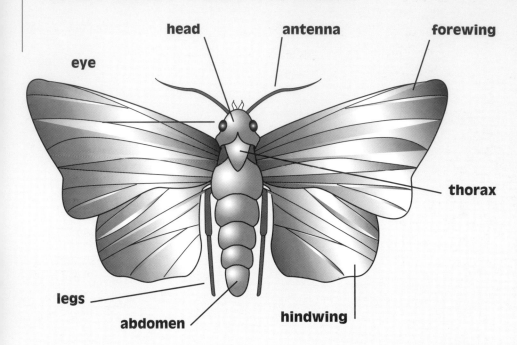

eye — head — antenna — forewing — thorax — legs — abdomen — hindwing

It's easy to see why some people mistake moths for butterflies. After all, they both flutter by when they fly. They both have wide, interesting wings. And they both sip nectar or water from flowers or puddles.

But in many ways, moths and butterflies are entirely different.

Most moths, for instance, spin a fluffy, silken cocoon when they get ready to change from a caterpillar to an insect with wings. Scientists call that change *metamorphosis* (met-uh-MOR-fuh-sis). Most butterflies, though, go through the change inside a *chrysalis* (KRIS-uh-lis), a tough, hard shell formed from the butterfly caterpillar's skin.

Also, adult moths usually have fatter, furrier bodies than butterflies. Compared to most moths, butterflies are sleek and slender and streamlined.

Another good clue is whether the insect is flying during the day or in the evening. Almost all butterflies fly only during the day. The brighter and sunnier the day, the more butterflies you'll see. A really gray, cloudy day is enough to keep butterflies from taking to the skies.

Most (not all, but most) moths, on the other hand, fly only at night. The "mothiest" nights happen when the sky is cloudy and pitch dark, with no light shining through from the moon or stars.

If you watch carefully, you'll see that moths and butterflies hold their wings differently too. A butterfly resting on a flower or twig holds its wings straight up and down. From the side, the wings look a bit like a sail on a boat. But when a moth is resting, it folds its wings down flat, level with its body, like a little roof.

Also, butterflies are usually more brightly colored than moths. That's because butterflies need to use colors and patterns to keep birds and other daytime creatures from eating them. Have you ever noticed that some butterfly wings have spots that look like eyes? The spots give birds a fake target, away from the butterfly's body. Many moths have eyespots, too. But since most moths are out only at night, their wing colors are usually duller, to match their after-dark surroundings.

Not all butterflies and moths fit all these rules. Some kinds of moths, for instance, have wings that shimmer with bright, beautiful colors. And skippers, one of the most common families of butterflies, have fat, furry bodies and dull brown- and rust-colored wings, just like a moth. That's why some scientists say skippers aren't "true" butterflies, but something somewhere between a butterfly and a moth.

One of the best ways to tell whether an insect is a skipper, a "true" butterfly, or a moth is to study its feelers, or antennae. Almost all butterflies have slender, smooth antennae that get rounder and thicker at the end. They look like little clubs. Skippers have slender antenna that curve back at the ends, like small hooks. And moths have short, feathery antennae that almost always taper to a sharp point.

Next time you see a "butterfly," take a closer look. It just might be a moth in disguise!

Accordion-Fold Nature Journal

If you want to make a record of a wonderful unfolding such as the growth of a plant, the blooming of a tree branch, or the changing of a tadpole into a frog, an accordion-fold journal is the perfect place to do it.

What You'll Need

4 or 5 sheets of 8-½-by-11-inch
    unlined paper, such as typing
    or copier paper

A ruler

A pencil

Scissors

A glue stick

2 pieces of cardboard or poster
    board, 4 inches by 5 inches
    each

2 pieces of decorated paper, 8
    inches by 9 inches; use wallpa-
    per, wrapping paper, or plain
    colored paper on which you
    can draw a design

What to Do

1. Fold the 8-½-by-11-inch paper in half the short way, so that you have two 5-½-by-8-½-inch sections. Cut each page along the fold.
2. Glue the pages to each other to form a long, skinny strip of paper. **1** and **2**

3. Fold the long piece of paper into 4-inch-wide sections, beginning at one end. Make each section the exact size as the one before it, and fold back and forth, like an accordion, until the whole strip is pleated. Cut off any leftover paper. **3**, **4**, and **5**
4. Next cover the two pieces of cardboard with the decorated

paper. To do this, place each piece of cardboard in the center of a piece of decorated paper. Make corner marks. **6**

5. Cut along each corner mark to make flaps.

6. Spread glue on one side of the piece of cardboard, and place it on the inside of the cover paper, within the corner cuts. Put glue on the flaps, and bend them over the cardboard. Smooth the paper over all of the surfaces. Any small lumps or wrinkles will disappear as the glue dries and the paper shrinks. **7** and **8**

7. Fold up the accordion paper strip. Slip a piece of scrap paper between the top page

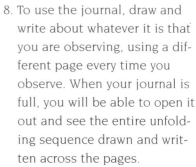

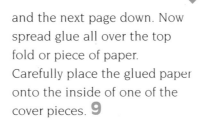

8. To use the journal, draw and write about whatever it is that you are observing, using a different page every time you observe. When your journal is full, you will be able to open it out and see the entire unfolding sequence drawn and written across the pages.

and the next page down. Now spread glue all over the top fold or piece of paper. Carefully place the glued paper onto the inside of one of the cover pieces. **9**

Repeat this step with the other cover and the other end of the accordion strip. **10**

Seashell Wind Chime

Wondering what to do with all the shells you've collected at the beach? Make a seashell wind chime. It will tinkle softly in the breeze and remind you of the days you enjoyed at the seashore.

What You'll Need

Seashells that are lightweight and somewhat flat, such as scallop shells and clam shells

Several feet of very thin, flat satin ribbon, ⅛ inch wide

A 10-to-12-inch-long wooden dowel

About 18 inches of dental floss or other strong, light string

An awl

Scissors

White craft glue

What to Do

1. Tie the dental floss to each end of the dowel with double knots, and hang the dowel around a doorknob.

2. Work out a design for your shells by moving them around on a table. Try placing them one below another on a couple of lengths of ribbon or at the ends of several different lengths of ribbon. When you have a design that you like, cut pieces of ribbon about 6 inches longer than you want the length of each hanging shell to be. Turn the shells inside up, and run a thin bead of glue down the length of the inside of each shell. Be sure to follow any curves completely.

3. Press the ribbon down along the glue, following the curves of the shells. For some shells

it might be possible to drill a small hole at the top with the awl. If you are able to do this, slip the ribbon through the hole before gluing it to the inside of the shell. Slipping a ribbon through a hole in the shell makes it hang a little better, but it's okay to skip this step and just use glue. Let all the glue dry overnight.

4. Tie the ribbons of seashells onto the dowel while the dowel is hanging from the doorknob. Arrange the ribbons close enough to each other so that the shells jingle against one another when you move the dowel. Adjust the balance of the ribbons of shells by sliding them along the dowel carefully. When everything is in good balance, put a drop of glue over each ribbon to hold it in place where it is tied to the dowel.

5. Hang your mobile in a breezy spot indoors or on a deck, patio, or porch.

What Are Shells and Where Do They Come From?

Have you ever walked along a beach and noticed how many shells there are, and how many different shapes and colors? Shells are the empty homes of soft-bodied animals called *mollusks*. There are more than 100,000 kinds of mollusks in the world, and almost all of them have their own special sort of shell.

A few mollusks, such as garden snails, live on land. But most mollusks live in the sea. There are countless millions of shelled sea creatures living on or under the ocean floor. Some tunnel into the sand; others creep or crawl or swim. As you walk along the seashore, you can't easily see these animals. But you know they're there—because of all the shells other mollusks just like them left behind when they died.

Some mollusks live in single shells that are cone-shaped or that spiral round and round and come to a point or form a sort of cap, like a turban. These are the snails, or *univalves*. They all have a head and tentacles and creep around on a muscular "foot," just as land snails do. When danger approaches, they pull their bodies into their homes and shut the "door," a hard covering called an *operculum*. Some univalves gobble up small plants or algae. Others are meat-eaters. Have you ever found a shell with a small, round hole in it? A univalve ate the creature inside. First it used its rough tongue, call a radula, to drill into the shell. Then it sucked the meat out. Some univalves just pry the shells open with their strong foot.

Univalves have some of the world's most beautiful shells, with graceful, swirling patterns or rows of colorful lines or dots. Conchs, whelks, cowries, and moon snails are examples of univalves.

Other mollusks (such as oysters, clams, mussels, cockles, and scallops) are called *bivalves* and have two shells connected by a hinge. The shells can open and shut like a book. The squishy creature inside eats and breathes by sucking water through its gills. The gills trap bits of food and take oxygen out of the water.

Some clams and other bivalves bury themselves deep in the sand. Their only connection to the outside world is a tube, called a *siphon*, that reaches up to the surface to suck in water. Have you ever noticed small holes bubbling in the wet sand as you walk along a beach? Those are siphon holes. Somewhere down there beneath each hole is a hungry clam!

Most bivalves crawl around and dig by pushing a narrow, muscular "foot" forward between their two shells. A cockle actually kicks and jumps along the bottom by pushing down hard with its long, powerful foot. And scallops are jet propelled! To move from one place to another, a scallop opens its two shells and then quickly snaps them shut. Jets of water squirt out between the shells and send the scallop sailing in the opposite direction. Mussels and oysters hardly ever move at all. Mussels anchor themselves to objects with tough, stringy hairs. Oysters make a kind of cement to fasten themelves to rocks, coral, and other oysters.

As mollusks grow, their shells grow with them. If you look at a shell carefully, you might see rows of growth rings. The more rings, the older the shell. The largest shell ever found was from a marine giant clam discovered near Okinawa, Japan. The double shell was 45-1/2 inches long and weighed over 750 pounds!

Fern Picture Frame

Make a special frame for your favorite spring vacation photograph. If you collect ferns or flowers from the place where you vacation, the frame as well as the photo will be a reminder of the fun you had there.

What You'll Need:

An 8-by-10-inch plastic box frame
A collection of pressed ferns,
    leaves, or flowers
White craft glue
A 1-inch-wide flat paintbrush
A 9-by-11-inch sheet of white
    tissue wrapping paper
Scissors
Rubber cement

What to Do:

1. Take the cardboard backing section out of the frame. Put the plastic frame part aside for now. Arrange the pressed ferns, leaves, or flowers around the edges of the cardboard.
2. Place the sheet of tissue carefully over the leaves, ferns, or flowers. Paint the entire tissue with glue. Be sure to brush out

all bubbles and wrinkles. Glue the edges down tight, too.
3. While the glue is still wet, trim the edge of the tissue where it hangs over the edge of the cardboard. Brush the cut edges smooth.
4. Let the tissue dry completely.
5. Put a few dabs of rubber cement on the back of the photograph, and press it into

place in the center of the cardboard. Put the cardboard section back into the plastic cover. You can either hang the frame on the wall or stand it on a table or desk or shelf.

Willow Whistles

In the days before television, people used to sit around in the evenings and carve things such as this whistle. It takes some patience and some willingness to make a few duds before getting it just right, but once you get the knack, you'll enjoy making a variety of whistles with different tones.

What You'll Need

A green willow branch about $\frac{1}{2}$ inch in diameter and 4 inches to 5 inches long *

A wooden or rubber mallet or a stick about 1 inch in diameter and 1 foot long

A pan of water

A sharp pocketknife

A chopping block or board

The branch should be as smooth as possible and free of knots or side branches. It MUST be cut fresh, in the spring, when buds are just beginning to sprout. If you can't find willow, try any other smooth-barked branch.

What to Do

1. Cut a ring about $\frac{1}{4}$ inch wide out of the bark or skin of the branch all the way down to the inner wood. The ring should be about 2 inches from one end of the branch. **1**

2. Soak the branch for a few minutes to get it thoroughly wet.

3. Pound the 2-inch-long bark-covered section thoroughly, on all sides, along its entire length. You can use a mallet, a stick, or the side of your closed up knife. Be careful in pounding not to crack or bruise the bark; yet, you need

to pound hard enough to
loosen the bark.

4. After a few minutes of pounding, hold the branch with both
of your hands and twist the
pounded bark-covered section.
If it has been pounded
enough, you'll hear a soft snap
and feel the bark give way.
Then you can slip the tube of
bark off the inner wood in one
piece. If it won't come off yet,
pound some more until it
does.

5. Slip the bark back onto the
inner wood, and lay the branch
on the chopping block. Cut a
slant from the loose-bark end.
2

6. Cut the loose-bark piece off
the rest of the branch. **3**

7. Now cut straight down just
behind the slant a short
distance, and then make an
angled cut to form an air vent
opening in the bark. Be careful
not to make this vent too big.
4

8. Slip the inner wood out, and
cut it off at the vent. This

smaller piece is now the whistle's reed. The outer bark will
be the whistle. **5**
Cut a thin slice from the top of
the reed to make an air space.
6

9. Push the small wooden reed
back into the bark. Cut a ¼
inch piece from the end of the

remainder of the leftover piece
of inner wood. Slip this piece
back into the other end of the
whistle. **7**

10. There are several things you
can do to adjust the tone of
the whistle. Try cutting a
longer end-plug and pushing it

all the way in to shorten the
air chamber. Try enlarging the
air space by trimming slightly
more off the top of the mouth-
piece.

11. Once you've gotten the knack
of whistle making, try making

different lengths of whistles for different tones. Try making a flute: make a 6-inch- or 7-inch-long whistle and drill some holes along the barrel with an awl or a nail. Try making a long end-plug and pushing it in and out to vary the tone. Try putting a dried pea in the barrel to make a warble.

12. When you aren't using your whistle, store it in a pan of water to keep it from drying out. Shake the water out of it before you use it again.

Hey, Bud!

In winter and early spring, a tree is a leaf explosion just waiting to happen. Give it a few weeks of warm spring days and—poof!—out pop thousands of new leaves, fresh and green.

Actually, though, those new leaves have been there all along, even before the tree lost its old leaves in autumn. Take a good look at a bare tree branch before the leaves come out. See those roundish, pointed things sticking up along the sides? Those are *leaf buds*. Each one is a bundle of tiny leaves or flowers-to-be all wrapped up in a protective winter coat of *bud scales*: the outer part you can see. The scales keep rain and snow and frost away from the baby leaves inside. When the leaves start growing in spring, they become too big for their winter coat and burst out. The bud scales fall off.

If you look very carefully at a leaf bud, you might also see a light-colored place just below it, with several little holes inside. That's a *leaf scar*, where a leaf was attached the year before. And those holes are *vein scars*, where water and sap moved back and forth between the branch and the leaf!

See the *end bud* at the very tip of the twig? Inside are all the fresh tissues the branch will use to grow longer this year. When it opens in spring and the bud scales fall off, it will leave a ring around the twig. If you look back along the twig, you'll see the ring left by last year's end bud. The space between the two rings is how long the twig grew in one year.

Most people look at a tree's leaves to figure out what kind it is. But with a little practice, you can tell just by looking at a bare twig. Each kind of tree has its own special sort of twigs and buds.

Some tree buds, for instance, are covered by only one scale, while others have two or more. The bud scales might be brown or green or red, smooth or fuzzy, sticky or shiny. And different kinds of trees have differently shaped leaf scars with different numbers of vein scars.

A black ash tree has smooth, gray twigs with black, fuzzy buds that grow opposite one another. Beech buds are almost an inch long and pointed, and have eight or more bud scales. They grow up the twig in a zigzag pattern. Sycamore buds have sharp-looking points and are covered by just one bud scale each. Tulip tree twigs are light gray and have an extra-large end bud shaped like a duck's bill! Oak has clusters of buds at the tip. Black walnut twigs are dark and rough and have a stubby gray end bud. The leaf scars are heart-shaped with three circles of tiny vein scars.

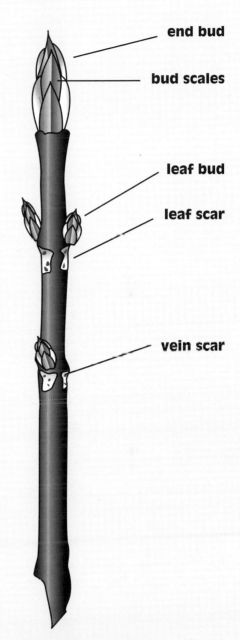

end bud

bud scales

leaf bud

leaf scar

vein scar

Horse Chestnut Twig

Garden Edge Bricks

Many people use bricks or stones to edge their gardens. Some people pay a lot of money to buy fancy edge bricks. You can make your own with a few inexpensive tools and materials. When other gardeners see your bricks, they may want you to make some for them. You might find yourself in the business of making and selling custom-made bricks!

What You'll Need

- A plastic bucket with smooth, straight sides, such as a dry-wall bucket or a paint-mixing bucket
- A fine-tipped permanent marker
- A hacksaw
- 3 pieces of 6-by-15-inch corrugated or other stiff cardboard
- A razor knife
- Aluminum foil
- Cellophane tape
- Petroleum jelly or motor oil
- A bag of ready-mix sand mix concrete
- A 1-lb. bag of red concentrated mortar color *
- A garden trowel or small shovel
- A hose with a spray nozzle
- A galvanized tub or a wheelbarrow to mix concrete in
- A piece of plywood or other scrap wood about 3 feet by 5 feet
- A large piece of plastic sheeting, such as an old shower curtain
- Rubber gloves
- Sticks, old dinner knives and spoons, and other tools for drawing designs in bricks

You can buy mortar color at a place that sells concrete.

What to Do

1. First make brick molds from the plastic bucket. Hold the marker flat on top of a 3-inch- high can or box so that the tip touches the side of the bucket. Holding the pen flat and keeping the tip in contact with the side of the bucket, slowly turn the bucket so that the marker makes a straight horizontal line all around the circumference of the bucket. **1**

2. Make a second horizontal line 3 inches up from the first line using the same process as in step 1, but this time with a 6-

inch-high can or box or by stacking two 3-inch-high cans.

3. Ask an adult to help you use the hacksaw to saw the bucket into three rings along the lines. Then saw the bottom off the bottom ring by sawing about ¼ inch up from the bottom. **2**
   If there is a handle on the bucket or any kind of stiffening lip,

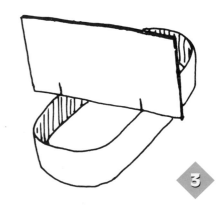

saw it off just below it in the same manner.

4. Press one of the rings into an oval, and hold the oval against one of the pieces of cardboard. Mark the cardboard where the sides of the oval ring cross it. **3** Cut slots on both marks. The slots should be as deep as the sides of the ring are high. **4**

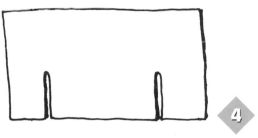

4

5. Cover the front and back of the cardboard with aluminum foil. Tape the foil in place.

6. Repeat steps 4 and 5 for the other two rings and pieces of cardboard.

7. If your bucket had tapered sides, which most buckets do, each ring will have a small circle side and a bigger circle side. *Set the rings on the plywood with the bigger circle side down*. It is very important that you look carefully and figure out which side has the bigger circle,

because if you put the smaller circle side down, it will be very hard to unmold the bricks without breaking them.

8. Slip the pieces of cardboard over the rings so that the cardboard pieces hold the rings in oval shapes. Push the cardboard all the way down so that the oval is divided into two parts. Each part will make one brick.

9. Grease the inside of each mold with petroleum jelly or motor oil.

10. Now to make bricks! First you will mix the concrete. Pour a 3-inch-deep layer of concrete mix into the galvanized tub or wheelbarrow. Use the trowel to pile the dry mix into a hill. Dig a crater in the center of

the hill and put in about 2 cups of water. Mix the dry concrete into the water, gradually adding more water as you need it. Be sure to scrape the edges and bottom often in order to mix in all the dry powder. 5

5

To test the consistency of concrete, make a v-shaped cut in a small mound of the mixture with the edge of the trowel. If the mix is too dry, the cut will crumble. If it is too wet, the cut will melt back together. If the mix is just right, the cut will hold. You may need to add more water or more concrete to get the mix to the right consistency.

11. After the concrete is mixed, add about ½ the bag of color. Mix in the powder until the color is even. You may need to add a little more water. **6**

12. Fill the molds with colored concrete. Pat and smooth as you go so that the bricks will be even and smooth on their sides and bottoms as well as their tops. When the bricks are about 1-½ to 2 inches thick, smooth the top surfaces with a stiff piece of cardboard or with your rubber-gloved hand. **7**

13. After all the molds are filled, drape the piece of plastic over everything. The pieces of cardboard will hold the plastic up off the bricks. Let the bricks dry for an hour.

14. After an hour, check the bricks. Try carving and scraping designs in them with old knives and spoons and sticks. Gently brush off crumbs with your gloved hand. If the brick is still too wet to hold a design, let it dry for another half hour. Check the bricks every half hour so they don't get too dry to carve. **8**

15. After two to three hours, you

can unmold the bricks. Simply lift up the cardboard, which will release the plastic circles. You can then lift off the rings. **9**

16. After unmolding the bricks, lightly spray them with water and cover them up again so they'll continue to cure and dry slowly. If the weather is dry, spray the bricks several times a day during the next three or four days while they are drying. Depending on the weather, the bricks should be completely dry and ready to use in five to seven days.

17. Clean your hands and tools with water before the concrete dries.

Stepping Stones

Have you ever wondered what to do with the pretty rocks or shells that you keep finding and bringing home? One way to use them is to decorate stepping stones with them. Then every time you take a stroll through the garden, you'll remember the wonderful places where you found these natural treasures.

What You'll Need

A plastic bucket with straight, smooth sides, such as a dry-wall bucket or a paint-mixing bucket *

A fine-tipped, permanent marker

A hacksaw

Petroleum jelly or motor oil

A bag of ready-mix sand mix concrete

A galvanized tub or a wheelbarrow to mix concrete in

A garden trowel or small shovel

A hose with a spray nozzle

A 3-by 5 foot piece of plywood or other scrap wood (larger if you will be making more than 3 stones at a time)

Pretty rocks and shells

A flat smoothing tool, such as a mortar trowel or a piece of heavy cardboard

Rubber gloves

A large piece of plastic sheeting, such as an old shower curtain

The diameter of the bucket will be the diameter of the stepping stones. One bucket will make 3 stones. If you want to make more than 3 stones at a time, you'll need more buckets.

What to Do

1. First make stepping stone molds. Hold the marker flat on top of a 3-inch-high can or box

so that the tip touches the side of the bucket. Holding the marker flat, and keeping the tip in contact with the side of the bucket, slowly turn the bucket so that the marker makes a straight horizontal line all around the circumference of the bucket. Look at the photograph marked 1 on page 42.

2. Make a second horizontal line 3 inches up from the first line using the same process as in step 1, but this time with a 6-inch-high can or box or a stack of two 3-inch-high cans.

3. Ask an adult to help you use a hacksaw to saw the bucket into three rings along the lines. Then saw off the bottom of the bucket from the bottom ring by sawing ¼-inch up from the bottom. Look at the photograph marked 2 on page 42.

4. Place the molds down on the plywood. If the bucket you used had sloping or tapering sides, each ring will have one circle slightly larger than the other. (This will be the circle that was higher up on the bucket.) It's important that you put the molds on the plywood with the bigger circles facing down; otherwise, it will be very

hard to lift the molds off without crumbling the concrete.

5. Now mix the concrete. Pour a 3-inch layer of dry concrete mix into the tub or wheelbarrow. Pile the concrete mix into a hill, and make a crater in the top of the hill. Pour around 2 cups of water into the crater. Mix the dry concrete into the water, adding more water as you need to. Be sure to scrape the sides and bottom to get all the dry powder mixed in. **1** To test the consistency of the concrete, make a v-shaped cut in a small mound of the mix with the trowel. If the mix is

46

5

too dry, the cut walls will crumble. If the mix is too wet, the cut will melt back into the mound. If the mix is just right, the v-shape will hold. You may need to add more concrete or more water until you get the right consistency.

6. Grease the inside of each mold with petroleum jelly or motor oil.

7. Fill the molds with concrete mix, patting and smoothing as you go so that the bottoms and sides of the molds will be as smooth as the tops. When the molds are around 1-½ inches to 2 inches thick, smooth the tops. **2**

8. Now you can decorate the cement with shells and/or rocks. Press down hard enough so that the rocks or shells are partly buried in the concrete. **3**

9. Drape the sheet of plastic over the molds. **4** After two or

Watching Bugs and Other Small Critters

Your yard is full of tiny interesting creatures that crawl, slither, hop, skitter, and scurry. Most of them carry on their lives out of sight, hidden in grass or beneath rocks or logs or among leaves on the forest floor. One way to get a better look is to catch them in a pitfall trap.

To make one, you'll need a medium-size can or jar at least six inches deep. (A wide-mouth quart jar—the kind used for canning vegetables—is perfect.) Now dig a hole and bury the jar so that its open end is exactly even with the ground. Be sure to firmly press the dirt down all around the jar right up to the rim. Next, make a roof for the trap; place three or four rocks around the hole, and lay a board or large flat rock over them so that it rests about one-half inch over the jar's mouth.

Insects and other ground creatures will crawl under the roof, fall into the jar, and won't be able to crawl out because of the trap's smooth sides. The roof helps keep rain out of the container, and stops mice and birds from stealing your catch.

Check your traps every few hours to see what's inside. Do you capture more bugs in the morning, afternoon, or evening? Do you catch different kinds at certain times of the day?

Try putting traps in several places—the garden, the woods, under bushes, at the edge of the lawn. What sorts of creatures do you find in each one? Put bits of bread, cheese, or fruit in the jars. Which baits are most popular?

Don't forget to check your traps at least once a day, and always be sure to let the captives go once you've had a chance to study them. Also, when you're done with a trap remember to take the jar out of the ground and fill the hole with soil.

three hours, you can remove the stones from the molds. Simply lift up the rings. **5** Then lightly spray the stones with water, and cover them up again with the piece of plastic. Put the molds under the plastic to help hold it off the stepping stones. It will take five to seven days for the stepping stones to cure and dry completely. If the weather is dry, spray the stones with water several times a day while they are drying. Keep them covered with plastic so they don't dry too fast. Slow drying makes stronger concrete.

10. Clean your hands and the tools with water right away before the concrete dries.

Mint Leaf Candies

These are the coolest, most delicately flavored mints you'll ever taste, and you can make them in a just a few minutes with fresh mint leaves from your garden.

What You'll Need

Fresh mint leaves, picked on a
sunny morning after the dew
has dried
The white of 1 egg
2 bowls
A fork
1 cup of granulated sugar
Waxed paper
A tin with a lid

What to Do

1. Beat the egg white with the fork until the white becomes slightly bubbly.
2. Make sure each mint leaf is dry. Then dip it in egg white so that the leaf is completely coated on both sides.
3. Now dip each wet leaf in sugar until it is completely coated.
4. Lay the sugary leaves on waxed paper to dry. Cover them with another piece of waxed paper. You can dry them in a warm, dry room for a couple of hours, or you can put them in a slightly warm oven (225 degrees F.) with the door left ajar for about 15 minutes, and then let them finish drying in a warm, dry room.
5. When the leaves are dry and brittle, store them between layers of waxed paper in a tin with a lid.

Herbal Vinegars

Herbal vinegars make salads and cooked vegetables taste extra special. They are a nice way to save a little bit of summer to give to your family and friends during the winter. It takes six weeks to make this vinegar, so start early if you want to give bottles away as Holiday gifts

What You'll Need

A clove of garlic

A nonaluminum, 2-quart or larger pot

A large canning jar with a lid or a screw ring

Several perfect fresh sprigs of whichever herb you want to use *

A wooden spoon

Plastic wrap

A quart of white wine or apple cider vinegar

3 or 4 glass bottles with corks that fit them

Tongs

A small plastic funnel

A paper coffee filter

Harvest the herbs early on a sunny morning. Rosemary, thyme, oregano, fennel, tarragon, and basil are some herbs that make good vinegar.

What to Do

1. Simmer the clove of garlic in a little water in the pot for two minutes. Put the garlic clove into the canning jar. (It will kill any bacteria that might spoil the vinegar.)
2. Add the herb sprigs to the jar. Crush them with the wooden spoon to release their flavor.
3. Heat the white wine or apple cider vinegar in the pot (empty out the garlic water first) until it begins to boil. Pour the hot vinegar on top of the herbs in the canning jar.
4. Place a piece of plastic wrap over the jar opening before screwing on the ring or lid. (The plastic wrap is necessary to keep the vinegar from rusting the metal lid.)
5. Put the jar of vinegar in a cool dark place for six weeks.
6. After the six weeks are up, sterilize the three or four glass bottles by boiling them in an upright position for 15 minutes in a large pot filled with water. Be very careful handling hot bottles. Ask an adult to help you lift them out of the water with tongs.
7. When the bottles have cooled enough that you can handle them, strain the vinegar into the bottles through a funnel lined with a paper coffee filter. This will be a slow job.
8. Add a fresh sprig of herb to each bottle, and then tightly cork the bottles.

Rose Petal Jam & Decorated Lid

Rose petal jam sounds like something from a fairy tale! You'll enjoy the delicate rose-honey flavor of this jewel-colored delicacy. The recipe makes one small jar of jam. If you want to make enough to save or to give away, triple the recipe, and be sure to sterilize the jars and lids by boiling them in a large pot of water for 15 minutes before filling them.

What You'll Need

4 cups of red or pink strong-smelling rose petals from roses that have NOT been sprayed
A large bowl
Water
Several paper towels
A 1-quart-size pot
¼ cup sugar
⅓ cup honey
Juice of ½ a lemon
A large spoon
A clean jar with a lid
A 5-by-5-inch square of heavy wrapping paper or wallpaper
A pencil
Scissors
12 inches of fancy string or ribbon

What to Do

1. Pick the petals from the roses, breaking off the white part of each petal where it was joined to the rose.
2. Put the petals in the bowl, and pour water over them to clean them. Spread them on a piece of paper towel to dry.
3. Put the petals in the pot with about ¼ cup of water, and simmer them for about five minutes, until they are tender.
4. Add the sugar, half the honey, and the lemon juice; simmer

this mixture until the jam thickens a little. This will take about 15 minutes.

5. Remove the pot from the stove, and stir in the rest of the honey. The jam will thicken as it cools.

6. Spoon the jam into the jar. Screw the cap on the jar and store it in the refrigerator.

7. If you want to make a fancy cap for the jar, cut a circle about twice as big as the circle of the lid from a piece of wrapping paper or wallpaper. **1**

8. Center this circle on the lid.

Hold it down with one hand while you fold pleats all around the part of the paper circle that sticks out beyond the jar lid. **2**

9. Tie string or ribbon around the side of the jar lid over the paper, holding the pleats in place.

10. Trim the edges to even them up if necessary. Turn the brim of the pleated cap up or down.

Incredible (But True!) Hummingbird Facts

Who says you have to be big to be impressive? Hummingbirds are the smallest birds in the world. And almost everything about them is amazing!

The tiniest bird on earth is the Cuban bee hummingbird. From the tip of its bill to the end of its tail, it's only about two inches long. And it weighs just 1/16 of an ounce—less than a U.S. penny!

Even an average size hummingbird is very small. Black-chinned and ruby-throated hummingbirds (the two most common kinds in North America) are just over three inches long and weigh about as much as three paper clips.

Hummingbirds are the only birds in the world that can fly not only forward but also backward and sideways and can hover (stay in one place in the air) like a helicopter. To make a quick getaway, a hummer can even flip over and fly upside down!

The wings of a hummingbird beat so fast humans can't see them. In the time that it takes you to say the word "hummingbird" (about one second) a hovering hummer beats its wings 55 times. And when it's flying fast, its wings beat 200 times a second!

The hummingbird's heart is the largest (compared to its body size) of all warm-blooded animals. It beats 500 to 1,200 times a minute. (Yours beats 60 to 100 times a minute.)

To keep their fast-moving bodies fueled, hummingbirds eat almost constantly. Every day, a hummingbird visits between 1,000 and 2,000 flowers and drinks more than half its weight in nectar. It also gobbles up small insects and spiders. If a grown man burned energy as fast as a hummingbird, he'd have to eat 285 pounds of hamburger a day to keep from losing weight!

A hummingbird's tongue is forked and fringed at the tip, and twice as long as its bill. It slurps up nectar at a rate of 13 licks a second!

In very hot weather, hummingbirds cool themselves by panting like a dog.

Hummingbird eggs are half an inch long and look like small beans. Brand-new baby hummingbirds are the size of a bumblebee. By the time they're three weeks old, they're almost as big as the mother and ready to start flying.

A hummingbird's nest is a tiny cup made of moss and plant fluff woven together with spider's silk. At first, it's about an inch high and one or two inches wide. But as the baby birds inside it grow, the nest stretches to make more room. By the time the birds are ready to fly, the nest is almost flat.

Even though they're small, hummingbirds are tough. To defend their territory, they'll fight hawks, owls, cats, or even people. Some live 15,000 feet up in the Andes Mountains. Others fly very long distances. Ruby-throated hummingbirds fly 500 miles nonstop across the Gulf of Mexico to migrate to and from North America. And twice a year, rufous hummingbirds travel 2,500 miles between Central America and Alaska!

There are 340 different kinds of hummingbirds in the world, and they all live only in the Western Hemisphere. Europeans had never seen a hummingbird until a French explorer spotted one in the New World in 1558.

Garden Trellis

Tomatoes and peas are some of the plants that do well when given something to climb on. This garden trellis is easy to make out of branches that you can collect around your yard or neighborhood. Green branches are necessary for the rounded arches. If you are saving up branches and are afraid your arch pieces might dry before you have enough wood to build the trellis, tie the ends of each green branch together so the branch will dry in an arch shape.

What You'll Need

A saw

Heavy-duty branch clippers

3 straight pieces of branch, each about 2 inches in diameter and about 3 feet long

A shovel or a posthole digger

A piece of plastic, such as an old shower curtain or a large garbage bag

Scissors

About 100 feet of jute or similar rope

2 fairly straight branches, each about 1-½ inches in diameter and 6 feet to 8 feet long *

3 flexible green branches about 1 inch in diameter and 8 to 10 feet long. **

If you can't find branches this long, you can use 4 branches, each about 1-½ inches in diameter and 4 feet to 5 feet long.

**Thick grapevines or wisteria vines work very well, also. If you want to change the design of the trellis, make a drawing of what you want the arches to look like, and collect however many and whatever length of flexible arch branches you will need. Remember to tie arch-branch ends together, if you need to store them for a while before building the trellis.*

What to Do

1. This project should be done with one or preferably two friends to help you. The first step is to dig three 10-inch-deep holes about 6 inches wide in the location where you want the finished trellis to be. (Adults are pretty useful for getting a hole started). **1** Place the trellis in a sunny garden, leaving enough space in front of it for full-grown tomato or other plants.

   The three holes need to be dug in a straight line, spaced 4 feet apart. As you dig, place the soil from each hole on the piece of plastic, which you

have spread out on the ground nearby. After you've dug the hole and have placed one of the 3-foot pieces of branch upright in it, it will be easy to scrape the soil back into the hole and press it around the upright branch. Step on the filled-in soil to press it around each branch. The branches should not wiggle but should stand firmly. **2**

2. Cut the rope into eighteen 6-foot lengths.

3. With your friend or friends holding the first long cross branch in place, tie one end of that branch near the top of the first upright branch.

4. Now tie the same cross branch to the middle and other end upright branches. **3**

5. Repeat steps 3 and 4 with the other long cross branch. If you are using two shorter cross branches, tie the first to one end and the middle upright. **4** Tie the second one to the middle and other end upright. Repeat this step for the other two 4-foot branches.

6. Tie the arch branches so that they form curving arches between the uprights. Be sure to pull all knots tight so that the branches are firmly tied together. **5** and **6**

7. As your plants grow, use soft twine or thin strips of rags to tie them loosely to the trellis.

Hooray for Flying Fur!

There are lots of different kinds of mammals in our world—mice, foxes, tigers, whales, elephants, walruses, and people, just to name a few. But did you know that of all the types, or species, of mammals on earth, one out of every four is some sort of bat? There are over 1,000 kinds of bats. And each one is different.

Bats are the only animals with fur that fly. (Flying squirrels don't really; they just glide from a high place to a lower place.) Most bats have furry bodies that are either brown or gray. But others have orange, black, tan, or even white fur. Some bats have long, pointed ears or wrinkled, odd-shaped noses (or both!). A few have cute teddy bear faces, while others look more like weird winged aliens from far-away galaxies.

Sometimes you can get an idea of what a bat looks like by the name people have given it, such as spear-nosed bat, dog-faced bat, mustache bat, horseshoe bat, hammer-headed bat, bulldog bat, and slit-faced bat.

The biggest bat in the world weighs over three pounds and is called the giant flying fox. It has reddish fur and a foxlike face, but it also has something no fox ever dreamed of: huge wings nearly six feet wide from tip to tip! The world's smallest bat lives in Thailand and is called Kitti's hog-nosed bat. Its wings measure only six inches. And its body is the size and weight of a jelly bean!

Bats are shy creatures, and most kinds come out only at night. So you may never have seen one. But unless your home is in the Arctic or Antarctic, there are almost surely bats living near you. They live almost everywhere in the world.

Don't let the idea of fuzzy flyers flitting through the skies over your backyard at night frighten you, though. Bats may look scary, but they're actually quite harmless. It's true there are a few kinds called vampire bats that bite animals and then suck up small amounts of the blood, like oversized mosquitoes. But they live in remote parts of the world. And besides, they almost never bite people.

Some species of bats sip nectar and pollen from flowers. A few kinds that live in Mexico and South America swoop down over water and catch fish for their meals. But most bats just eat insects—lots of insects. Scientists say that bug-eating bats gobble up about half their body weight in insects every night. If you had as big an appetite as a bat and weighed about 80 pounds, you'd eat 40 pounds of food for supper. That's a lot of pizza!

Moths, mosquitoes, and beetles are favorite bat food. A single little brown bat (one of the most common bats in North America) can eat 600 mosquitoes in just one hour. The 20 million bats that live in the world's largest bat colony, in Bracken Cave, Texas, eat more than 200 tons of insects every night! And remember, there are billions of bats on earth.

It's a good thing our world is such a batty place, or we'd be up to our ears in bugs!

Garden Markers

Use these markers at the head of each row of vegetable seeds that you sow. They are a weatherproof and attractive way to remind you what you planted where.

What You'll Need

1 each of the vegetables you plan
   to grow in your garden
A sharp knife
A cutting board
Acrylic paints
A brush
Paper towels
Scratch paper
¼-Inch plywood, smoothly sanded,
   cut to 4 inches by 5 inches,
   1 piece for each marker
A flat stick 10 inches long for
   each marker
Sandpaper
Waterproof glue
Urethane varnish
A brush for varnish

What to Do

1. Slice the vegetables in half lengthwise. Be very careful to make a perfectly straight cut. The cut vegetable will print best if it is perfectly flat.
2. Paint the flat surface thinly with acrylic paint. If your vegetable has both leaves and roots, paint the leaves one color and the roots another.
3. Press the vegetable down on some scratch paper. Press over it with a paper towel. Lift the vegetable and check the print. Experiment until you like the way the print looks.
4. Now make prints on the smooth plywood. Let them dry.
5. Sand the edges of each marker.

6. Glue a stick to the back of each marker. Make sure you glue at least 3 inches of the stick to the plywood.

7. Paint urethane varnish over both the sides and all the edges of the marker and stick to protect them from wet weather.

Wild Vegetables

You'd never know it to look at them, but those mild-mannered vegetables you see in supermarkets and backyard gardens have a really wild past. In fact, all the vegetables we eat today started out as wild plants.

Early humans soon learned which plants were good to eat. So as tribes roamed from place to place hunting and fishing for food, they also kept an eye out for their favorite vegetables, seeds, berries, bulbs, and roots.

Nobody knows exactly how these ancient wanderers learned to grow their own vegetables. Maybe someone tossed leftover roots or seeds on a garbage pile and noticed the plants that sprouted seemed especially healthy. Rotted garbage, after all, makes good fertilizer (today, we call it compost). Perhaps, later, someone in the tribe figured out how to plant crops by poking a hole in the soil with a stick and putting a seed there.

Eventually, people were able to stay in one place and raise their own food instead of constantly searching. Each year, they would save the seed from the biggest and best plants in their gardens to grow the next year. That's how wild plants gradually became tame. It's also why today's vegetables are much bigger and tastier than were their long-ago ancestors.

When ancient people did travel, they took their favorite vegetables or seeds with them. In this way vegetables from one part of the world came to be planted in other places far away.

Early explorers helped to spread the world's once-wild vegetables too. When Columbus returned to Spain from the New World in 1493, for instance, he brought all sorts of food plants that people in Europe had never seen.

One of those plants was corn. Seven thousand years ago, natives in central Mexico ate wild corn. The cobs were just an inch long and had only about a dozen kernels! By the time Columbus arrived in the New World, though, native Americans were growing corn that looked similar to today's corn.

Spanish explorers also found potatoes and tomatoes in the New World. Both vegetables started out as wild plants growing in the mountains of Peru. Wild tomatoes were red or yellow and not much bigger than a marble. In South America today, there are still hundreds of different kinds of wild potatoes, in all sorts of shapes and sizes and colors. Some are purple and the size of a Ping-Pong ball. Some are brown or black and look like sausages. And they're all relatives of the big, white, tame potato most of us now eat.

In fact, the wild cousins of many supermarket vegetables can still be found in their homelands. Celery grows wild in marshes in Asia and northern Africa. Cucumbers thrive in the foothills of the Himalaya mountains. Wild asparagus is so common in some parts of western Asia that cattle eat it just like grass. And in India, wild eggplants are thought of as weeds.

Next time you see vegetables in a garden or grocery store, think about their wild past. Here are some other common vegetables and the surprisingly far-away places they came from.

Vegetable	Came From Wild Plants In
Beets	southern Europe
Broccoli	northern Mediterranean coast
Carrots	central Asia
Kidney beans	central Mexico
Lettuce	Egypt, eastern Mediterranean coast
Lima beans	Peru
Peanuts	Brazil, Peru
Peas	southeastern Europe and western Asia
Peppers	South America
Radishes	China
Soybeans	India
Spinach	Iran, western Asia
Squash	Mexico, South America
Turnips	eastern Europe, Siberia

Potpourri

Potpourri was used to sweeten the air inside homes long before anyone invented air fresheners. To make potpourri, first collect and dry materials that both smell and look good. The natural materials listed below are favored in making potpourri but don't stop there! Let your own nose and eyes be your guides.

What You'll Need

Materials that smell good, such as roses, peonies, lavender, rosemary, spearmint, thyme, basil, sage, pine needles and cones, bay leaves, orange and lemon peels, cloves, scented geranium leaves, cinnamon sticks, and vanilla beans

Materials that look good, such as woodruff, black-eyed Susan flowers, marigolds, cornflowers, lamb's ear leaves, money plant, berries, tiny cones, and statice flowers

Rubber bands

An old window screen or a large, flat and wide basket

A large shoe box

Aluminum foil

Tape

5 cups of borax (available in the grocery store where detergents are sold)

5 cups of plain white cornmeal (NOT self-rising or cornmeal mix)

A large bowl

A wooden spoon

A teaspoon measure

A 1-cup measure

Fragrance fixative such as ground orris root—1 teaspoon for each cup of dried material *

Jars with lids

Small baskets and bowls

You can get orris root at natural food stores and at craft supply stores.

What to Do

1. Collect materials to dry on sunny mornings right after the dew has dried. Pick flowers and leaves that are as near to perfect as you can find, without insect damage or bruises.

2. Dry the materials in these ways:

Hanging

Rubber band several flowers or herb sprigs together, and hang them from nails, upside down, in a shady, dry, airy place such as a screened porch.

Depending on the humidity and on the kind of material, it will take between one and three weeks to dry materials this way.

Air Drying
Spread blossoms, petals, or leaves in a single layer on an old window screen or in a wide, flat basket. Place the screen or basket in a shady, dry, well-ventilated (but not breezy) room for a week or two.

Borax and Cornmeal Drying
Tape aluminum foil to the inside of a large shoe box. Mix the borax and cornmeal in a large bowl. Spread a 1-inch-deep layer of this mixture in the bottom of the shoe box. Lay flowers on top of the mixture,

with their stems going the same way. Fill in around the flowers with more borax and cornmeal, being sure to pour the mixture inside large blossoms. The mixture should touch all surfaces so that it can absorb moisture from all parts of the flowers. Be sure the flowers don't touch each other. You can make several layers of flowers. Cover the box and check it every week. Most flowers take between one and three weeks to dry completely.

3. When your materials are dry, mix them together in the large bowl. Add different materials as well as powdered spices until the potpourri looks and smells good to you.

4. Add 1 teaspoon of ground orris root for every cup of

dry materials. Stir the mixture gently.

5. Store potpourri in closed jars until you want to use it. Set it out in baskets or bowls to sweeten the air in a room.

Fancy Covers for Potpourri Jar Lids

If you plan to give your fragrant potpourri as a gift, you'll want to find a pretty jar to store it in, and then dress up the lid. Pressed flowers are a nice way to make a fancy cover for the lid. See page 73 for instructions on how to press flowers.

What You'll Need

An assortment of pressed flowers
A pencil
A sheet of white (or light-colored) paper
Scissors
A 12-inch-long piece of clear self-adhesive paper
White craft glue
A piece of raffia or ribbon, or 12 inches of white plastic tape

What to Do

1. Trace around the lid you want to cover on the piece of white or light-colored paper. Cut out this circle, and arrange pressed flowers on it.
2. Cut out a circle of clear self-adhesive paper, 1 inch bigger all around than the jar lid.
3. Peel the backing from the sticky paper, carefully center it above the paper circle, and lay it down, pressing the flowers to the paper circle. Press the clear paper down over the flowers so that it sticks to the paper circle and the flowers. **1**
4. Lift the circle, and make a series of cuts from the edge of the clear paper to the edge of the white or light-colored paper. Remove the jar lid from the jar. Place the paper circle centered over the lid. Press the clear plastic tabs that you cut around and under the lid to attach the cover to the lid. Screw the lid back onto the jar.
5. Glue a piece of raffia or ribbon around the rim of the lid, or cover it with a piece of plastic tape. If the rim of the lid is a color that you like, just tie a ribbon around the neck of the jar. **2**

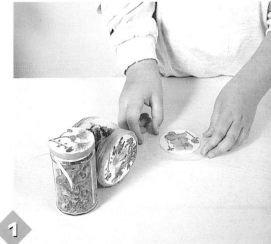

Why Do Flowers Have Colors and Different Shapes?

People use flowers to make their homes and yards cheerier and more colorful and fragrant. But in nature, a flower's main purpose in life is to make seeds that will grow new plants. To do that, most kinds of flowers need help. They need an insect or bird or some other creature to carry pollen from one flower to another of the same type. Biologists call that *pollination*.

Here's how it works: An insect lands on a flower to sip nectar. While it's drinking or looking for the nectar, it bumps into the pollen-making part of the flower called the stamen, and gets some dusty pollen on its body. Later, the insect flies to another flower of the same sort to slurp up more nectar. As it's crawling around, it brushes against a special flower part called the *stigma*. Some of the pollen on its body rubs off and gets stuck on the stigma. Presto. That flower becomes pollinated and is now able to make seeds.

Nothing at all happens, though, if the insect is the wrong size or shape to brush against the right parts of the flowers. And nothing happens, either, if the insect gets pollen from one kind of flower and then brushes it off onto a different kind. No pollination. No seed. The pollen is wasted.

That's why different types of flowers use color, shape, and other tricks to attract just the insects or other creatures that "fit" their parts and won't waste their pollen. Flowers that depend on bees, for

instance, open during the day (when bees are out), and are usually brightly colored—yellow, blue, white, or pink. That's because bees have excellent color vision. In fact, bees can see some colors, called ultraviolet colors, that people can't. Flowers that look plain white to us are blue-green to bees.

One color that bees and many other insects can't see is red. Most red flowers are pollinated by hummingbirds instead. The flowers hide their nectar way at the back or in deep tubes, where only a hummingbird's long tongue can reach. As the tiny bird zips from flower to flower poking its beak into the blossoms, it picks up pollen on its head or breast.

Moths and butterflies also have a long tongue, called a *proboscis* (pro-BAH-sis), for sipping nectar. They use it like a drinking straw. Flowers

pollinated by moths and butterflies often are shaped like a bell or funnel, and store their nectar too far back for shorter-tongued insects to reach.

Butterflies are attracted to most colors, but they especially like yellow, purple, and blue flowers. Plants that are pollinated by moths open their flowers at night and are white or some other light, easy-to-see-in-the-dark color. Sometimes the flowers have a strong aroma, too, to help moths find them.

Some flowers even give their pollinators a treasure map that points the way to nectar. The patterns of spots, stripes, or lines on flowers are known as "nectar guides". They lead to the part of the blossom where the nectar is located. When an insect lands in search of a snack, it just follows the dotted line to a sweet treat!

Fish Print T-Shirts

You and a friend can have lots of fun on a rainy afternoon making fish print T-shirts. Print a jumping fish, two fish chasing each other, or a whole school of fish dreamily swimming over the shoulder of your shirt!

What You'll Need

A 100% cotton T-shirt (white or light-colored)

1 or 2 fish, cleaned and scaled, but with the heads on *

Acrylic paints

3 or 4 soft paintbrushes of different sizes, from a 1-½ inch flat brush to a round, fine-tipped brush

A container of water

A palette made out of an old aluminum baking sheet or pie pan

A stack of old newspapers opened out and torn in half lengthwise along the center fold

A spray bottle of water

Order whole fish from the seafood department in a grocery store or from a seafood store. Sometimes you can get these fish for a good price if you let the seafood person know that you will be using it for a craft project and don't plan to eat it.

What to Do

1. Slip a piece of newspaper flat inside the T-shirt so that the paint from the print won't bleed through to the back of the shirt.

2. Place two pieces of newspaper side by side on your worktable or countertop. Place the fish on one of the pieces. Keep the other piece clean for now.

3. Mix paint colors on the palette; use them straight from the tubes without adding any water. If the paints begin to dry while you are working, lightly spray the whole palette with water.

4. Paint the entire top surface of the fish. Use a thin, even layer of paint, except where you want to emphasize something; there you can use a slightly heavier layer of paint. Don't use too much paint, though, or

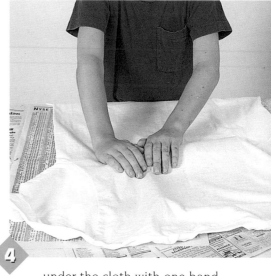

the print will smear. **1** Use the thin pointed brush to lightly encircle or paint the eye. To paint the fins, use your fingers to fan them out while you brush paint on. Work quickly before the paint dries. **2** If you are using two fish, it helps to have a friend working with you so you can get both fish painted before the paint dries.

5. When the fish is completely painted, carefully lift it by the tip of the tail and under the mouth, and place it on the clean piece of newspaper that you have saved. If you are using two fish, arrange them the way you want them to be on the T-shirt.

6. It's a good idea to do a few practice prints on old T-shirts or on soft rags, such as cut up old bed sheets. It takes a bit of practice to figure out how to get the effects you want. After each print, either paint right over the fish, or, if there is too much wet paint on the fish, wash it off under running water and blot it dry with paper towels before going on to the next print.

7. Once you have the hang of fish printing and are ready to print on a T-shirt, hold the shirt and the newspaper inside it by the shoulders with its back facing you (if you want to print on the front). Position the shirt over the fish, being careful not to crease or fold the cloth. Gently drape the T-shirt over the fish. You cannot move the shirt once it has touched the fish. **3**

8. Rub the T-shirt over the fish with your hands. Press gently all over the fish. **4** Wherever you can feel the fish, rub and press gently. You can reach

under the cloth with one hand to fan out the fins and carefully rub them with the other hand. Be careful not to shift or move the shirt! You can check the progress of the print by carefully peeling back one corner at a time while holding the rest of the shirt in position.

9. When you have completely rubbed or burnished the fish,

Fins, Gills, and...Yipe! What's That Stripe?

Look at almost any fish, and what do you see? Eyes and a mouth, for seeing and eating. Fins for helping to push and steer through water. Gills for getting oxygen from water to breathe. And . . . what's this? A thin line or stripe that runs from head to tail along both sides of its body. What's that for?

At first you might think it's only a decoration, a sort of fishy racing stripe. Or maybe you'd guess it's just a simple marking, like a leopard's spots or the rings on a raccoon's tail. But actually, that thin stripe marks an important sixth sense that only fish have. Scientists call the stripe the *lateral line*.

If you looked at it under a microscope, you'd see that the lateral line is really a row of small holes, or pores, in the fish's skin. The pores lead to a shallow groove just beneath the skin. The groove is full of tiny sense organs that are connected to the fish's brain.

Fish use the lateral line to sense movements and vibrations in the water around them. Everything that moves in water makes waves, just like you make a wave when you're in the bathtub and move your hand (or wiggle your toes) underwater. The lateral line can feel even very slight waves or changes in pressure in the water. Fish don't have good eyesight. But they do have lateral lines to help them "see" the waves and vibrations created by other creatures, so they can tell if an enemy is nearby. And they can find smaller fish and other food to eat, even in dark or muddy water.

Scientists think the lateral line also helps keep a fish from bumping into things. When a fish swims, it makes its own waves. When those waves hit an object and bounce back, the fish can sense the vibrations and can then steer in a different direction. That explains why fish in an aquarium never run into the glass walls and why even blind fish don't crash into obstacles. They use their lateral lines as radar.

Have you ever watched a school of fish? They all swim together at exactly the same speed and stay exactly the same distance apart—even if they're startled and suddenly turn in a different direction. That's because, in a way, they're all connected by their lateral lines: each fish can sense the waves and vibrations created by its neighbors. So when one schoolmate changes speed or direction, its buddies know it and all change too, instantly.

Lateral lines come in lots of shapes and patterns. Some are silvery, some are dark, and others look like dots or dashes. A few are impossible to see without a microscope. Some lateral lines, such as the great white shark's, are super-straight. The bluegill's is curved, to match its saucer-shaped body. All lateral lines, though, serve the same purpose: not as the snazzy decoration that most people think, but to help fish survive.

peel the shirt off and spread it out to dry. Remove the newspaper from inside the shirt after the print is dry. **5**

10. The print will dry completely in about 30 minutes. It will probably smell a little fishy. Wait 24 hours before washing it in cold water with a mild detergent in a washing machine. It's okay to put it in the dryer.

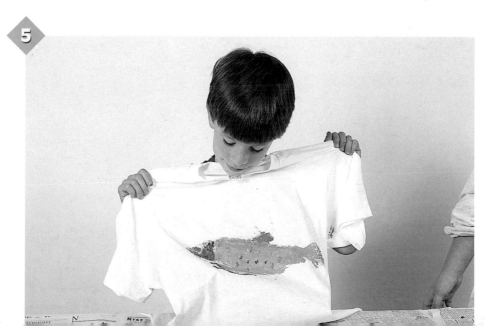

Twig Wreath

Celebrate spring or summer with a wreath that you've made out of flowers and twigs.

What You'll Need

About 80 twigs, each about 4 to 5 inches long, with lots of forks and interesting bends and shapes

16 stems of dried flowers (see directions on page 59 for drying flowers)

16 small rubber bands

A roll of thin, green floral wire

Scissors

Plant pruners

A wire coat hanger

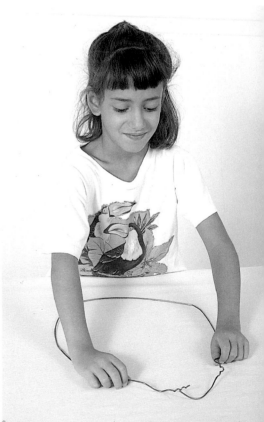

1

66

What to Do

1. Bend the coat hanger into a circle. Unwind the hook, and twist the wire from the hook to form a closing for the circle of wire. Or, you can bend each end to form a small hook and interlock them to make the circle. **1**

2. Assemble 16 bunches of twigs, each with five twigs and one stem of dried flowers. Cut twigs with pruners so each is about 6 inches long. Fasten each bunch with a rubber band at the stem end. **2**

3. Attach the bunches to the wire circle with floral wire. **3** Overlap each bunch so that it hides the rubber band of the bunch next to it. Work around the circle so that the entire circle is covered with bunches of twigs and flowers. If there are any places where the rubber bands show, poke in extra dried flowers to hide them.

4. Make a loop of floral wire at the top to hang the wreath from.

Blackberry & Onion Skin Dyes

Natural basketry materials have beautiful colors of their own, but sometimes it's fun to add color for a particular effect. You can dye materials yourself using harmless natural dyes. The colors won't be as bright as those from commercial dyes and they will fade somewhat over time, but the colors from natural dyes are beautiful and perfectly suited to natural basketry materials.

What You'll Need

Materials to dye, such as daylily leaves, cattail leaves, or iris leaves *

3 cups of ripe blackberries OR a couple of handfuls of red or yellow onion skins **

3 tablespoons of alum ***

A 2-cup glass measuring cup

A tablespoon measuring spoon

A very large enameled steel or oven-safe glass pot (1-gallon size)

An old long-handled wooden spoon or stick to stir with

A potato masher

A quart-sized cooking pot

A 5-gallon plastic bucket

A quart-sized jar with lid

A plastic funnel

A package of cheesecloth (available at the grocery store)

Scissors

A soup spoon

With this recipe, you can dye enough materials to make a hat or a medium-sized basket. To dye more materials, double the recipe or dye materials in different batches.

*** Clean out the onion bin at your local grocery store.*

*** Alum is the short name for potassium aluminum sulfate. You can buy it at a craft supply store or from a pharmacist.*

What to Do

1. First you must prepare the basketry materials so that the dye will bond to them. This process is called *mordanting*.

The mordant that you will use, alum, is not as harmful as many mordants, but you should still be careful not to

taste either dry or liquid mordant, and to keep it out of your eyes. Ask an adult to help you with mordanting.

Dissolve 3 tablespoons of alum in ½ gallon of water in the gallon-sized pot. Heat this until it just begins to boil, and then remove the pot from the heat.

2. Pour 1 gallon of hot tap water into the bucket. Add the dissolved alum and water. Stir the resulting mixture with the wooden spoon or stick. Place the basketry materials in the pot. Use the stick or spoon to spread out the materials so that they are all under the alum water and not clumped together. Let this sit for 12 hours or overnight.

3. Prepare dyestuff (either berries or onion skins) by placing them in the quart-sized cooking pot and adding just enough water to cover them. The less water you use the stronger the dye liquid, so just put in enough water to cover the materials. Heat the dyestuff until it comes to a boil; then turn down the heat and simmer the berries or onion skins for about 45 minutes. Add more water if the mixture gets too dry.

4. After the berries have simmered for a few minutes, you can use the potato masher to break them up and help the juice come out. Keep simmering the dyestuff until the liquid in the pot is dark, and then let it cool for half an hour.

5. Place the funnel in the glass jar. Cut a double thickness of cheesecloth about 12 inches by 12 inches. Put the cheesecloth into the funnel as a lining.

6. Pour the berry or onion mush into the cheesecloth-lined funnel. Use the cooking spoon to help press the mush so that the dye liquid strains into the glass jar.

7. Remove the basketry materials from the alum water and wash out the bucket. *Do not rinse the basketry materials.*

8. Fill the bucket with enough hot tap water to just cover the basketry materials (probably about 3 or 4 inches deep). Add the hot dye liquid to this water. If the dye has cooled off, reheat it to simmering before adding it to the water in the bucket. Stir with the wooden spoon or stick to thoroughly mix the dye liquid with the hot water.

9. Now place the basketry materials in the bucket of hot dye. Use the wooden spoon or stick to arrange the materials so that they are spread out and not clumped together. You can dye the material in batches if it seems too crowded.

10. Let the materials sit in the dye for 24 hours. Then rinse them in cool water until the water runs clear. Dry the materials (unless you are going to use them right away) by hanging them over a coat hanger or the back of a chair. Be sure they are completely dry before storing them in a paper bag.

Daylily Leaf Hat

Woven hats are fun to wear and not very hard to make. You can use many kinds of flat dried leaves, as long as they are strong and flexible when wet. The leaves from irises, cattails, and daylilies all work well. To see if a leaf is long enough to use, drape it over your head. Any leaf that drapes from shoulder to shoulder will do very well!

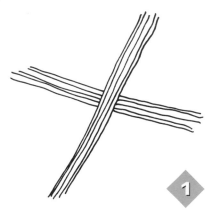

weaver. Fold this weaver in two. Make the fold about one-third of the way down from one end. **2**

You will do a weave called *twining* for the first part of the hat:

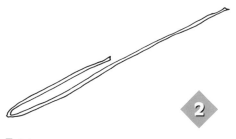

Twining

What You'll Need

About 100 daylily leaves *
A bucket or tub full of water
Something the size of your head
    to shape the hat on **
Scissors

Gather dry leaves from the base of daylily plants after some of the leaves have turned brown. Pull gently and the leaves should come away easily. Store dry daylily leaves in an open paper bag in a dry, shady place. If any leaves are damp, lay them out on a table or countertop to dry before storing them.

** *Try a polystyrene foam wig stand, a large rounded bowl turned upside down, a ball, or another hat.*

What to Do

1. Pick out 32 of the longest, thickest leaves and soak them for about five minutes.
2. Divide the wet leaves into two bunches of 16 leaves each. Straighten the leaves in each bunch so that the ends are together and all the leaves are arranged in the same direction.
3. Make an X by placing the center of one bunch over the center of the other bunch. **1**
4. Put the rest of the leaves in the water to soak while you work. After a few minutes, select a leaf to be the first

a. Slip the folded weaver over one of the crossed bunches of leaves so that the bunch is caught between the folds of the weaver. **3**
b. Twist the weaver around the bunch of leaves one time. **4**
c. Catch the next bunch of leaves

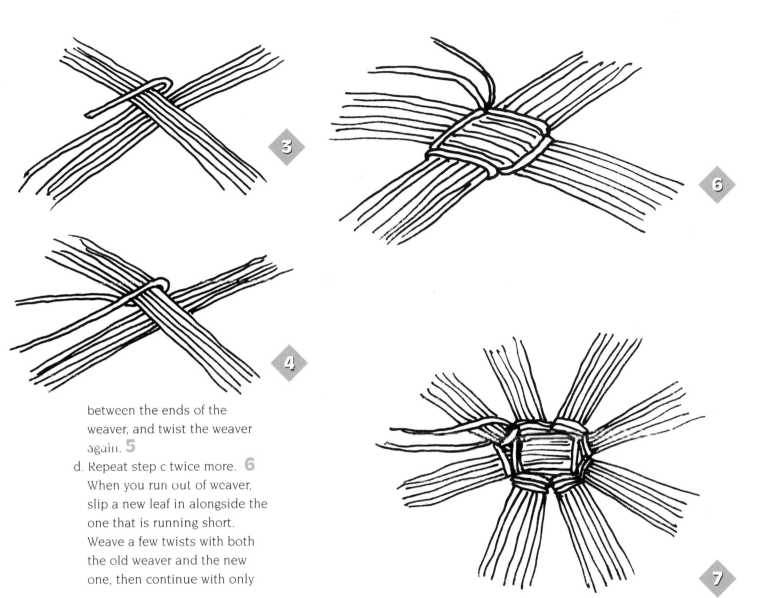

between the ends of the weaver, and twist the weaver again. **5**

d. Repeat step c twice more. **6** When you run out of weaver, slip a new leaf in alongside the one that is running short. Weave a few twists with both the old weaver and the new one, then continue with only

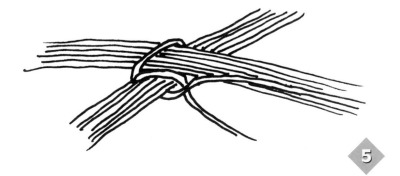

the new weaver when the old one runs out. You should add only one weaver at a time.

3. Do another round of four twin-ings. On the next round after that, divide each bunch of eight leaves into two bunches of four. There will now be eight twinings to a round. **7**

4. Place this hat center on top of your hat form, and twine about 10 more rounds. Press the hat

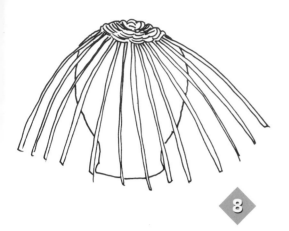

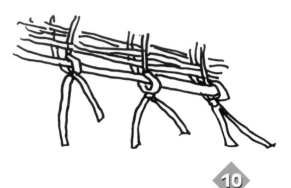

to the form as you work. The form will let you know how loose or how tight the weaving needs to be.

5. On the next row, divide the bunches of four in half again, so that you are now twining 16 bunches to a round. There are two leaves in a bunch now. After a few rounds, you should be ready to begin coming down the sides of the hat form. Adjust the tightness or looseness of your weaving to shape the hat. **8**

6. Once you've begun the sides of the hat, you'll do plain *over-under weaving*. Let one of the two twining weavers run out without replacing it. Now continue with one weaver, going over one bunch and under the next. **9** Add weavers the same way you did when twining.

Over-under Weaving

When doing plain over-under weaving, be sure that you go over one bunch and under the next, and that on the next round you go under the bunches you went over on the last round. If you get the pattern mixed up, fix it by going over the next TWO bunches, and then continuing over one, under one. It doesn't matter if there are some mistakes in the weaving as long as the weave doesn't get too loose and fall apart.

7. If you need to widen the hat, divide the bunches again so that you are now weaving over and under single leaves.

8. When you get to the place where you want to begin the brim of the hat, pick up another weaver, (just stick one end of the leaf in and out a few times so that it is held firmly next to the other weaver) and do two rounds of *twining* to lock in place the weaving you've done so far.

9. If you haven't yet broken down the bunches to single leaves, do so now. Set the hat on a

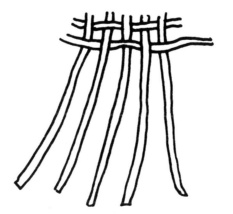

table or countertop to work, with the brim leaves spread out all around the hat. This arrangement will help you shape the flat brim. Weave the brim in plain over-under weave.

10. When the brim is as big as you want it, or when only 2 inches remain of the leaves, stop weaving and tie off the brim. To do this, first finish off the weaver and do not replace it. Then tie each brim leaf to the one next to it in a double knot. If the leaves are dry and brittle, set the whole hat in water for a few minutes to soften the leaves again. Trim the leaf ends to 1 inch. **10**

11. Finish off the hat by sticking a few feathers or a flower in it or by tying a ribbon around the place where the brim starts. If you want to change the shape of the hat or brim, set the hat in water for a few minutes, then shape it with your hands, and let it dry completely.

Pressed Flower Note Cards

These delicate note cards look like you've captured the beauty of summer flowers under a light wrapping of parchment. Pressed flowers come in very handy for a lot of craft projects when you want flowers and leaves that are both dry and flat. The easiest way to press natural materials is to lay them on a paper towel, cover them with another paper towel, and stack a heavy book on top. If you leave them for several days to a week, they should emerge dry and flat—ready to add a touch of the outdoors to many different projects. For other pressed flower and leaf crafts see page 163.

What You'll Need

(For each note card)

2 pieces of 12-by-12-inch waxed paper

Pressed flowers

1 white facial tissue

A soft camel hair lacquer brush (1 inch wide)

A cup or small bowl

White glue mixed half and half with water

A brown paper grocery bag

Scissors

An iron

A piece of 8-½-by-11-inch light-colored drawing or writing paper (or smaller for smaller cards)

A piece of thin satin ribbon or fancy cord 12 inches long

What to Do

1. Lay a piece of waxed paper flat on a countertop or table. Arrange pressed flowers the way you want them to look on the front of the card. Be sure that the flower arrangement is either in the center of the bottom half of the paper or in the center of the right hand half of the paper because you will be folding the paper in half to make the card. **1**

2. Place a single ply of the piece of facial tissue over the waxed paper. Be careful not to move the pressed flower arrangement.

3. Carefully paint over the tissue, flower arrangement, and waxed paper with the mixture of glue and water. In order not to tear the delicate tissue paper, use small, light strokes and don't try to go back over any of the tissue. Be sure to paint the entire tissue, even where there are no flowers.

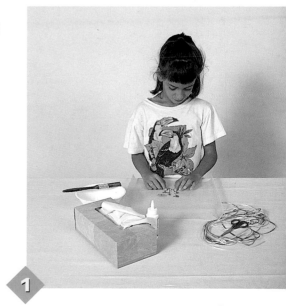

1

The tissue will wrinkle some. The wrinkles will make the paper look like fancy hand-made paper when it is dry. **2**

4. Let this dry overnight.

5. Cut a slit down one side of the grocery bag. Cut off the bottom of the bag so that you can fold it in half and it will lie flat. Place the other piece of waxed paper between the two layers of brown paper. Iron this paper sandwich with a warm iron so that some of the wax will transfer from the waxed paper to the brown papers. **3**

6. Remove the waxed paper from between the sheets of brown paper. Fold the dried tissue paper/flower/waxed paper sandwich in half the way the finished card will be folded. Place it between the sheets of brown paper.

7. Again iron the brown paper. This time the wax will transfer from the brown paper to the tissue paper sandwich and give it a smooth finish.

8. Remove the folded tissue paper sandwich. Fold the piece of colored drawing or writing paper in half and slip it inside the tissue paper sandwich. Trim the tissue paper to fit if necessary. **4**

9. Cut two small v's in the fold of the card about 1 inch apart. **5**

10. Thread ribbon or thin cord through the holes, and tie a bow on the outside of the note card. **6**

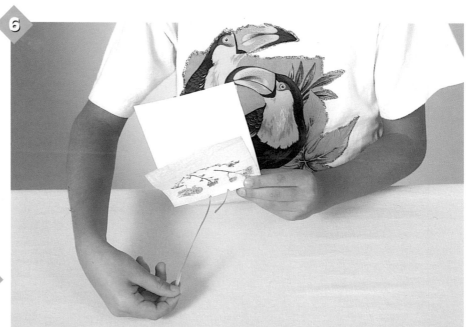

Nature's Papermakers

Most books will tell you that paper was invented in China about 1,800 years ago by a man named Ts'ai Lun. Well, Ts'ai Lun was the first *person* to make real paper. But insects—wasps—have been making paper for millions of years!

Have you tried making the potato paper on page 120? All paper is made pretty much the same way. Wood chips or bits of other plants are crushed and broken up into thousands of stringy pieces, or fibers. Then the fibers are stirred together with water to make pulp, and the gunk is spread out in a thin layer to dry. When the pulp does dry, an interesting thing happens. All the plant fibers stick tightly together.

The result is a strong, flat sheet of we're-not-letting-go-unless-you-pull-us-apart plant fibers: the stuff we call paper. If you tear some paper and look at the ragged edge through a magnifying glass, you can see the fibers.

Wasps go through the same steps to make their paper nests. Worker wasps use their powerful jaws to chew up mouthfuls of wood from dead trees, rotten fence posts, old boards, and other woody materials. As they chew, the wood fibers mix with the wasps' saliva to make— you guessed it: pulp. Then the wasps fly back to the nest and plaster the pulp in place. They spread the pulp out carefully with their jaws, stopping every few minutes to test the layer with their feelers to make sure it's the right thickness.

As each wasp works, it turns its body slightly. That's why paper wasp nests have hundreds of small curved lines on them.

When the pulp dries, it turns into paper tough enough to protect the wasps from rain and wind. In fact, it's so strong you can write or type on it. If you ever find an abandoned wasp nest (make sure it's empty, or you'll get stung!) tear a strip of the paper off and flatten it under a book overnight. Then use a pen or marker to write a note to a friend on it. Also, look at the paper through a magnifying glass. See all the fibers stuck together?

Paper wasps make a simple, open nest that looks like a round upside-down honeycomb hanging from a short stem. (Wasps don't make honey, though; they use the combs for raising young.) Other wasps— hornets and yellow jackets—build layers of combs, one below the other, and surround them in walls of paper. A hornet nest looks like a gray paper ball with a hole in the bottom (or side). Some hornet nests are as big as beach balls and contain thousands of busy wasps!

Because wasps get the wood fibers for their nests from different places, the paper is streaked with different shades of black, gray, and white. Have you ever seen a wasp nest with bands of red or some other bright color? That happens when wasps chew up pieces of painted wood. One kind of South American wasp decorates its home on purpose. It makes a brown paper nest shaped like an upside-down cupcake, and then frosts it with layers of red, pink, and green. And another tropical wasp uses thin bits of mica—a see-through mineral—to give its paper house another invention we humans say we thought of: windows!

Lotus Book

This wonderful book is perfect for keeping a collection of things that make you remember nature—pressed flowers, seeds, bark rubbings, feathers, poems, drawings, or photographs.

What You'll Need

Sheets of 8-½-by-11-inch paper *
2 pieces of 4-½-by-4-½-inch
   corrugated cardboard
A glue stick
2 sheets of 6-by-6-inch
   wrapping paper or other
   decorated paper
2 feet of thin, flat ribbon
Scissors

Typing or copier paper work well. You can get colored sheets from an office supply store.

What to Do

1. Square each sheet of paper by folding. **1** Cut off the leftover piece across the top of the triangle. **2**
2. Each square piece will have a diagonal fold (from corner to corner) from when you

squared it. Fold the paper back
along this fold and press the
crease with your finger to
make it sharp.

3. Unfold the paper and fold it
sharply in half from top to bottom. Press the crease. **3**

4. Keeping the paper folded, fold
it in half the other way. Press
the crease. **4**

5. Unfold the paper. It now has
three creases. Fold it again
along the diagonal crease,
but this time fold it the opposite way.

6. Open out the paper. You'll see
four boxes made by creases.
Two of the boxes have diagonal creases and two don't.
Pinch gently on the sides of
the diagonal creases so that
the two plain boxes fold up
toward each other. **5**

7. Push the two diagonal folds
toward the center and toward
each other. You'll be able to
flatten the two plain boxes
over the creases. **6**

8. Repeat steps 2 through 7 for
each sheet of paper.

9. Place a folded page on the
table in front of you in a diamond position. Keep the two
folded edges to your left and
the open, unfolded edges to
your right.

10. Rub glue stick over the entire
top sheet of the diamond.

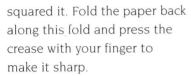

Place another diamond exactly on top of the first one with the edges in the same position. Press down to glue them together.

11. Repeat step 10 until all pages are glued to each other. **7**

12. Cover the two cover boards by placing the cardboard in the middle of the cover paper and drawing tab marks. Cut the cover papers along the tab lines (see page 34, figure 6).

13. Put glue over one entire side of the cardboard and place it, glue side down, centered among the tabs.

14. Put glue on each tab and fold it to glue it to the cover (see page 30, figures 7 and 8).

15. Place the two covers, right sides down, on a table with two of their corners ½ inch apart. **8**

16. Put a strip of glue from corner to corner across the two covers. Place the ribbon across the strip of glue. Be sure to leave ½ inch between the two covers. **9**

17. Put glue all over the top sheet of the pile of glued pages, and press it against the inside front cover. The ribbon will be sandwiched between cover and pages. Repeat this step with the back page and cover.

18. When you open the book, the pages will flower open, giving you four petals on each page for poems, drawings, photos, rubbings, or whatever you want to collect.

Tree Branch Hideaway

There's something wonderfully satisfying about building a shelter for yourself out of natural materials. The directions here are for a simple tipi-shaped hideaway that you can build quickly and easily, especially if a friend works with you. Once you've built it, you may want to invent a bigger shelter. Try using longer upright sticks. Then arrange them in a bigger circle or in an oval instead of a circle. Experiment with different kinds of branches and vines. You'll love sitting in your shady, sweet-smelling hideaway.

What You'll Need

- A pointy-tipped shovel or hand trowel
- 10 sturdy, straight branches, about 5 feet long and 1-½ to 2 inches in diameter
- 3 feet of rope
- Heavy duty long-handled branch pruners
- About 30 (or more for a bigger hideaway) green, freshly cut branches, 1 inch or less in diameter at the thick end; each branch should be at least 4 feet long *

We used pine branches, but other types of trees will work well, too. Don't take all the branches from one tree. Never cut branches from a tree on someone else's property without first asking the owner's permission. It might be best if an adult identifies which trees to prune and helps you cut the branches. If you notice neighbors pruning their trees, you could ask them for some of the branches they are cutting off.

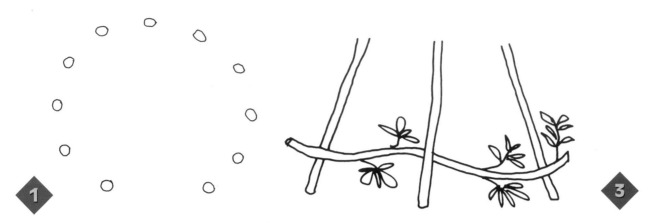

What to Do

1. Select a place to build your hideaway. Then dig 10 holes in a circular arrangement, each hole about 2 inches deep and 1 foot apart. **1**

2. Stand the 10 big branches in the holes, all leaning toward each other in the center so that they form a tipi shape. Tie all 10 together at the top with the rope. **2**

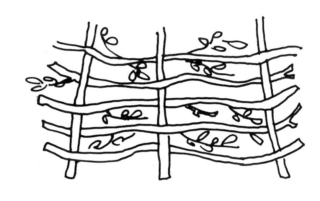

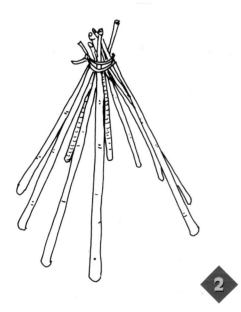

3. Weave the other branches in and out around the tall branches. **3** and **4** Leave a space between two branches in front for a doorway. If you want to have a window, simply leave a space without woven branches. **5**

4. To finish the hideaway, poke in short branches to close up gaps and holes. Trim any branch ends that stick out. Decorate the hideaway with pinecones, interesting branches, or dried seedpods or flowers.

How Big Is Your Favorite Tree?

Do you have a favorite tree in your yard or neighborhood, one that's especially big or beautiful? Trees are the largest forms of life on earth. Fossils tell us that there have been trees on earth for more than 200 million years!

Foresters use a special instrument called an *Abney level* to measure trees exactly. You can get a good idea of the size of your favorite tree using just a tape measure, a yardstick, some wooden pegs or stakes, and a hammer. Also, you'll need a friend to help you hold and read the tape.

You'll need to take three measurements because trees are big (or small) in more ways than one.

1. How Big Around Is It?

First, measure 4-½ feet up the trunk from the ground. That's what tree experts call *breast height*, and that's where they always measure a tree's trunk. Just wrap the tape around the trunk at that point and measure how big around your tree is.

2. How Tall Is It?

A tree's official height is the distance from the bottom of the trunk to the highest twig. You and your tape measure probably can't reach that far, but you can use a yardstick to help.

First, hold your hand straight out in front of you, at arm's length and level with your eye, and make a fist. Use the yardstick to measure the distance from your hand to your eye. Now hold your arm out and level with your eye again, but this time hold the yardstick in that hand, too, straight up and down. Slide the stick up or down so that the part showing above your hand is as long as the distance from your hand to your eye.

Ready? Now line up the top of your hand with the bottom of the tree's trunk and, staying on level ground, slowly move back away from the tree. Stop when the top of the stick is even with the tree's top. You should be able to see over your hand to the tree's base and, without moving anything but your eyes,

over the top of the stick to the tree's top.

Measure the distance between you and the tree. That's the tree's height (give or take a few feet).

3. How Wide Is It?

The distance that a tree's branches reach from one side to the other is called its *crown spread*. Make an outline on the ground of the tree's crown by pushing stakes (or sturdy sticks) into the ground beneath the outer tips of the branches. Then, using the tree's trunk as a middle point, measure the distance between the two stakes farthest apart on opposite sides, and the two closest together. Add the two measurements, and divide by two. That's the average crown spread.

Some National Champion Big Trees

Here are the measurements of some of the National Champion trees listed on the American Forestry Association's official National Register of Big Trees. Do the trees in your yard measure up?

	Inches Around Trunk (at 4-1/2 ft.)	Height (feet)	Average Crown Spread (feet)
Common Apple	183	44	49
American Beech	222	130	75
Black Cherry	181	138	128
Flowering Dogwood	110	33	42
Eastern Hemlock	224	123	68
American Holly	119	74	48
Red Maple	222	179	120
White Oak	374	79	102
Peach	72	18	32
Eastern White Pine	186	201	52
Western White Pine	394	151	52
Giant Sequoia	998	275	107
Blue Spruce	186	122	36
Sycamore	582	129	105
Black Walnut	278	130	140
Weeping Willow	309	117	116

The world's *tallest* living tree is a coast redwood in Humboldt Redwoods State Park, California. The giant tree measures 365 feet from base to tip. That's taller than a 30-story building!

The world's *biggest-around* tree is a Montezuma cypress in Oaxaca, Mexico. Its trunk measures 117-1/2 feet (1,410 inches) around.

The world's *oldest trees* are bristle-cone pines, which grow in deserts in Nevada and southern California. Some living bristlecone trees are at least 4,000 years old. A dead bristlecone discovered on Mount Wheeler in eastern Nevada was found to be 5,100 years old.

The world's *most massive* tree is the General Sherman sequoia, in California's Sequoia National Park. The giant tree is 275 feet tall and its trunk is 83 feet around. Foresters have figured out that the General Sherman sequoia weighs around 2,756 tons—that's heavier than a herd of 450 African elephants!

The *smallest* tree in the world is the dwarf willow. Some full-grown dwarf willows are only two inches tall!

The *loneliest* tree in the world has to be the poor Norwegian spruce growing all by itself on Campbell Island, Antarctica. Its nearest neighbor trees are in the Auckland Islands—138 miles away!

Gathering Basketry Materials

You can always go to a craft store and buy reed to make baskets. But if you gather your own wild materials, your baskets will be the one-of-a-kind creations that result only when a basket maker is willing to let the materials have some say over the way the basket turns out.

What You'll Need

Long-handled branch pruners

Small pruning shears

Garbage bags to help carry materials home

Gardening gloves

Paper grocery bags or cardboard boxes to store materials

What to Do

1. You will be gathering two kinds of materials: *stakes* (the ribs of baskets—the strong pieces that you weave onto) and *weavers* (the material that goes over and under the stakes to fill in the walls of the basket). Materials for weavers need to be tough yet flexible, and the longer the pieces are, the better. To test whether or not a material is tough and flexible enough to collect for weavers, wrap it around one of your fingers. If it snaps, it's either too stiff and fragile, or else it's too dry. Material for stakes also should be tough and flexible, but it can be stiffer than weavers and should be thicker. Stake material can be shorter than weaver material.

2. Although you can gather materials any time of year, the best times to collect are fall and winter. During these seasons,

vines, grasses, and branches are tougher. In spring and summer, plants grow fast and are full of water and new cells, which make them softer and more fragile. So try to do most of your gathering in the fall or winter. Of course, if you come upon some wonderful materials in the summer, you can collect them too. **1**

3. You may be lucky enough to find basket materials right in your own backyard, or your neighbor may let you gather plants from her yard. Never collect materials from private property without first getting permission to do so. Also, it's important that you gather only materials you are certain grow wild in great quantities. If you are unsure how common a plant material is to that area, don't pick it. Some plants species, like certain animal species, are becoming endangered due to over-collecting. Help ensure that all types of plants will continue to grow in abundance so that others can enjoy them too.

4. Here are some suggested materials and where to look for them. But don't stop here. Try out whatever looks good to you. Just be sure to learn to recognize poison ivy and stay away from it, even in the winter!

Vines	Where To Find Them
Honeysuckle	Along fences and hedgerows
Grapevine	Often grows up tree trunks and along fences and hedgerows; you can always tell grape by its curly tendrils
Bittersweet	Has bright yellow and orange berries in fall; look for it in trees and along hedgerows or growing over bushes
English ivy	On the ground, along fences, and up tree trunks
Wisteria	Along fences and over arbors

Leaves	Where To Find Them
Daylily	In gardens; along roadsides in ditches
Iris	In gardens; near the edges of ponds
Palm and palmetto	From low trees
Cattail	In ditches along roadsides and in swampy, boggy places; at the edge of ponds

Grasses	Where To Find Them
Beach grass	From dunes (check to be sure what you want to pick is not a protected species, such as sea oats)
Other tall grasses	Fields; along roadsides

Branches	
Willow	In damp, boggy areas; along streams
Birch	In woods and hedgerows; along streams

Other Interesting Materials	
Corn husks	In cornfields and gardens; in the grocery store
Philodendron sheaths	(look in potted philodendron plants for the brown sheath that covers new leaves before they emerge)

5. When you get the materials home, remove leaves from vines and cut them into single, long strands. Coil them loosely and store them on nails or on open shelves. **2** and **3**

6. Store grasses upright in open paper bags or in open cardboard boxes in a dry, shady place.

7. You can store materials for a very long time as long as they stay dry and out of the sun. If they get damp and begin to mold, add a cup of chlorine bleach to the water when you soak them before using them.

Wild Basket

A basket made with wild materials that you've found yourself is always something of a surprise. You may start out with an idea such as, "I want to make a long basket to put bread in." Then you see what kind of materials you can find. When you begin working, you learn that the materials have their own ideas! You might say, "This stake needs to bend right here." But the particular piece of grapevine you've chosen for the stake wants to curl the other way. So you say, "Okay, that looks good, too. Maybe this stake COULD bend here instead." As a result of this conversation between you and your materials, the basket becomes an entirely new creation, one of a kind, impossible to copy, and usually more interesting than the first idea you had.

What You'll Need

Stake materials: 4 pieces of flexible vine, about the thickness of a pencil, each about 24 inches long; 7 pieces of the same kind of vine, each about 18 inches long

Weaver materials: lots of thin, flexible vine, such as honeysuckle, bittersweet, or wisteria. Each vine should be as long as possible. Remove all leaves and side branches.

A large washtub full of water

Scissors or pruning shears

A craft knife

A piece of thick cardboard to put under the knife while cutting

What to Do

1. Soak all stake materials overnight.
2. When you are ready to work, roll the weaver materials into loose circles and put them in the soaking water.
3. Lay out the seven short stakes. Ask an adult to help you cut a two-inch-long slit down the center of each short stake. **1**

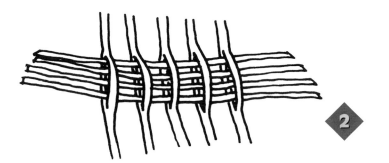

4. Lay the four long stakes side by side. Slide the four long stakes into the slits in the short stakes. Leave about 1 inch between each short stake and its neighbor. **2**
5. You will be using a weave called *twining*. To do this weave, you'll use two weavers at once. Begin by selecting a long, thin weaver and folding it in two around any stake. (But don't make the fold in the middle of the weaver. You want one of the resulting two ends to be longer than the other so you don't run out of both pieces at the same time.) **3**
6. Twist the ends of the weaver tightly across the stake. Catch the next stake between the two ends of the weaver, and twist tightly again. **4**
7. Continue twining all the way around the basket, catching each stake in turn and twisting before going on to the next stake.
8. When one weaver gets ready to run out, slip the end of a new weaver alongside the last 2 or 3 inches of the old weaver, and work both together. When the

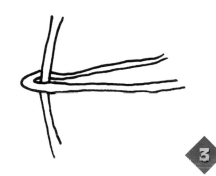

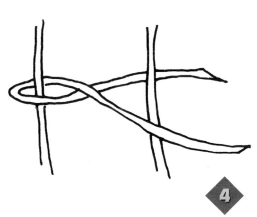

old weaver ends, continue with the new one. **5**

9. To shape the basket, press in on the stakes as you twine. Bending stakes up from the bottom of the basket to form the sides is called *upsetting* the basket. To make upsetting eas-

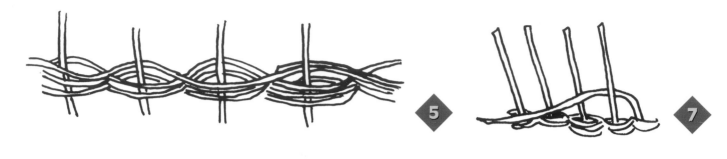

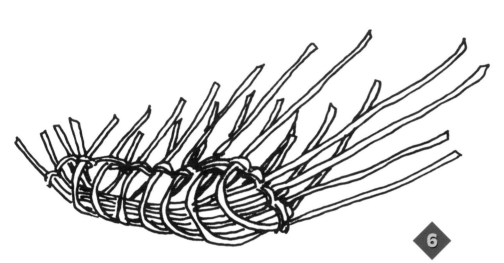

ier, try turning the basket on its side to work the opposite side. **6** If the basket begins to dry out and get stiff, dunk the whole thing in the soaking tub for a few minutes; then continue working.

10. When the basket is the size you want it to be, you'll need to finish off the edges. First put the basket upside down in the tub of water to soak the stake ends again. Let it sit for at least 30 minutes.

11. When the stakes are flexible and can bend without snapping, set the basket on its bottom. Starting with any stake,

bend that stake in front of the stake next to it and then back behind the next stakes. **7**

12. Do the same thing with the next stake. **8**

13. Continue with the other stakes. Push firmly to keep the bent stakes close to each other.

14. When there are only two stakes left, bend the second to last stake behind the last one; then tuck the end of the second to last stake under an already folded stake.

15. Bend the last stake, and then tuck it under an already folded stake.

16. You now have a braided rim and a lot of stake ends sticking out from the basket. You can either tuck these ends back over the rim toward the inside of the basket and then trim them, or you can trim them now on the outside of the basket.

17. To finish the basket, poke in any loose ends of weavers, or trim them off. **9**

88

Nature's Icing

Have you ever looked out your window on a cold, clear morning and discovered that all the leaves and grass were covered with a thin white icing? If the weather's really cold, even your window might be coated with lacy patterns of ice. Where does this thing called frost come from, and how does it make such beautiful designs?

Frost is really just the cold-weather cousin of morning dew. To see how dew forms, look at a glass of ice water on a warm day. See those small beads of water, or dew, on the outside of the glass? The cold glass made the layer of air around it a bit cooler. All air contains water in the form of a gas, or *vapor*. But cool air can't hold as much water vapor as warm air. So when the glass chilled the air, the vapor condensed: it turned into drops of liquid water that collected on the glass surface.

The same thing happens outdoors on clear, still evenings. Without the sun to warm them, trees and leaves and grass on the ground become colder than the surrounding air. The chilled plants make the layer of air right next to them cooler. So the vapor in that air condenses.

If the air temperature is well above freezing, the vapor condenses as tiny drops of dew. But if the air temperature is below freezing or close to it, the moisture condenses as ice crystals: frost.

The lacy patterns of ice on a cold window are called *fern frost*. The beautiful, feathery designs start out as tiny ice crystals that form along scratches or around bits of dust on the windows. Then the crystals grow outward from there, creating all sorts of delicate, lacy figures.

Gardeners often blame frost for killing their plants in cold weather. But that's not exactly true. Frost is a layer of ice crystals that forms on the outside of plants. A hard or killing frost is actually a *freeze*. It happens when the night is so cold the water inside leaves and stems freezes and bursts the plants' veins.

In fact, a light layer of frost actually insulates and protects plants from chilly temperatures. Frost and dew are helpful in other ways, too. They help wash dust and dirt off plants. And they're the main source of drinking water for most insects, birds, and animals!

Gourd Dipper

Since prehistoric times, gourds have been used to make dippers, ladles, and spoons. Today, at some farms around the country, you can still find gourd dippers hanging by the pump or well. You can hang your own gourd dipper by an outdoor faucet so you can easily drink cool water on a hot day.

What You'll Need

Long-handled dipper gourd, cured
    and dried so that the seeds
    rattle when you shake it
    (can be found at farmer's mar-
    kets or vegetable stands)
Steel wool
A bucket of water
A pencil
A keyhole or fine-toothed saw
Medium-grit sandpaper
A cork from a wine bottle
An awl
A 6-inch piece of heavy string
Cream-type shoe polish, either
    burgundy or oxblood
A shoe brush or polishing cloth

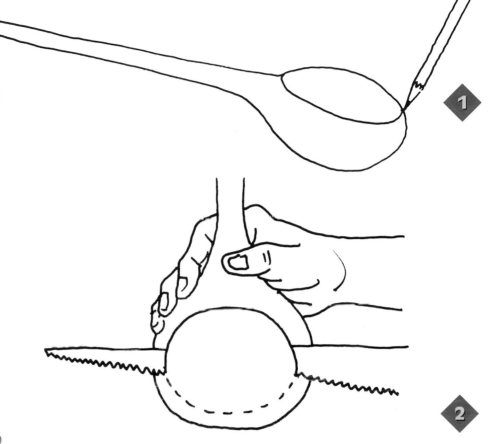

What to Do

1. Soak the gourd in water for 30 minutes; then scrub with steel wool to remove all dirt and mold. Some marks will stay on the gourd even after you've cleaned it. These marks will add a nice touch to your dipper.
2. Let the gourd dry overnight.
3. With the pencil, mark a circle where you want the opening of the dipper to be. **1**
4. Holding the gourd by the bottom of the handle, saw across the gourd to cut out the circle. **2** Sawing a gourd is hard at first because the saw slips until you've made a groove. To do this, pull the saw several times in one direction across the place where you want the groove. Then it will be easy to saw a slice off the gourd along both sides of the circle at once. (You may want to ask an adult to help you with this step.)
5. Remove all pulp and seeds from inside the gourd. Clean the inside with soapy water and steel wool. Let the gourd dry completely. (Save the seeds to plant or to make a gourd seed necklace like the one on page 98.)
6. Let the gourd dry overnight again.
7. Sand the edges and inside wall of the gourd.
8. Use the awl to poke two holes in the skinny end of the handle. Poke string through these holes, and tie it to make a loop for hanging up the dipper.
9. To decorate your dipper, rub shoe polish all over the OUTSIDE of the dipper. Let it dry for a few minutes, then shine it with a shoe brush or polishing cloth.
10. Place the cork into the neck of the gourd to prevent water from flowing into the handle.

Gourd Drum

A big fat gourd makes a wonderful drum. You can make several of them of different sizes to get different tones

What You'll Need

The biggest, fattest gourd you can find, ideally one that's 8 to 10 inches across at the wide end (can be found at farmer's markets or vegetable stands)

A large tub of water

Steel wool

A pencil

A keyhole or fine-toothed saw

Medium grit sandpaper

A piece of chamois about 15 inches by 15 inches (This is a soft leather that is sold in automotive supply stores.)

A piece of television antenna wire long enough to wrap around the fattest part of the gourd

A package of fancy upholstery tacks

Cream-type shoe polish, either burgundy or oxblood

A small rag

A shoe brush or polishing rag

What to Do

1. Soak the gourd in water for 30 minutes. Use steel wool to scrub off all dirt and mold. Some marks will stay on the gourd even after you've cleaned it. These marks will make your finished drum look very attractive. **1**

2. Let the gourd dry overnight.

3. Draw a line all the way around the gourd where you want the top of the drum to be.

4. To saw off the top of the gourd, start by making a cut about 2 inches long, and deep enough to go all the way through the wall of the gourd in one spot. The saw will slip at first, but if you keep pulling it only in one direction until you cut a groove, the job will be easier. (You may want to ask an adult to help you with this step.) **2**

5. Once you have a hole in the gourd, stick the point of the saw into it, and continue sawing all along the pencil line until you've cut off the top of the gourd.

6. Sand the edges of the cut area to smooth them.

7. Clean out all the seeds and dried pulp from the inside. Clean the inside with soapy

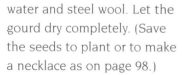

water and steel wool. Let the gourd dry completely. (Save the seeds to plant or to make a necklace as on page 98.)

8. Soak the chamois in warm water for 5 minutes.

9. Squeeze as much water as you can from the chamois. Then flatten it out and stretch it over the opening of the gourd. It should stick to the sides of the gourd. Pull out all wrinkles.

10. Wrap the antenna wire over the chamois all around the rim, about ½ an inch down

from the cut edge. Use upholstery tacks to hold the two ends of the wire in place. (You may have to put some muscle into pushing the tacks into the gourd.) Trim the wire as needed. Be sure to stretch the wire tightly against the chamois and the side of the gourd. **3**

11. Push the tacks in all around the wire, about 1 inch apart. **4** Stretch the chamois as you work to be sure there are no

wrinkles and that the chamois is pulled tight.

12. Trim the chamois about 1 inch all around the bottom of the wire. As the chamois dries it will shrink a little, pulling itself even tighter.

13. Rub shoe polish all over the gourd (but not on the chamois or wire), and let it dry for a few minutes. Then buff the gourd with the shoe brush or polishing cloth until it glows with warm color.

Shakeree

A shakeree or chequeree is a rhythm instrument made from a gourd. It is used in Latin and African bands. Players shake the beads against the gourd to make a beat. Another way to play a shakeree is to hold the instrument by its neck and pull the tail so that the beads tap against the gourd.

What You'll Need

A large bucket or tub
Steel wool
A bottle gourd, about 12 inches to 15 inches tall (can be found at farmer's markets or vegetable stands)
A keyhole or fine-toothed saw
Medium grit sandpaper
60 wooden beads with holes big enough for two thicknesses of seine twine to fit through at the same time
A ball of seine twine
Scissors
Cream-type shoe polish, either burgundy or oxblood
A shoe brush or polishing rag
A small rag

What to Do

1. Soak the gourd in the tub of water for 30 minutes. Scrub off all the dirt and mold using steel wool. Some marks will stay on the gourd even after you've cleaned it. These marks will make your finished shakeree look very attractive.
2. Let the gourd dry overnight.
3. Use the saw to cut an oval or rectangular opening about 1 inch high by 3 inches wide midway down one side of the fat part of the gourd. To make the cut, first saw across the

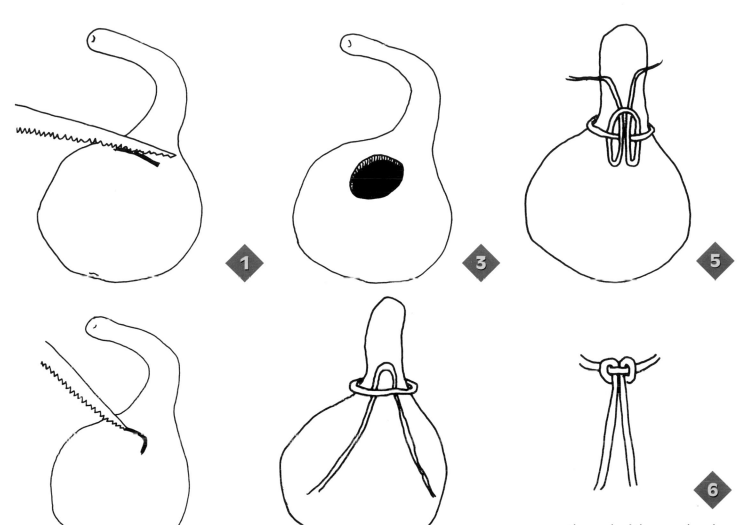

top of where the opening will be. **1** When you have cut all the way through the wall of the gourd, stick the tip of the saw inside, and finish cutting the hole that way. Sand the edges of the cut area to smooth them. (You may want to ask an adult to help you cut through the gourd.) **2** The drawing marked **3** shows the finished hole.

4. Clean out the pulp and seeds from the inside of the gourd.

Clean the inside with soapy water and steel wool. Let the gourd dry completely. (Save the seeds to plant or to make a seed necklace as on page 98.)

5. Put shoe polish all over the gourd. After a few minutes, buff the gourd with the brush or polishing rag until the gourd glows with rich color.

6. Cut a piece of seine twine about 10 inches long. Tie it into a circle big enough to fit

over the neck of the gourd and rest at the top of the fat part of the gourd. Tie a double knot. Slip the circle of twine over the neck of the gourd.

7. Cut 12 pieces of seine twine about 40 inches long each. Fold each piece exactly in half.

8. Hold one piece of twine near its fold. Slip the fold under the twine circle that is on the neck of the gourd. **4**

9. Tuck the two ends of this piece of twine over the neck circle and through the fold. **5** Pull on the two ends to tighten the knot. **6**

7

8

9

10. Tie the other 11 pieces of twine onto the neck circle in the same way. Space them evenly around the neck circle. **7**

11. You'll notice that each knot has two lines hanging down. Pick up one line from one knot and one line from the knot next to it. Tie an overhand knot in these two lines, about 1 inch down from the first row of knots. To tie an overhand knot, place your index and middle fingers of one hand under the pair of lines, close to the neck circle. Wrap both lines together around your two fingers, making a loop, and pull the ends of the lines through the loop. Push the knot up as you tighten it so that it sits about 1 inch below the row of knots that go around the neck circle. **8**

12. Continue tying knots around the circle until you have tied every line to its neighbor. You should end up with 12 knots.

13. Slip a bead over the ends of every pair of lines that you

have tied together. Push the beads up until they touch the knots.

14. You'll see two lines coming out of each bead. Take one line from one bead and one line from the bead next to it. Slip a bead over the ends of both these lines together. Push the bead up until it is about 1 inch below the first row of beads. Continue slipping beads over pairs of lines until you have made another row of 12 beads. **9**

15. Make three more rows of beads.

16. At the end of the fifth row of beads, tie an overhand knot below each bead.

17. You should now have a ring of tails hanging below the last row of beads. Gather the tails together loosely at the bottom of the gourd. Use a piece of twine to bind all the tails tightly into one tail. Be sure to leave enough room between the tail binding and the bottom of the gourd to pull the tail and click the beads against the shakeree. **10**

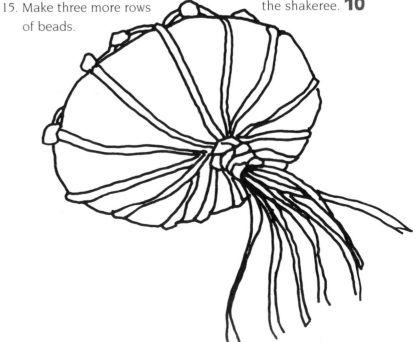

10

Great Gobs O' Gourds!

What vegetable tastes terrible and is blue, green, gray, yellow, red, black, smooth, bumpy, wrinkled, warty, long, round, short, striped, spotted, and almost any other shape or size or color you can imagine? You guessed it: gourds. Gourds are nature's way of saying that not all garden plants are meant for eating. In fact, gourds are used for almost everything under the sun *except* eating!

People have used hollowed-out gourds as cups, baskets, jugs, and all sorts of other containers for thousands of years—long before pottery was invented. In Mexico, gourd bottles more than 8,000 years old have been found in ancient cave kitchens. What's that? You need a new set of pots and pans? Just plant some gourd seeds, and stand back!

The two most common kinds of gourds in northern countries are thin-skinned *ornamental* gourds (the small, many-colored gourds used in holiday decorations) and hard-shelled *bottle gourds* (the ones used to make dippers, spoons, containers, and other crafts). Ornamental gourds grow on vines with yellow flowers. Bottle gourd vines always have white flowers.

In Mexico and South America, gourds also grow on trees. *Tree gourds* are round, grow to about the size of a small soccer ball, and have a hard thick shell just like bottle gourds.

All over the world, people grow gourds for all sorts of reasons.

In Central and South America, Indians use gourds as floats for their fishing nets. Sometimes they lash as many as 100 gourds together and put a floor on top, to make a sturdy raft.

When you shake a dried gourd, the seeds inside make a pleasant sound. Gourd rattles (and drums, like the one on page 92) were among the first musical instruments. In Africa, the rattles are also used for scaring birds away from the garden and for sending messages. Two of the most famous kinds of gourd rattles are *maracas* (muh-RAH-kuhs) from South America and *uli ulis* (OO-lee OO-lees) from Hawaii. People in many other countries make instruments from gourds, too, including horns, lutes, flutes, and the most popular instrument in India, the sitar.

Some gourds are as big as or bigger than a person's head. So in some places, people use them as hats. Native tribes in Hawaii, New Zealand, and the United States carve fancy slip-over-your-head masks out of gourds for special dances and ceremonies.

In ancient China, tiny, pear-shaped gourds with beautiful decorations were used as cages for pet crickets. And have you ever seen a picture of Sherlock Holmes with his famous curved pipe? That's called a *calabash pipe*, because it's made from a calabash: another word for gourd!

Seed Necklace

If you've made anything out of a gourd, you know that each gourd contains enough seeds to plant several hundred gourd plants! Another use for gourd seeds is to make a terrific necklace.

What You'll Need

About 200 gourd seeds
1 teaspoon red food dye, if you
    want to dye the seeds
A baked enamel or glass
    cooking pot
A slotted spoon
White waxed dental floss
A sewing needle
Scissors

What to Do

1. Pull any remaining gourd pulp off the seeds.
2. The necklace in the photograph was made with half plain seeds and half dyed seeds. If you want to dye some or all of your seeds, cook food dye in 1 cup of water for 5 minutes. Add the seeds to the dye and let the seeds sit in the dye until they are slightly darker than you want them to be.
3. Rinse the dyed seeds with cold water, and spread them out on a counter or table top to dry.
4. Thread the needle with a piece of dental floss about 36 inches long.
5. Push the needle through the center of one seed, and pull the floss until 3 inches of it stick out of the other side of the seed.

6. To tie off one end, tie the short end of the floss to the long end by looping around the first seed.
7. Continue stringing seeds until the necklace is the size you want it to be. If you have trouble getting the needle through the seeds, try pushing the nee-

dle part way into the seed, then stand the needle on its eye end and push on the sides of the seed to slide it down the needle.
8. Tie the two ends of dental floss together, and clip the ends to about ½ an inch.

Rutabaga Lantern

You can carry this scary glowing face with you (perfect for Halloween!) or plant the candle end in the ground or in a clay flowerpot filled with stones or soil.

What You'll Need

The biggest, fattest rutabaga you
    can find at the grocery store
A sharp paring knife
A stainless steel spoon
A 12-inch candle

What to Do

1. Slice the rutabaga straight across the stem end to flatten it. **1**

2. Set the rutabaga on its stem end, and make cuts with the knife straight down in the center of the top. Stay at least ¼ inch in from the edges at all times. What you are doing is breaking up some of the meat inside the rutabaga so that it will be easier to scoop out.

3. Now begin scooping out the meat. This is a hard job because rutabaga flesh is tough. If you turn the spoon so that your thumb presses in the bowl of the spoon, you can use the back and bottom edge

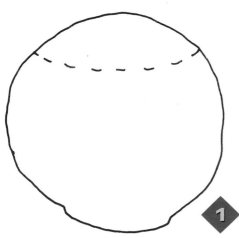

Roots and Vegetables

Not all roots are the same. A *taproot* is a large, fleshy root, sometimes with branches coming out of it, that stores nutrients for the plant to use in winter and early spring. You can find taproots outdoors—or in a grocery store. Rutabagas, turnips, radishes, and carrots all are taproots.

Fibrous roots spread out in a tangle of small roots and root hairs in search of water. The grass in your lawn has fibrous roots. A corn plant has fibrous roots that reach six to eight feet deep.

Some of the foods that we call root vegetables aren't really roots at all. Most people think a potato is a root, but actually it's an underground stem, with its own buds and leaves. The potato's "eyes" are its buds. If you

don't eat a potato, it will eventually sprout a new "branch" from each eye.

Onions aren't roots, either. They're flower bulbs—like the tulip bulbs people plant in gardens. The fleshy white part that people eat is actually layers of leaves wrapped around a stem in the center. If you cut an onion crosswise, as if you were slicing it to put on a hamburger, the leaves look like rings. But if you cut an onion in half lengthwise, from top to bottom, you can see the short, stubby stem down at the bottom, with its circles of white leaves around it. The onion's roots are at the very bottom, outside the papery brown husk. If you let an onion grow, the stem sends up a hollow green flower shoot.

of the bowl of the spoon to scoop. Continue stabbing and scooping until the inside is hollowed out and the wall of the rutabaga is between 1/2 and 1/4 inch thick all around. (Younger kids may want to ask a grown-up for help with this step.) **2**

4. Turn the rutabaga over and make three jabs with the knife in a triangular shape right in the middle of the circle where the stem of the rutabaga was. **3**

5. Press on the cut triangle with your finger, stick in the knife a few more times, and wiggle the triangle until you can poke it through to the inside of the rutabaga.

6. Set the rutabaga on its stem end, and turn it around to find the best place to carve a face.

7. To carve the face, turn the rutabaga on its side with the face surface upwards. Stick the knife into the wall of the rutabaga to outline the eyes, nose, and mouth. Then push, jab, and wiggle the cut-out shapes until you can push them into the hollow center of the rutabaga. Clean out the pieces.

8. Push the wick end of the candle into the triangular cut in the stem end of the rutabaga. Push until the candle is held snugly in place. Light the candle, and watch the eerie glow!

Root Power

People and animals have legs to help them move around in order to find food. Birds have wings. But plants? They don't need to move around. Their "legs" reach out and grab food for them.

To a plant, roots are legs, drinking straws, and food gatherers all in one. Each day, they "walk" a little farther, underground, in search of water and minerals: the nourishment plants need to grow .

Pushing your way through soil and sand and over and around rocks every day is hard work. To help, the tip of each root is protected by a tough, slippery root cap. Just behind the cap, on the inside, the root grows and become longer, pushing the tip forward in a sort of corkscrew motion, like a drill. Roots can actually press hard enough to break through a cement sidewalk or driveway!

While the root tip is growing and pushing, millions of tiny, almost invisible hairs along its surface gather water and food. Each hair wraps itself around a grain of soil and sucks up the moisture, along with dissolved minerals. From there, the water and nutrients travel through the main part of the root, up the plant's stem, and on to its leaves.

As roots grow, they branch out, just like the branches of the plant aboveground. Each new root tip searches for water. If its root hairs touch any moisture, the tip grows in that direction. If it doesn't find water, it grows downward. That's why plants in dry places have very deep roots that reach far down into the earth for water. Plants in moist areas, where water is closer to the surface, have shallower roots that branch out to the side.

As a root grows and branches and lengthens, the older parts farther back become tough and woody. Their job is to help hold the plant in the ground. Have you ever looked up at a really tall, heavy tree and wondered why it didn't just fall over? It's because, however huge the tree may be, its underground root system is even huger. A full-grown oak tree has hundreds of miles of strong, tough roots beneath it.

Even small plants have lots of roots. A scientist once measured the roots from just one winter ryegrass plant. He found 378 miles of roots and over 6,000 miles of root hairs!

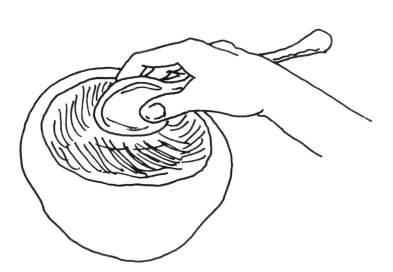

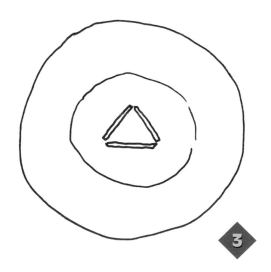

Chili Pepper Garland

When you grow peppers in your garden, you usually have too many to eat all at once. If you hang the extras up to dry, you can enjoy dried peppers as you need them all winter long.

What You'll Need

Peppers: jalapeno, chili, or banana peppers—
all with stems
Waxed dental floss
A large-eyed needle

What to Do

1. Begin by threading the needle with a piece of dental floss about 30 inches long.
2. Pierce the stem of the first pepper, bringing the threaded needle all the way through. Tie a knot.
3. Pierce the stems of all the rest of the peppers one at a time, threading them onto the dental floss. Push the peppers close together, but leave enough space so that air can circulate around the peppers to dry them.
4. When you run out of peppers, tie a loop in the dental floss, and hang the garland in a dry, shady place in your kitchen. (Be sure to wash your hands when you are finished: even a hint of chili pepper on your finger can burn if you rub your eye.) The peppers will gradually turn from green to red and become somewhat shriveled and leathery. You can soften them up when you want to use them by soaking them in water for a few minutes.

What's So Hot About Chili Peppers?

Bite into a hot chili pepper and—yeeeow!—it bites you back. Your mouth burns, your forehead sweats. Your lips feel like they're on fire. Other vegetables don't do that. What makes chilies so unchilly?

The answer is the hollow inside of the pepper, up at the top, where the white part that holds the seeds starts. If you look there closely through a magnifying glass, you'll see what seem to be tiny blisters. Actually, they're glands that make a stinging chemical called *capsaicin* (cap-SAY-uh-sin). Capsaicin is the stuff that sets the inside of your head ablaze when you eat a chili. You can't taste it or smell it. But you sure can feel it! Capsaicin is really powerful. Just one drop of capsaicin mixed with 100,000 drops of water still makes your tongue burn.

The top half of a chili is always hotter than the bottom half because the top's where the most capsaicin is. And the white tissue inside is zingiest of all—it has 16 times more capsaicin than the rest of the pepper. That's why cooks usually remove the white part (and the seeds attached) before using chilies in recipes.

All chili peppers bite, but some bite hotter than others. In 1912, a scientist named Wilbur L. Scoville figured out a way to rate chili peppers on a scale of "Scoville Heat Units." A sweet green bell pepper rates a 0, because it produces no heat units. Fiery *jalapeño* (hahl-uh-PEEN-yo) chili peppers rate a 5, and measure up to 5,000 heat units. And at the top of the firecracker food list, with a rating of 10 and a tongue-scorching 200,000 to 300,000 heat units, is the world's most sizzling chili pepper: the *habanero* (hah-ben-AIR-o). Some especially strong habaneros are 100 times hotter than jalapeños!

Nobody knows exactly why, but chili peppers grown in very warm climates tend to be spicier than the same kind of pepper grown in cooler weather. Different soils effect a chili pepper's heat too. Long ago, gardeners used to believe that chili peppers grew best and came out hottest if the person planting them was angry or had red hair!

What should you do if you bite into a too-hot chili? Many people reach for a glass of water to put out the fire. But water is actually the least effective chili extinguisher because it just spreads the heat around. Scientists have found that eating chocolate, beans, nuts, or starchy foods such as rice or bread helps. And the fastest cooler-offers are dairy products. When a chili bites you back, quick: grab some yogurt, a glass of milk, or—best of all—a big bowl of ice cream!

Ahhhhh....relief!

Seed Drying Frame

When autumn comes, it's time for seed gathering. Saving seeds from your garden to start next year's garden and to give to friends is an old custom. To make the job easier, build a seed drying frame and save the seeds in packets (instructions on page 107).

What You'll Need

2 small cardboard boxes with bottoms about 10 inches by 8 inches

A ruler

A pencil

A craft knife

A piece of nylon screen cloth 12 inches by 10 inches

A stapler

Colored plastic tape

Self-adhesive plastic shelf paper

A sheet of white paper to fit the bottom of one of the boxes

Cellophane tape

What to Do

1. Measure and make marks 1 inch up from the bottom of each box on all four corners of the box.

2. Connect the marks, using the ruler to help make straight lines. **1**

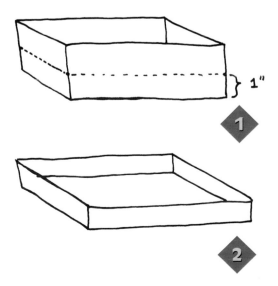

3. Use the craft knife to cut the boxes along the straight lines. You will end up with two shallow boxes. **2**

4. Cut a rectangular opening in the bottom of one box, 1 inch inside of all four sides. This box will become the frame part of the seed drying frame. **3**

5. Cut a rectangle of screen cloth 1 inch longer and 1 inch wider than the rectangular opening of the frame. Lay the screen over the opening on the inside of the frame, and tape it in place with plastic tape, stretching it tightly as you tape.

6. Tape the piece of white paper to the inside of the bottom of the other box with cellophane tape. This box will become the seed box part of the seed drying frame.

7. Cover both frame and box with self-adhesive paper, leaving uncovered only the screen and the white paper.

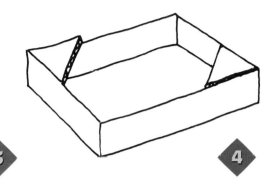

8. Cut two triangles out of scraps of cardboard. Place one in each of two opposite corners of the box and tape them into position with strips of self-adhesive paper. **4**

9. To use the seed drying frame, set the frame section on top of the box with the screen cloth side down. Place dead flower heads or seedpods in the frame. As the flowers continue to dry, seeds will fall through the screen and gather in the box. You can then empty the seeds out of the box into packets (see page 107), and remove the seed heads and other dried material from the top of the frame. This sifter works only for small seeds, ones that can fit through the screen. But you also can use the frame as a drying frame for plants with larger seeds.

105

The Mighty Acorn

You've probably heard the saying, "Tall oaks from little acorns grow." It's true, of course: curled inside every acorn is a miniature tree-to-be, with its own little root, trunk, and two tiny leaves. In autumn, after the acorns have dropped, the forest floor is covered with thousands of future oak trees, each wrapped in a shiny brown shell.

Most acorns, though, never get a chance to sprout and become tall trees. Instead, they help the forest grow in another important way. They provide food and nourishment for the birds, animals, and other wildlife that live there. Without acorns, many forest creatures couldn't survive.

Acorns are a perfect high-energy food. They're jam-packed with B vitamins, protein, and complex carbohydrates—the sort of high-power fuel athletes eat before a big game.

For wildlife, though, living in the outdoors—especially during winter—is no game. They need acorn energy just to get by.

Did you know that a single gray squirrel eats about 100 pounds of food every year? There are plenty of seeds, berries, and other foods to snack on during the summer and early fall. But come winter, squirrels, chipmunks, and mice live mostly on the nutritious acorns they've stored in burrows or buried in the ground.

Other birds and animals gobble up acorns all year round. Blue jays and white-tailed deer would rather eat acorns than almost any other food. Black bears roam the forest all summer devouring huge amounts of the nuts, fattening up for the winter. Wood ducks, wild turkeys, quail, gray foxes, crows, woodpeckers, and dozens of other creatures also rely in a big way on the little acorn.

In times past, people ate lots of acorns too. Native Americans and early colonists boiled the nuts to remove the bitter taste and then ground them into flour for baking.

The sweetest, least bitter acorns come from trees in the white oak family. Most birds and animals eat them first. Then they eat the not-quite-so-tasty acorns from the red oak family. You can tell the difference between these two oaks by looking at the trees' leaves. Red oak leaves have sharp-looking points all around. White oak trees have leaves with rounded "fingers" or "toes." Another way to tell is to pick up an acorn and pry off its cap. If the cap is smooth on the inside, the nut probably is from a white oak; if it's fuzzy, it came from a red oak.

When you picked up an acorn, did it have worm holes in it, or bugs crawling on it? Birds and animals aren't the only creatures that are nuts about acorns. Ants, slugs, weevils, wasps, caterpillars, millipedes, and a parade of other creepy-crawlies join in the feast too. If you're a bug or worm, an acorn is a real find. Once you get inside, it's a meal *and* a roof over your head!

No wonder so few little acorns ever become tall oaks. Of the 5,000 or so acorns an oak tree makes in a year, only about 50 escape being eaten long enough to sprout. And of those, only about 20 survive to become trees. Maybe the old saying should be, "Tall oaks from *lucky* little acorns grow!"

Seed Packets

These packets are handy for saving seeds from this year's garden to use in planting next year's garden. They also make nice gifts for family and friends who enjoy gardening.

What You'll Need

Pressed flowers from the same kind of plant as the seeds are from
Clear plastic zipper-type bags
Clear plastic self-adhesive paper
Scissors
Seeds

What to Do

1. Lay the plastic bag flat on a table or counter top.
2. Arrange pressed flowers on the top surface of the bag. (See page 73 for instructions on how to press flowers.)
3. Cut a piece of self-adhesive paper big enough to cover the flowers and to have at least 1 inch of space all around.
4. Peel off the backing and carefully lay the plastic with the sticky side on top of the flowers and the bag at the same time. Press to smooth out any wrinkles or air bubbles.
5. Fill the packet with seeds. The pressed flowers will tell you what kind of seeds are in the bag. If you want to add information, such as when and where to plant the seeds, write it on a small piece of paper, and put the paper in the packet.
6. Seal the packet.

107

Save Those Seeds!

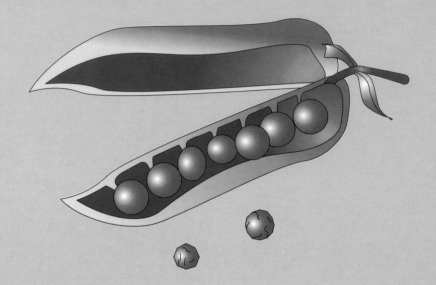

Seeds are more than just future plants. They're tiny time capsules. When a seed sprouts and becomes a plant, it will have some of the traits its ancestors had—just like you might have your grandmother's button nose or your great-grandfather's curly hair. Maybe the plant will be super tall or leafy. If it's a vegetable, maybe it will be extra tasty or have a special color or shape.

That's why many gardeners save the seed from their favorite kinds, or varieties, of vegetables each year. They want to be sure to be able to grow crops with the same special qualities the next year.

Some vegetable varieties have been saved by gardeners for dozens, or even hundreds, of years. They're not sold in most garden stores or seed catalogs. Gardeners call these antique vegetables *heirloom* (AIR-loom) plants.

Some have been grown in gardens since the 1600s. If people through the years hadn't saved and replanted the seeds each season, the varieties would be extinct by now. We'd never get to taste a squash like the ones American Indians grew, or the peas early pioneers ate when they traveled West. Planting an heirloom seed is like keeping a little bit of history alive for another year.

Many heirloom varieties have interesting names, such as Lazy Wife beans, Purple Calabash tomatoes, and Cut And Come Again beets. Some, such as Bird Egg bean or Tennis Ball lettuce, describe what the vegetable looks like. Moon And Stars watermelon has dark skin with a bright yellow circle (the moon) and dozens of tiny spots (the stars). Other heirlooms, such as Uncle Quimby beans, are named for the person who first grew and saved the seed.

Can you guess how Howling Mob sweet corn got its name? The corn was said to be so good any farmer who came to town to sell it would be surrounded by a crowd of eager buyers—a howling mob!

It takes a lot of practice and special care to raise pure heirloom vegetables that are exactly like their ancestors. But you can start learning how to save seed right now.

Peas and beans are the easiest vegetables for seed saving. Just keep the pods on the vine until they turn brown and dry. Shake one of the pods. If the seeds inside make a rattling noise, they're ready. Break the pods open, pick out the seeds, and put them in a dry place in a paper bag for a few days. Then store the seeds in a tight jar.

If you don't pick and eat them, radish and broccoli plants will flower and make seedpods, too. After the pods turn brown or yellow, pick them and dry them a few days on a screen or frame (such as the one on page 104). Then break the pods open, separate the tiny seeds, and store them in seed packets like the ones on page 107, or in paper envelopes.

Apple Crisp

On chilly autumn days, nothing tastes better than a bowl of warm, crunchy apple crisp.

What You'll Need

5 or 6 apples (Any variety will taste delicious!)

¼ cup water

½ cup rolled oats

½ cup flour

1 cup brown sugar

½ cup butter or margarine

1 teaspoon cinnamon

A pinch of salt

A medium-sized glass baking dish

A large mixing bowl

Measuring cups and spoons

A large spoon

What to Do

1. Butter the baking dish.
2. Preheat the oven to 350 degrees F.
3. Slice the apples but don't peel them. Pick out the seeds as you slice.
4. Put the sliced apples in the bottom of the baking dish.
5. Mix all the other ingredients together. To mix in the butter, crumble it with your hands.
6. Crumble the mixed ingredients over the apples.
7. Bake the apple crisp without a cover for 30 minutes. For an extra treat, serve ice cream on top.

Gathering Wood

Several of the projects in this book require gathered wood. Gathering wood can be an adventure in which you not only learn to recognize trees but also the special properties of their wood. When you see a piece of wood growing, imagine how it would look as part of a shelf or a bench or a birdhouse. Is that curve the perfect place to rest your arm? Is that just the branch you need to finish off the doorway of your playhouse?

What You'll Need

A small saw, such as a pruning
   saw or a short cut saw
Heavy-duty, long-handled pruning
   shears
Small pruning shears
Heavy garden or work gloves
Large garbage bags for collecting
Crates or boxes for storage

What to Do

1. It's possible to use all kinds of wood and to mix different kinds of wood in the same piece of furniture. By experimenting, you'll learn which woods are easiest to work, which are flexible, and which are strongest. Here are some places to scout for fresh cut wood that has not dried (is still green): brush piles, newly-cut-down trees, small wooded areas in your neighborhood, hedgerows, and vacant lots.

2. The best time of year to cut wood for furniture is winter or late fall when the sap is down,

but you can cut wood all year long. The main point is to gather wood when it's available. If you want to peel the bark off the wood for a particular project, then you should gather this wood in late spring or summer. Wood cut then will be much easier to peel.

3. Before you hunt through your neighbor's brush pile or go wood gathering in someone else's woods, be sure to ask the owner if it's all right. If you gather wood from a brush pile, put everything back the way you found it when you're finished. If you will be trimming saplings or branches, be sure to ask an adult to help you because trees must be cut in a certain way or they will be damaged.

4. Don't cut wood from trees that are endangered species. If you aren't sure, ask. Some good trees to cut are silver maple, dogwood, hemlock, willow, sycamore, large grape vines, birch, and elm. Pine isn't a good wood to use unless you plan to dry it thoroughly, because it oozes sticky sap for a long time after it's cut and is messy to work with. It's fine for building sim-

ple shelters, however. (See page 79.)

5. If you find a nice tree or branch on the ground, check first to be sure it isn't rotten. Often wood that falls from trees is dead and quickly rots once it hits the ground. Wood that has been on the ground for a while is almost always in the process of becoming a meal or a home for insects, and won't make strong furniture. Try bending the branch. If it crushes or breaks easily, or feels soft and has a damp, mildewy smell, leave it for the bugs.

6. If you live near the beach you might be able to find interesting pieces of driftwood. Some driftwood is strong and good for building, but some is full of mildew or other fungi. Test driftwood the same way you would test wood that has been on the ground.

7. When you've found wood that looks promising, cut it, and then trim off any parts you don't want (side branches, leaves, etc.). Keep branches as long as possible. You can always cut them shorter later, after you know what you'll be using them for.

8. You can use fresh cut wood right away, as long as you plan on nailing your furniture together (rather than using hole and peg joints). You can also store and dry your wood. As wood dries it shrinks and may warp or twist. For this reason, you may want to dry your wood before building with it. The traditional rule is that wood will air dry at a rate of 1 inch in diameter a year. This means that a big branch 2 inches in diameter will take two years to dry. Even a small twig as big around as a pencil will take a few months to dry completely.

If you don't want to wait, and you don't mind your furniture changing shape slightly as it dries, go ahead and use fresh cut wood. As long as you nail the joints together, that's fine. The projects in this book all have nailed joints and are designed to use fresh cut wood.

9. Store wood in a cool, dry place where water can't get to it. Keep it off the ground. Don't ever pile wood against the side of a building.

111

Rustic Twig Shelf

Furniture made from branches and twigs is called rustic furniture. It can be simple and rough-looking or very intricate and polished. People who make rustic furniture search carefully for branches to fit the ideas they have. Sitting in a chair made of branches can make you feel as though you're perched in a tree. The rustic shelf in this project is perfect for a summer camp or a beach cottage, and will make even your bedroom feel woodsy.

What You'll Need

A pruning saw or a short cut saw
Large branch cutters
Pruning shears
A tape measure or yardstick
12 straight unpeeled green or dried branches each 27 inches long and about 1 inch in diameter *
48 straight branches 23 inches long and ½ inches to ¾ inches in diameter
4 branches 30 inches long and 1 inch to 1-½ inches in diameter
4 straight branches 60 inches long and 1-½ inches to 2 inches in diameter
3 branches 60 inches long and 1 inch to 1-½ inches in diameter
8 branches 20 inches long and 1 inch in diameter
A roll of masking tape
A hammer
1 pound of 1-½-inch common nails or masonry nails
1 pound of 1-inch common nails
Scissors
A roll of jute cord

When the word "straight" is used, cut branches that are as straight as possible. If the word "straight" is not used, it's okay to use branches that curve slightly or have interesting angles.

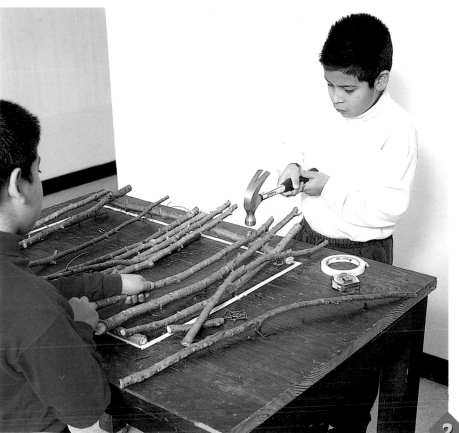

What to Do

1. Sort and pile up the branches that you will use according to size. See page 110 to learn how to gather wood for rustic furniture.

2. Begin by making four shelves. To make sure these end up the same size, make a 27-by-20-inch rectangle out of masking tape on the floor or table where you'll be working. To make sure the corners are square, use the corner of a book to line up the tape. **1**

3. Lay a 27-inch long stick on each 27-inch long piece of tape. Nail twelve 23-inch sticks evenly spaced across the 27-inch sticks. Use 1-inch nails. **2**

4. Turn the shelf over and nail a 30-inch branch from the upper left-hand corner to the lower right-hand corner to brace the shelf. **3**

5. Repeat steps 3 and 4 three more times. Now you should

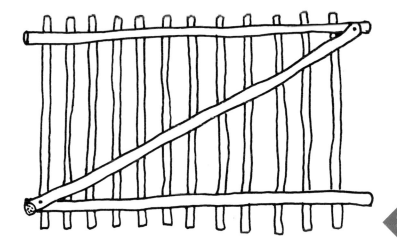

have four shelves that are all the same size.

6. Next make the two sides of the piece. Lay two 60-by-1-½- or 2-inch in diameter sticks side by side on the floor with 18 inches between them.

7. Nail four 20-inch side support sticks across the two long sticks, beginning 12 inches down from the top, and placing a new stick every 12 inches, ending 12 inches from the other end. **4**

8. Turn the side piece over. Make a diagonal brace by nailing

113

first stick.

12. With your friends still holding the sides in position, nail a 30-inch stick across the two long sticks that are NOT on the ground, 22 inches down from one end. **7**

13. Nail another 30-inch stick across the same sticks, 27 inches down from the first stick. **7**

14. Now CAREFULLY stand the construction up. It will be wobbly, so your next job is to stabilize it by making a diago-

one of the 60-by-1- or 1-½-inch sticks from the top left to the bottom right.

9. Repeat steps 7 and 8 for the other side piece.

10. The next steps are the trickiest in this whole project. You will need a friend or two to help. Ask your friends to stand the two side pieces on their long edges, side by side, with the diagonal braces facing out, with 26 inches between them. **5** While your friends hold the side pieces in position, nail a 30-inch stick across the two sides 16 inches down from one end, across the two sticks that are lying on the ground. **6**

11. Nail another 30-inch stick across the same two sticks, 14 inches down from the

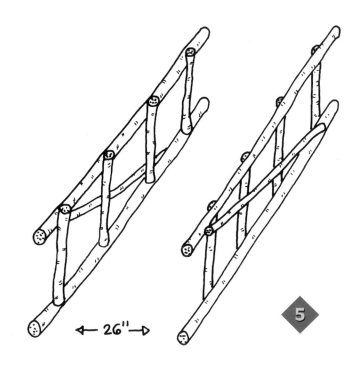

← 26" →

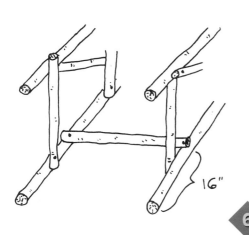

6

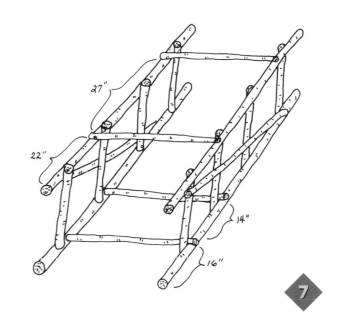

27"

22"

14"

16"

7

nal back brace. Walk around to the back of the construction. (The back has cross pieces 16 inches up from the bottom and 14 inches up from the first stick.) Carefully nail the remaining 60-inch stick from the top of the back left support stick to the lower end of the back right support stick. **8** To make this job easier, first drive the two nails all the way into the ends of the 60-inch stick; then pound the stick into position. **9** and **10**

15. Lift each shelf and fit it into position. The diagonal shelf brace must face downward. The ends of the 27-inch-long shelf sticks will be supported by the 20-inch side crosspieces.

16. To complete the construction, tie the corners of each shelf to the side pieces with 24-inch pieces of jute cord. Wrap the jute tightly around each stick several times; then tie it with a double knot. **11**

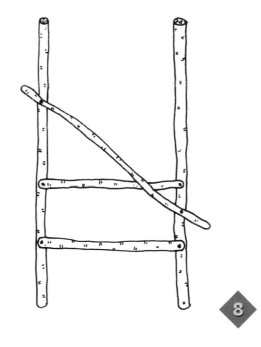

8

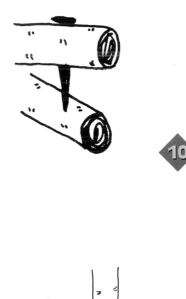

10

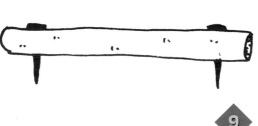

9

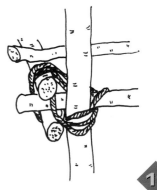

11

115

Evergreen Wrapping Paper

Wrapping paper with printed evergreens shows off some of nature's prettiest patterns.

What You'll Need

Evergreens such as pine, hemlock, spruce, and boxwood

Nuts, shells, and pods (optional)

Old newspapers

Sheets of tissue paper, white or colored

Acrylic paints

A large, soft paintbrush

An old pie tin to hold paint

A cup or jar of water

What to Do

1. Spread newspapers over the table or countertop. Lay a single unfolded sheet of tissue over the newspaper.
2. Squeeze out 1 inch of paint into your pie tin, and work it up with the brush until it is easy to spread. Hold an evergreen sprig down by pressing on the end of its stem with one finger. Brush paint over the entire surface of the sprig.
3. Place the sprig, painted side down, on the tissue paper. Be careful not to move it once you've set it down. Lay a small piece of newspaper over the entire sprig. Press and rub the sprig through the top sheet of newspaper.
4. Peel off the top sheet of newspaper and the sprig of evergreen. You can use the same sprig many times; just repaint it each time you print it. Use a clean top sheet of newspaper each time you print the sprig.
5. Experiment with different colors and designs. Try using several different sprigs on the same sheet of tissue. Try using some nut shell halves or seed pods. When you use a new color of paint, rinse and dry the sprig first to remove the old color. Dry it by pressing it gently between pieces of newspaper.
6. Spread sheets of tissue out to dry for at least an hour before using them to wrap your holiday gifts. Clean up everything with water.

Seashell Candles

The glow of these candles on a chilly winter night will remind you of a warm beach in summer.

What You'll Need

Old newspapers
A large tin can, such as a
    2-pound coffee can
A pot that is larger than the can
Several lumps of beeswax,
    paraffin, or bits and pieces
    of old candles
Old broken, peeled crayons
    (optional)
Oven gloves or 2 heavy
    pot holders
A large seashell for each candle
Small birthday candles, preferably
    the same color as the beeswax
    or paraffin
Scissors

What to Do

1. Half fill the pot with water and put it on the burner of a stove. Put the wax or paraffin in the tin can, and set the can in the pot of water. This arrangement is called a double boiler. Wax and paraffin are very flammable, so it's important never to put them in a pot directly over the heat source. Always melt wax or paraffin in a double boiler.

2. If you want to color the wax or paraffin, add crayons to the tin can.

3. While the water is boiling and the wax is melting, use a stick to scoop out old wicks if you are using old candles.

4. Lay several thicknesses of newspaper on the countertop near the stove. Set the shells on the newspaper. Prop them up using wads of newspaper so that they don't tip when you pour in the wax.

5. Ask an adult to help you slowly and carefully pour the melted wax into each shell. Let the candles cool for about five minutes until they begin to look frosty on top.

6. Poke a birthday candle down into each candle where you want the wick to be. If the birthday candle is too tall, pull it out right away and trim some off the bottom with scissors; then poke it back in. It's okay if the birthday candle is a little too tall. The first time you light the candle it will burn down to the right height.

7. Let the candles cool before lighting them.

Fantastic Floating Water

Think of the ice covering a pond in winter. The smooth white surface glistens beautifully in the sun. Maybe you can even skate on it. But all in all, it's just ice, right? Nothing special about it, right?

Wrong! Ice is one of the strangest, most unusual substances in the natural world. Why? Because it floats. And according to all the laws of science, it shouldn't.

Almost everything else in nature contracts, or shrinks, and becomes heavier as it gets colder. For example, cold air is heavier than warm air. That's why a room is coldest near the floor and warmest near the ceiling: the warm air expands and grows lighter while the cold air shrinks and gets heavier.

But water is an oddball. It doesn't behave. At first, as water cools it gets heavier just as it should—but only until it reaches a temperature of 39.2 degrees F. Then, as it grows even colder, something strange happens: it starts to expand and become lighter again! The colder the water gets, the lighter it becomes. When it freezes and turns to ice it's so light that it floats.

So what? Think of that winter pond again. If ice and water followed the rules, the coldest water would be the heaviest and would sink all the way to the bottom. The pond would freeze from the bottom up. Sooner or later it would become

solid ice, and everything in the pond—fish, frogs, plants, and all—would freeze and die. The same thing would happen in all of earth's lakes and oceans!

But instead, really cold, near-freezing water rises. Ice forms at the top of a pond and acts as a blanket to keep the water near the bottom from getting colder than 39.2 degrees F. Fish and other water life can survive in the bottom water until spring.

Ice is interesting in other ways, too. Have you ever wondered why ice is so slippery? Ice almost always has a thin layer of liquid water just a few hundred molecules thick on its surface. When you push on ice or rub across it, a little more ice melts and the water layer gets thicker, creating a sort of slick

watery "oil" perfect for a sliding skate blade.

Icicles happen when water drips slowly from a roof, branch, or other place into below-freezing air. At first the icicle is just a tiny sliver of frozen water. But as more water travels in a thin film down the sides of the icicle and freezes at the tip, drop by drop, the icicle grows longer. The outside film slowly freezes too, a little at a time, making the icicle thicker.

Ice comes in all sorts of other forms: frost, snow, sleet, hail, glaciers, underground ice, icebergs, and more. Scientists say there are at least 80 completely different kinds of ice crystals. More than one-fourth of our planet is covered by ice. In parts of Antarctica, the ice layer is almost three miles thick!

Make Your Own Icicles!

If you live in a part of the world where winter temperatures dip below freezing (32 degrees F), you can create your own homemade icicles. You'll need a plastic milk jug, a push pin or sturdy needle, some wire (such as from a coat hanger), and some water.

Use the tip of the push pin or needle to make a tiny, pinprick-size hole in the bottom of the jug, about an inch back from the corner opposite the handle. Then, on an evening when the temperature is below freezing, fill the jug with water—don't cover it—and use the wire to hang the bottle from its handle on a tree branch. The water should just barely drip out, a drop at a time. (If it comes out faster, try making a smaller hole in another jug.)

The next day, a brand-new "jugcicle" should be gleaming in the morning sun! If the day stays cold, you can try adding more water to make a longer icicle.

To create really unusual icicles, add a half-teaspoon of food coloring to the water before you hang the jug. Or try making several icicles at a time. Each one will be completely different!

Potato Paper

When the adults in your house make vegetable soup, ask them to give you a few uncooked potatoes and some carrot peelings so you can make potato paper.

What You'll Need

A blender

5 or 6 large potatoes (uncooked) *

Scraps of old paper torn into
    small pieces; soft, thick paper
    is best

A grater

A large bowl

Water

A plain wooden picture frame, 8
    inches by 10 inches or larger

A piece of metal window screen,
    12 inches by 14 inches or larger

Metal shears or scissors to cut the
    screen

A staple gun

A large plastic dishpan

Some clean rags, at least
    15 inches by 15 inches

Old newspapers

A rolling pin

Spray starch

An iron

Optional: A few cups of onion skins, a cup of carrot peels, a handful of chopped parsley or dried parsley flakes, a few pinches of dried red pepper flakes

What to Do

1. Peel the potatoes and grate them into the bowl. Save the peelings. **1** Add an equal amount of torn paper to the bowl of potatoes. Add enough water to cover the potatoes and paper. Let this mixture soak while you go on to Step 3.

3. Cut a piece of screen 2 inches longer and 2 inches wider than the picture frame. Stretch the screen over the frame, and staple it into place.

4. With your fingers, squash the potato-paper mush in the bowl until it's completely mixed. **2** When it feels soft, fill the blender container about ⅓ full

of mush, add 1 cup of water, and blend until smooth. **3** (Be sure to hold the lid on the blender while it's blending!) If the blender seems to be straining or smells hot, stop the motor and add more water to the container. If you want your paper to have color flecks, add a handful of potato peels or carrot peels to the container for the last few seconds of blending. This is also the time to add onion skins, parsley, or pepper flakes.

5. Pour batches of the mush into the dishpan or tub, adding a little water if it seems too thick, until you have about 6 inches of mushy water in the dishpan. If you want larger flecks of color in your paper, add potato or carrot peels or parsley or pepper flakes now.

6. Dip the frame under the mush, screen side up. **4** Then, holding the frame level, shift it back and forth under the mushy water until a layer of mush settles evenly over the surface of the frame. This layer

should be no more than ½ an inch thick.

7. Without tilting the frame, lift the frame and mush layer out of the dishpan. Hold the frame over the pan to let the water drain out. **5** If the mush clumps together or if there are holes, put the frame back under the mushy water and try again.

8. As soon as you have drained most of the water from the mush on the frame, place a clean rag over the top of the drained mush layer. Press down gently, squeezing out more water. **6**

9. Lay a few pieces of newspaper down on a table. Carefully turn the frame, wet paper, and rag upside down onto the newspaper, and lift off the frame. **7** Cover the wet paper with another rag. You now have a sandwich of a rag, a layer of wet paper, and another rag.

10. Roll the sandwich with the rolling pin to press out as much water as possible and to flatten the paper. **8**

11. Carefully peel off the top rag. **9** Turn the wet paper and the bottom rag over onto a smooth counter or tabletop or a piece of glass (you can use a window for this), paper side down. Carefully peel off the remaining rag. **10** If you are using a window, don't worry about the paper falling off; it will stick there until it dries.

12. Let the paper dry overnight or longer.

13. If you want very smooth paper, spray the dry or almost dry paper with spray laundry starch, put a clean rag over the paper, and iron it with a slightly warm iron until the paper is dry. The starch will make the paper better for writing on too.

14. You can use your paper to make cards, wrap presents, cover handmade books, write notes, or draw on. Try using the prehistoric paints on page 129 to make a small painting on your handmade paper. Or use the fish T-shirt instructions on page 63 to make a fish print on your potato paper.

Warm, Snuggly Snow

It's not easy to think of snow as anything but cold. But when snowflakes pile up, they make a warm, fluffy blanket for the earth and many animals.

A layer of snow is made of billions of ice crystals surrounded by zillions of tiny air spaces. Snow contains so much air it's 10 to 30 times lighter than the same amount of water! The air in snow keeps cold out and heat in, the same way the air in a fluffy sleeping bag traps your body heat and shuts out nighttime chill. Earth's "body heat" is the planet itself. All that rock and soil hold the sun's warmth from the summer and slowly release it during the winter.

Snow is such a good insulator that, once there is at least eight inches on the ground, the temperature under the blanket almost never drops below freezing. That's good news for farmers, who depend on snow to keep the ground soft enough for plowing in early spring. And it's also fortunate for small animals that don't have a lot of fur or fat to keep them warm in winter. They depend on a warm snow "roof" to help them survive.

When snow falls, it doesn't cover every nook and cranny on the ground. It bends bushes and weeds and drifts over rock piles and logs, creating snow-covered chambers and tunnels. The earth's warmth, too, melts some of the snow closest to the soil, opening up more space. Scientists call this place under the snow but above the ground the *subnivean environment*.

Meadow voles, white-footed mice, and other small rodents live all winter long in this undersnow world, scurrying about from place to place and gathering food just as they do in summer. Their fluffy roof keeps them warm and hides them from foxes and other enemies. Even red squirrels, which live in trees all summer, spend most of the winter under the snow blanket, eating nuts and pinecones that they buried in the fall!

124

Winter Berry Garland

This garland brings indoors the colors of winter: soft grays and browns, white, and jewel-like reds. Hang it on a wall or drape it across the top of a mantlepiece. You could also lay it on a table for a centerpiece. When you're finished using it in the house, hang it outside for the birds to enjoy.

What You'll Need

A wire coat hanger

About 50 twigs, 4 inches to 6 inches long, from a variety of trees, and in a variety of shades of gray and brown

About 10 sprigs of red berries such as red-berried elder, rose hips, winterberries, yaupon, pyracantha, and dogwood

A few sprigs of dried white or cream colored flowers, such as baby's breath

10 small rubber bands

A roll of floral wire

Scissors or pruning shears

What to Do

1. Unwind the twisted neck of the coat hanger, and straighten the wire. Bend a small hook on one end. Bend a few curves in the wire.

2. Gather between 10 and 12 bundles of twigs, each with 4 or 5 twigs and a sprig of berries and/or of white flowers. Fasten each bundle tightly at one end with a rubber band.

3. Attaching twig bundles to the wire is easier if you hang the wire by its hook from a nail in a wall. You can also do this job by laying the wire flat on a table. Begin by placing one bundle at the end of the wire away from the hook, with the

rubber banded end facing the hooked end of the wire and the twig ends covering the end of the wire. Wrap a piece of floral wire about 12 inches long several times around the bundle to hold it in place. If you have leftover floral wire, use it to attach the next twig bundle.

4. Lay the second twig bundle facing the same way as the first one so that the twig ends of the second bundle cover the rubber band of the first bundle. Fasten this bundle with floral wire.

5. Continue placing the rest of the bundles in the same way until the entire wire is covered, with only a couple of inches of wire and the hook sticking out.

6. Poke leftover sprigs of berries or flowers into bare spots.

Terrarium & Terrarium Stand

A carefully made and tended terrarium lets you bring a small bit of the outdoors inside. Choose your materials from a place that you especially enjoy visiting. Then, when you look at your terrarium, it will seem as if you are spending time there. The terrarium stand made of sticks will also remind you of being outdoors.

What You'll Need

A pencil and notebook
A large glass or plastic jar with a
    wide mouth *
A trowel
A spot outdoors where you can
    collect soil and plants
Plastic wrap
A rubber band
Scissors
22 straight sticks 6 inches to 7
    inches long
Wood glue

You can also buy a specially made terrarium tank or use an old aquarium tank.

What to Do

1. Select a place that you like to visit—a path in the woods, a boggy area in your backyard, a shady spot under some pine trees, the edge of a desert.

2. Spend some time studying this environment and making some sketches and notes. (See page 132 to learn about nature sketching.) The more you learn about this particular environment, the better you'll be able to reproduce it in your terrarium. Notice whether the place is shady or sunny, damp or dry. Notice the different kinds of plants: where are they growing? on rocks? in the soil? on decaying logs? Are any insects living there? Are there any signs of animal life? How might all the plants and animals act together? What is the soil like? Imagine what this place is like on a rainy day, a hot summer day, a cold winter night.

3. After you've made notes and sketches, begin collecting samples so that you can make a model of this environment, a mini-environment. First put a layer of pebbles or small stones in the bottom of the container to help drainage.

Then scoop down below the dead leaves or pine needles or whatever else is on the surface and get a couple of trowels of soil. Make a 2-inch layer of soil in your container. On top of the soil arrange some of whatever covers the ground— dead leaves, pine needles, grass, moss.

4. Now arrange rocks and sticks to reproduce a typical small section of the environment.

5. Select one or two samples of each of the different small plants—ferns, mosses, cacti, lichens—and place them in places similar to the ones in which they were naturally growing.

6. Pour about a ½ cup of water into the terrarium and cover it with plastic wrap and a rubber band. Trim the plastic wrap so that it doesn't show beneath the rubber band more than ½ inch or so. Poke a few holes in the plastic wrap with a pencil.

7. To make the terrarium stand, lay two sticks about 3 inches apart.

8. Put a small blob of glue about 1 inch from each end on the top side of each stick. Lay two other sticks across the first sticks, covering the glue. **1**

9. Repeat steps 7 and 8 four or five times so that you have a

stack of sticks with a space in the middle.

10. On the last layer of sticks, glue two sticks between the top two sticks: this layer is what your terrarium will sit on. **2**

11. To make a lid for your terrarium, glue together six sticks the way they look in the last illustration. Let all the sticks dry.

12. Place the terrarium in similar light and temperature conditions to those of the original environment. For the next few days, watch the terrarium carefully. The sides of the jar may become beaded with moisture, and drops of "rain" may actually collect on the plastic wrap and drop down. If the plants seem too dry, add water and replace the plastic wrap lid for one with fewer holes. If mildew (white cottony fuzz) appears on the surface of the soil, or the terrarium smells strongly of mildew or mold, leave the plastic wrap cover off for a few hours, and poke extra holes in it when you replace it.

13. Once you've regulated your terrarium, it will need very little attention besides an occasional watering. Of course, you'll want to study it, and adding and rearranging plants is fun. If your terrarium is in a very large jar or an aquarium

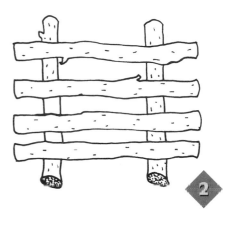

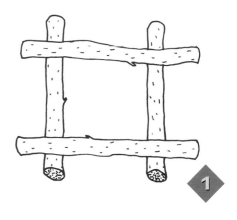

or terrarium tank, you might want to experiment with adding some insects and an amphibian or reptile or two. Be sure to add animals or insects that are naturally found in that environment, and provide a food and water supply. If you go back to the original spot to collect insects and amphibians and reptiles, you'll be certain to bring home the kind that belong there. You can also find out what they eat and what materials they need for shelter.

Winter's Invisible Wildflowers

Walk into a winter forest, and you might think all the plants are dead and gone. But—hey, watch out! You're stomping around on "invisible" wildflowers! You can't see them, but they're there just the same, hiding from you, sleeping the winter away beneath the ground.

In spring and summer, wildflower plants make food for themselves by soaking up the sun's energy through their leaves and water through their roots. They don't use the food they make all at once, though. They store some of it in special underground parts called *bulbs, tubers, corms,* and *rhizomes* (RYE-zomes).

In late fall or early winter, water in the soil freezes and can't be taken up by plant roots. The air is too cold for leaves. So the above-ground parts of wildflower plants dry up, turn brown, and wither away. But the belowground parts stay alive. They use the food stored during the warmer months to get them through the cold season.

Even before winter comes, the underground parts use some of their stored food to get a start on spring. They form the buds for next year's growth. And inside each bud is a whole new set of aboveground plant parts, leaves and all: an "invisible" wildflower.

Hidden beneath the soil, protected from hungry animals and icy winds, the flower-to-be waits for warmer days. When spring does come, the bud bursts open and uses its storehouse of saved-up energy to push a stem and leaves up through the soil and into a new season. Soon the wildflower unfolds, adding its brand-new blossom to the dozens of other fresh-from-a-winter's-sleep flowers carpeting the woodland floor.

Ah, another beautiful spring!

Flowering plants that live year after year are called *perennials* (purr-EN-ee-uhls). Different wildflowers use different kinds of underground food storage organs to help them survive the winter.

Bulbs are made of layers of fleshy leaves, or food-storage scales, wrapped around a flowering stem in the center. Most have a papery skin. Lilies and daffodils are bulb flowers.

Rhizomes look like thick, round roots, but actually they're underground stems. Most grow horizontally (side to side), at or just below the surface. Leaves and flower buds sprout along the top. Iris and Solomon's seal grow from rhizomes.

Tubers are swollen "barrels" of stored-up plant food that form along some kinds of underground stems. Their "eyes" are buds that sprout leaves and flowers. Buttercups and anemones are tuber plants.

Corms usually have a papery husk and grow upright, like bulbs, but they have a flattened shape and are solid inside. Several buds sprout from the top. Dutchman's breeches and trout lily grow from corms.

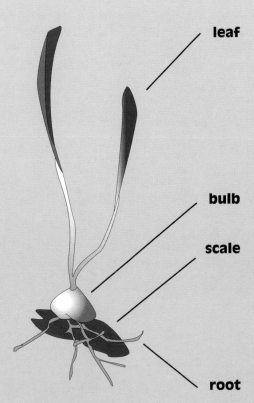

leaf

bulb

scale

root

Prehistoric Paints

The world's first artists painted graceful animals on the walls of underground caves using paints made of animal fat, burnt wood, soil, and ground rocks. You can make paints the same way and paint your own animal mural or painting.

What You'll Need

Small plastic bags

A trowel

A coarse garden sifter (not absolutely necessary, but helpful)

A mortar and pestle OR a large spoon and an old pie tin

The cheapest lard or vegetable shortening you can find—about ½ a cup for each cup of paint

A large spoon

Small jars, bowls, or aluminum cans to store paint in

Stiff bristle paintbrushes in various sizes (old or cheap ones work fine)

A large piece of shelf paper or mural paper

Masking tape

What to Do

1. Go for a walk around your yard or a vacant lot or a nearby wooded area, and scoop up a trowelful of as many different colors of soil as you can find. Look along creek banks for colored clays too. Store the different colors of soil in small plastic bags. Collect wood ashes from a fireplace or barbecue pit.

2. Sift (if you have a sifter) or pick out small sticks, leaves, pebbles, etc. from each sample.

3. Pour a handful of soil into a pie tin or a mortar. Add a spoonful of lard or shortening, and stir the mixture or grind it with the pestle or spoon. Mix and grind until the paint is as smooth as possible. Add more soil if the color is too light or too greasy. Add more fat if the paint feels too dry or stiff. Store the paint in a bowl or jar or can.

4. When all the paints are mixed, tape up the mural paper, and paint with stiff brushes, sticks, or your fingers. Make more colors by mixing paints together. This paint will last for thousands of years on the stone wall of a cool, dark, undisturbed cave. It won't hold up in the rain though; and if anything or anyone rubs up against it, it will smear. If you want a more permanent painting, paint on a piece of heavy paper. Then ask an adult to help you frame the painting behind glass with a double matt to keep the glass from touching the paint.

Earth's Amazing Caves

A cave is a hole in the ground—often a very big hole in the ground—hollowed out by nature. Some caves are ice caves, made by currents of warm air flowing through openings in glaciers or frozen mountaintops. Some are water caves, created by waves pounding against rock. Some caves were carved into cliffs by wind and blowing sand. Others were formed from hot, bubbling lava.

Most caves, though, are made of limestone, a rock found in much of the earth's crust. Limestone cracks easily and is so soft that rainwater trickling through the cracks dissolves the surrounding rock. Gradually, over many years, the cracks become tunnels and channels. More water flows through, dissolving more limestone. The channels widen and deepen. They join other channels, creating passageways. In some places, the rock collapses, forming rooms and chambers. This is how a cave "grows." As long as water seeps into it, it keeps growing and changing.

Water dripping from a cave's ceiling and across its walls contains dissolved limestone. As the water slowly evaporates, lime and minerals are left behind. They build up in layers and harden, creating shiny, curiously shaped formations. Rock "icicles" called *stalactites* grow drop by drop from the cave roof. Water dripping to the floor creates upside-down cones called *stalagmites*. Sometimes a stalactite and a stalagmite grow together, making a

column. Water trickling in sheets over cave walls forms rippled draperies known as "flowstone." Rows of stalactites grow together side-by-side, creating enormous hanging curtains. "Flowers" of mineral crystals sprout from walls.

There are thousands of limestone caves all over the world. Many are famous for their enormous size or awesome formations. Mammoth Cave, in Kentucky, is Earth's longest known cave system. It has at least 348 miles of underground passageways! In China's Daji Dong cave, there is a column known as the Flying Dragon Pillar that's 128 feet high—taller than a 10-story building! In Carlsbad Caverns in New Mexico, one of the chambers, known as The Big Room, covers 14 underground acres! In some places the stalactite-studded ceiling is 300 feet high!

Other caves are famous for their man-made beauty. In 1940, in the Lascaux Valley, in France, four boys

playing in a field discovered one of the world's most treasured caves. Its many beautiful cave paintings, created at least 15,000 years ago by Stone Age artists using natural earth pigments, are considered some of the world's finest art.

Humans have used caves as houses and for other purposes for at least 500,000 years. Because of their damp, dark conditions, some caves are still used today as underground mushroom farms and for aging wine and cheese.

Animals depend on caves, too. Some, such as bears and foxes, live in caves only part of the time. Bats stay year-round in caves, but come out each night to eat. Deep in the darkest parts of caves are the "true" cave creatures. They never leave their pitch-black homes. Most are ghostly white and blind. There are spooky-looking cave salamanders, cave crayfish, cave crickets, cave shrimp—and a dozen different kinds of blind cave fish!

Nature Sketching

Drawing something is one of the best ways to learn about it. If you want to really under-stand how a wasp nest is made, or how a plant scatters its seeds, or how the pattern of a seashell unfolds, make a careful drawing of it.

Drawing also helps us remember what we see. If you want to remember what that strange-looking insect on the back porch looks like, make a sketch of it, quickly, before it flies away. If you want to remember how the fields look under the first snowfall of the season, make a drawing. Nature sketching isn't just for artists. If you want to see better and remember more about the natural world around you, try your hand at nature sketch-ing. It can be enjoyed all year round.

When you sketch in the winter, you may be surprised to find how many beautiful and interesting things there are to draw. One advantage to drawing in winter is that, without the cover of foliage, it is easier to see the landscape and the shape of trees. Bushes draped in fresh snow make good subjects to draw, too. Be sure to wear clothes that will keep you warm and dry.

What You'll Need

A sketchbook, such as the one
    on page 136
A pencil
A pen
A small box of colored pencils
    (optional)
A magnifying glass
     (useful but optional)
A plastic garbage bag to sit on
A few small plastic bags to hold
    samples to draw at home
Something to carry everything in
    (a backpack or a jacket with
    big pockets will do)

What to Do

1. Drawing involves making many choices, and the first choice is selecting something to draw. There are some things that you will need to get very close to in order to draw. Here are some ideas for things to draw up close:

   an ice crystal
   a tree branch covered in snow
   a seashell
   a piece of moss or lichen
   a piece of wood
   a dried seedpod
   a flower
   an insect
   a twig
   animal tracks
   a bird's nest
   a leaf
   vegetables
   a wild mushroom
   a bone
   an animal skull
   an acorn
   icicles hanging from a boulder
   a pinecone
   a feather

2. The next choice in drawing is choosing which details, shapes, lines, and textures to include. You can't possibly draw everything about the object. What you must do is pick out the lines and shapes to put in the drawing that will show most clearly what you are seeing. The more you draw, the more and the better you will see. Compare the photograph of a sunflower **1** to the drawing of the same flower **2** When you draw something you can choose the details you want to stand out.

133

4. Here are some projects for close-up drawing; (some are better suited for summer and spring):

   a. *Go outside and tie a brightly colored piece of yarn or ribbon around the end of a twig on a tree. Make a careful drawing of the twig, putting in as much information as you can. What shape are the buds? Are they fuzzy or smooth? Does the twig have spots or other marks on its bark? Where are the marks located? How big are they? Draw the same twig several times over a period of weeks, recording all changes in it. Date each drawing.*

   b. *Pick out five things to draw that you could show to a friend to tell him or her about a particular place that you have visited.*

   c. *Draw a collection: every insect in your garden; one of every flower that you can find on a walk in the woods; or one of every kind of moss that you can find.*

5. There are some things that are usually drawn from a few feet away. Sometimes you can't get very close to what you want to draw. This is the case with most bird or animal drawings. When you draw from a few feet away, concentrate on drawing the main shape of the animal or bird. Show how it moves, how it normally stands. You won't be able to draw as many details as you can up close. One way to add information is to make some written notes on the drawing.

   The drawing marked **3** was done from memory, without looking at a bird. It doesn't tell you much about the way a real bird looks, and even less about the way a particular bird looks. See how much more information is in the second drawing marked **4**, which was made while looking at a bird.

6. Here are some projects for middle distance drawing:

   Birds at a feeder or birdbath
   Your pets
   Butterflies in the garden (You'll have to sit very still!)
   A squirrel
   Crabs at the beach
   A spider building a web, or ducks bobbing for food on a pond
   Animals or plants in a natural science museum exhibit

7. Sometimes you want to remember the way a place looks from a distance. As with all drawing, looking carefully is most important. Ask yourself where the main shapes and the lines are. Don't worry about details, since you can't really see them. Use different kinds of marks to show different textures such as grass, leaves, water, clouds, rows of corn.

8. Here are some ideas for distance drawings:

   a. *Your favorite scenes and places while on vacation. (You'll remember best the places that you've drawn.)*

   b. *A collection of cloud sketches*

   c. *Events, such as sunsets, rain, storms, an eclipse. Make a series of drawings for each event.*

   d. *The night sky, showing constellations at different times of the year*

   e. *The same outdoor scene each week during spring to show changes as the weeks go by*

   f. *A collection of water sketches— streams, ponds, puddles, lakes, the ocean*

3

4

What Big Eyes and Ears You Have!

Have you ever gone outdoors hoping to see lots of birds and animals—and ended up seeing almost nothing? Getting a look at wildlife isn't always easy. Birds and animals are much better at seeing and hearing people—and at hiding—than people are at seeing and hearing them.

With a little practice, though, you can give yourself more powerful eyes and ears for studying nature's creatures.

For starters, when you look for wildlife try using "wide-angle" vision. Don't focus on just one area. Instead, let your eyesight spread out, so that you're taking in everything you see around you, on both sides as well as in front, all at the same time. This might take some practice at first. If your eyes try to switch back to normal "narrow" vision, just let them relax and open up to the big picture again.

Now, using your wide-angle eyes, scan your surroundings. Don't expect to see a bird or animal standing out in the open. Instead, look for small or sudden motions or out-of-place shapes or colors in the bushes and trees and grasses around you. When you think you catch a glimpse of something, switch to normal vision and study the area closely. If it turns out there's nothing there, change back to "wide angle" and keep searching. But remember, wild animals are good at blending in. So look carefully. Perhaps you'll catch the

swish of a squirrel's tail, or the twitch of a rabbit's ear, or a bird's fluttering feathers.

When you do spot something and want a better look, use "body binoculars." Hold your hands circled in front of your eyes as though they were binoculars, with your thumbs on each side of your nose and your fingers curved together over your eyebrows. This helps you focus on the bird or animal and even magnifies your vision a bit. (Of course, if you have real binoculars you can use them instead.)

You can also boost your wildlife listening powers. Have you ever noticed that many animals have big ears that stand up or stick out? This helps them hear faint sounds and figure out what direction they're coming from. To give yourself bigger, more sensitive ears, cup your hands behind your ears and push them forward slightly with your thumbs and index fingers. You'll be surprised at how much more you can hear. Listen to a bird or cricket without your "new" ears, and then with them. Your giant-size sound catchers can be handy for helping you zero in on faint rustling noises or far-away bird songs.

You can try this anywhere—hiking in the woods or looking out an apartment window. The more you open your senses, the more you'll discover about the sights and sounds (and smells and tastes and textures) that make up our natural world.

Pocket Sketchbook

This is the handiest sketch/notebook you will ever find. It travels rolled up in your pocket or backpack, then unrolls and gives you a firm surface for sketching or writing.

What You'll Need

A single thickness of corrugated cardboard 5 inches by 11 inches *

10 to 12 sheets of drawing or writing paper, each 4-¾ inches by 10-½ inches

An awl or large nail to poke holes

A piece of thin jute cord 2 feet long

Scissors

A cardboard tube with a diameter slightly larger than a toilet paper tube

A craft knife

Colored plastic tape or colored self-adhesive shelf paper

A short pencil or a pen

* Measure with the ribs of the cardboard going the narrower direction. **1**

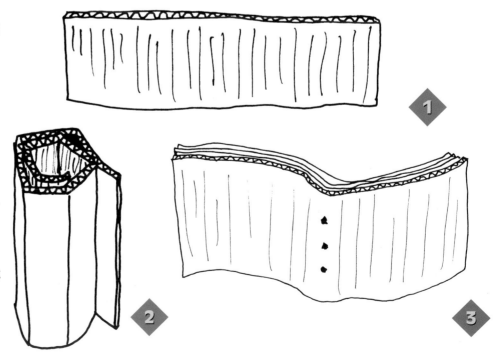

What to Do

1. Turn the corrugated cardboard so that one of its short ends faces you. Roll up the cardboard beginning at the 5-inch end that is nearest you. As it rolls, the cardboard will bend between the ribs. Keep rolling until you have a fat roll of cardboard 5 inches tall. **2** (It may be easier to roll first from one end and then from the other end, rolling both ends toward the middle, then to unroll and roll the whole thing from one end.)

2. Unroll the cardboard. (It will

stay bent and curly.) Fold
it in half.

3. Fold all the sheets of paper in half, and slip them inside the cardboard cover.

4. Use the awl to poke three holes through the cardboard and all the sheets of paper at once, around 1 inch apart, in the fold of the book. **3** Be careful not to shift the pages. The holes must stay lined up. Gently wiggle the awl to enlarge the holes until they are big enough to poke a shoelace through.

5. Make a "shoelace" out of the piece of jute by wrapping a 1 inch piece of tape tightly around one end. **4**

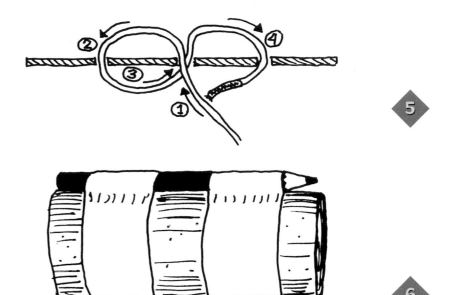

6. Poke the jute "shoelace" through the center hole from the outside of the book. Pull it through, leaving a 3- or 4-inch tail on the outside. Now, from the inside, poke it through one of the other holes and pull the cord tightly through, being careful to leave the tail hanging out.

7. Next, from the outside, and while holding onto the tail, poke the cord BACK into the center hole. (You may need to enlarge the hole with the awl to do this.) Pull the cord through to the inside of the book, holding onto the tail.

8. Now poke the cord into the remaining hole from the inside. **5** Pull it tightly and tie it on the outside to the tail. Make the tie as close as possible to the center hole. Tie a bow, and trim the ends of the cord.

9. To make the case, roll up the sketchbook and slide it into the cardboard tube to make sure it fits snugly. Then pull it back out. Hold the rolled up book alongside the tube and mark a section of tube the length of the book. Use the craft knife and scissors to cut the tube to exactly

the same length as the book You can decorate the tube with colored tape or self-adhesive paper.

10. To make a pen or pencil sleeve, cut two pieces of tape each 2 inches long. Lay them sticky side up on a tabletop. Put a 1-inch piece of tape in the center of each strip to make a sort of tape bandage. Tape one end of the first piece of tape to the tube. Hold up the other end of the bandage and place the pen or pencil under the part of the bandage that is not sticky. Pull the bandage over the pen or pencil, and stick down the other end. Repeat this step with the other tape bandage. You should be able to slide the pen or pencil smoothly in and out. **6**

Bird Feeder

This sturdy bird feeder will last for a long time in all kinds of weather. Hang it out of the reach of squirrels, and watch the birds feast. See pages 239 and 349 for other types of birdfeeders.

What You'll Need

A ruler

A pencil

2 feet of 1-by-4-inch wood

4 feet of ¼-by-1-½-inch wood

A piece of ¼-inch plywood, 6 inches by 24 inches

2 feet of ¼-inch dowel

A saw

Sandpaper

A hammer

A handful of 1-½-inch nails

A handful of 1-inch nails

A brace and bit

A ¼-inch drill bit

An auger bit that will make a circle 1-¼ inches in diameter

2 clear acrylic panels, 5 inches by 6-½ inches

A rag

A small can of wood stain

Birdseed

A cork with a small end diameter of 1-¼ inches

2 wire coat hangers

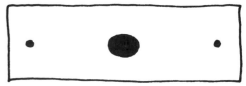

What to Do

1. Ask an adult to help you saw a piece of 1-by-4-inch wood 12 inches long. Sand all cuts after sawing. Then, using the auger bit, make a hole 1-¼ inches in diameter in the center of the piece of wood. **1** Drill a ¼-inch hole located 1 inch in from each end. **2** This is the top of the feeder. Put it aside for now.

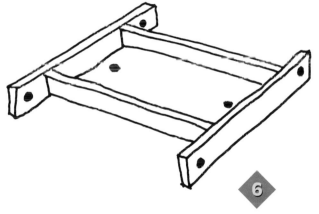

2. Next make the bottom. Cut a piece of 1-by-4-inch wood 10 inches long. **3** Then drill a ¼-inch hole at the center of each end of this board, 1 inch from each short end. Now cut four pieces of ¼-by-1-½-inch wood, each 10 inches long. Nail one of these pieces along each long side of the bottom board. **4** Drill a ¼-inch hole 1 inch from the end of each of the other two ¼-by-1-½-inch pieces. **5** Now nail these two pieces across the ends of the bottom of the feeder. **6**

3. To make the seed compart-ment, cut the following boards from the plywood:
   (2) 6-by-4-¾-inch rectangles
   (2) 6-by-3-⅛-inch rectangles
   (2) 6-by-⅝-inch strips of wood

4. Place the two 6-by-4-¾-inch rectangles flat on the table or workbench. You will nail three pieces of wood to each of

these pieces, creating slots that the acrylic panels can fit into. Nail a 6-by-3-½-inch piece and two 6-by-⅝-inch strips of plywood to each 6-by-4-¾-inch piece. Be sure to leave a slot between the pieces of wood big enough for the acrylic panels to fit into. **7**

5. Pound a 1-inch nail into each slot, ½ inch from what will be the bottom end. This nail will

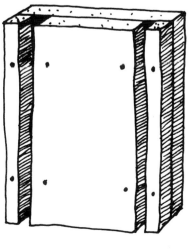

139

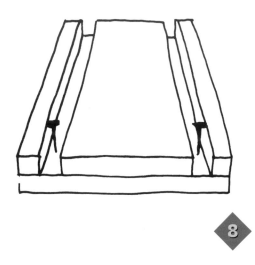

8

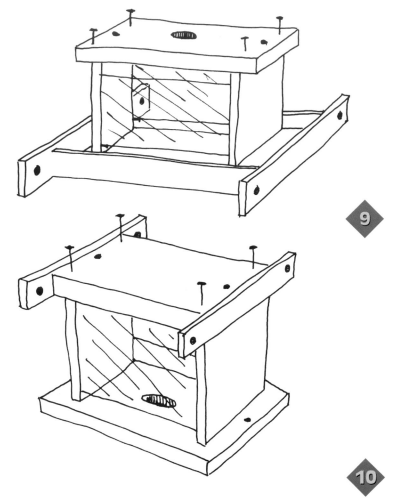

9

10

hold up the acrylic panels so that birdseed can fall out of the seed compartment into the feeding tray. **8**

6. Saw the dowel into two 12-inch-long pieces.

7. Before going any further, wipe wood stain on all pieces of wood. After you wipe the stain on, immediately wipe off any excess. Let the pieces of wood dry overnight.

8. To assemble the bird feeder, slide the two acrylic panels into the slots of both seed compartment sidewalls. You now have a box without a top or a bottom. Turn this box so that the nails in the acrylic panel slots are toward the bottom. Set the box inside the bird feeder bottom. Move it around until it is centered. DO NOT NAIL IT TO THE BOTTOM YET. Now carefully place the feeder top across the top of

the seed compartment. Move it until it is centered, being careful not to move the seed compartment from its centered position on the bottom.

Nail the top to the sidewalls of the seed compartment. **9** Next, carefully turn the bird feeder over and rest it on its top so that you can nail the bottom to the seed compart-

11

140

Bir-r-r-rd, It's Cold Outside!

Not all birds fly to warm sunny places in the winter. Some kinds stay right where they are, icy weather and all. And others fly to freezing cold places from places that are even *more* freezing cold.

How do these winter birds survive? How do they keep from starving? Why don't they freeze their little feet off?

Insect-eating birds such as swallows and flycatchers probably would starve in winter. After all, cold weather kills flying insects. That's why insect-eating birds migrate to warmer climates.

But cardinals, chickadees, sparrows, finches, and most other winter birds are seed eaters. They like berries and pinecone seeds and other foods that stay on trees and plants all year. Other cold-weather birds, such as woodpeckers and flickers, get their meals by poking around under tree bark for insect eggs and hibernating bugs.

Some birds even hide food for the winter, just like squirrels do! In fall, nuthatches, jays, and woodpeckers push nuts and seeds into holes and cracks in tree trunks, where they can find the snacks later.

Have you ever noticed how puffy and round small birds look on cold days? That's how they stay warm. They fluff up their feathers to trap their body heat underneath. Of course, their feet don't have feathers to puff up. But that's okay, because bird feet are mostly just bones covered by tough skin. The skin doesn't feel the cold the way your skin might. And it doesn't freeze, either.

Birds keep themselves warm at night by eating as much as they can during the day. They turn some of the food into body fat. Then they use the fat at night as fuel. Some birds can even feed themselves while they sleep! Just before sunset, they stuff a mouthful of food into a special place in their throats called a *crop*. Then, during the night, the food slowly travels to the stomach and digests.

On very cold nights and during storms, birds take shelter in places such as thick bushes and evergreens and in holes in tree trunks. Most winter birds sleep with their heads turned back and their beaks nestled under their shoulder feathers. Sometimes they snuggle together in groups to share heat.

Winter is never an easy time for birds, though. Finding food and water can be tough, especially when the temperature is below freezing for several days in a row. You can help the birds in your neighborhood. Put out a shallow pan of fresh water for them every day. And use a feeder (such as the one on page 138) to make sure your feathered friends get plenty of good food.

---

ment walls, just as you did the top. **10**

Finally, turn the bird feeder right side up and slide the dowels into the holes on either side of the tray.

9. Straighten the two coat hangers and make a hook on one end of each. Slide the straight ends through the holes in the top and bottom of the bird feeder, and bend the last inch or so of the wire to hold it in place. **11**

10. To fill the feeder, make a small cut across the corner of a bag of birdseed and carefully pour seed into the hole in the top of the feeder. Put the cork into the hole, and hang the feeder from a tree limb.

CEMENT BIRDBATH

What You'll Need

- A shovel
- A large plastic garbage can with a lid*
- Plastic wrap
- A 60-pound bag of sand mix concrete
- Water
- A trowel
- A 12-inch x 12-inch piece of chicken wire or hardware cloth
- Metal shears** or wire cutters
- A large plastic or metal tub (or a wheelbarrow) for mixing concrete
- Broken pieces of crockery or china, or seashells, pretty flat rocks,or beach glass for decoration

*Look for a garbage can lid that has a smooth inside with no plastic tabs or deep indentations.

**Metal shears are designed to cut metal. Any good hardware store will have them.

a

c

b

d

What to Do

1. Dig a shallow hole in the ground the size of the garbage can lid, for the lid to rest in. Be sure the hole is level.

2. Line the inside of the can lid with plastic wrap, and place the lid in the shallow hole.

3. Pour the concrete mix into the tub or wheelbarrow. Add a little bit of water at a time, mixing with your trowel as you add.

You can tell when the mix is right: make a hill in the concrete with your trowel, and slice the hill down the middle with your trowel. If the sides of the slice cave in, the mix is too wet. Add more concrete.

If the slice crumbles, the mix is too dry. Add more water.

If the slice stays put, the mix is just right.

4. Shovel an inch-deep layer of concrete into the lid and smooth it with the trowel.

5. Cut the chicken wire or hardware cloth to fit over the concrete, and an inch inside the edge of the concrete, and lay it flat on top of the layer of concrete.

e

6. Shovel in another inch-deep layer of concrete on top of the hardware cloth.

7. Set the garbage can in the center of the concrete. Put 4 inches of water in the can to hold it in place.

8. With the trowel, fill in concrete around the sides of the can, to form the rim of the birdbath. Smooth the edges.

If you want, you can place shells or pieces of broken pottery around the edge, for decoration.

9. Let the concrete set up for around an hour until it's hard enough to hold its shape. Then gently twist the garbage can to remove it. At this point you can press pottery shards or shells into the bottom of the birdbath to decorate it. Be sure to press the pieces in far enough so that the surface is level and there are no sharp edges that could cut a bird's feet.

10. Keep the concrete damp for three days while it sets up. Here's how to do that: Poke sticks into the ground around the birdbath, and drape a piece of plastic (such as an old shower curtain) over the whole project. The plastic will help keep the sun from drying out the concrete. Spray the concrete with water once a day.

11. After three days, when the concrete is hard, remove the birdbath from the mold. To do this, carefully peel the edge of the garbage can lid back in a few places. Flex the plastic to loosen the birdbath, then turn it over and lift the lid off. Peel away the plastic wrap.

12. Place the birdbath on an old tree stump or balance it on three flat rocks. You might also place it flat on the ground in your garden, or drive three pipes into the ground and rest the birdbath on the pipes. Fill it with water, and watch the birds enjoy it. And if you have a cat, you might want to put a bell on its collar, so it doesn't sneak up on the birds.

g

h

i

j

RAIN FACTS

■ It takes about nine days for water to evaporate from the oceans or the surface of the earth, condense as part of a cloud, and fall to earth again as rain or snow.

■ There are about one million cloud droplets in one raindrop.

■ The biggest raindrops measure about 1/4 of an inch across.

■ One inch of rain over one square mile weighs about 72,000 tons.

■ Scientists estimate that 40 million gallons of water in the form of rain, snow, or freezing rain fall on the earth every second.

■ The wettest place in the world is Mount Waialeale, on the island of Kauai, Hawaii. It rains there an average of 335 days a year, and sometimes as often as 350 days. The total amount of rain each year averages 460 inches, or more than 38 feet!

■ The driest places in the world are in Chile, South America. In Desierto de Atacama, virtually no rain fell for more than 400 years. In 1972, though, a downpour swept through and caused heavy flooding and mud slides. The village of Arica, in northern Chile, is almost always rainless. It gets an average of 3/100 of an inch of rain a year.

■ The greatest rainfall in one day (24 hours): 73 inches (that's over six feet!), in Cilaos, La Reunion, an island in the Indian Ocean.

■ The greatest rainfall in one year: 1,042 inches, at Cherrapunji, Meghalaya, India, between August 1, 1860 and July 31, 1861. Cherrapunji also holds the record for most rain in one month: 366 inches, in July, 1861. Most years, though, the village gets "only" about 425 inches of rain all together.

RAIN AND CLOUDS

Everybody knows that rain comes from clouds. But where do clouds come from? And why does rain fall from them?

Clouds are actually made up of trillions of tiny drops of water. Water is always in the air, in the form of an invisible gas we call water vapor. The warmer the air, the more water it can hold as vapor. The colder the air, the less water it can hold.

Whenever there's more water in the air than the temperature will allow it to hold, the water vapor condenses: It changes from gas to very small droplets of water. Together, those droplets make a cloud. That's why you can see your breath in the winter when you breathe out, but not during the summer. On a cold day, the air can't hold all the water in your breath, so the vapor condenses and makes a little cloud.

The same thing is going on when clouds form in the sky. Have you noticed that there are usually more clouds over mountains and hills? That's because when air passes over mountains, it's swept upward. The higher it gets, the colder it gets. The air can't hold as much water. So the water condenses and creates clouds.

The ocean is another place where you see a lot of clouds. That's because the air is so full of water from the sea that it condenses even when the air is quite warm.

Rain happens when water droplets in a cloud become heavy enough to fall. Sometimes enough cloud droplets bump into each other and stick together to make larger, heavier droplets that fall. That's usually the cause of short, hard showers during the summer or in tropical places. Long periods of rain or drizzle happen when the water vapor in very high, cold clouds sticks to ice particles and freezes, making heavier ice crystals and snowflakes. When the flakes drop down through warmer air, they melt and fall as rain. (Of course, in cold weather they don't melt, and drift to the ground as snow!)

BAROMETER

What You'll Need

- A glass jar with a wide mouth (2-1/2 to 3 inches across)
- Acrylic paints and a brush
- A 14-inch balloon*
- Scissors
- A piece of string about 12 inches long
- A plastic drinking straw
- Tape
- An 8-inch x 12-inch piece of posterboard
- Markers

*Check the bag the balloon comes in to find out its size. Most balloons are 9 inches; be sure this is a 14-inch one.

What to Do

1. With the brush and acrylic paint, paint designs on the jar. Let it dry.

2. Cut the skinny end off the balloon.

3. Stretch the balloon over the mouth of the jar. Pull it tight so that no bumps remain and the surface is as near perfectly flat as possible.

4. Wrap the string around the mouth of the jar, over the balloon, and tie the string, to help hold the balloon in place.

5. Cut both ends of the straw at angles.

6. Tape one end of the straw flat against the center of the balloon with a small piece of tape.

7. Fold the posterboard in thirds, and tape it into a long triangular column.

8. Stand the posterboard column next to, but not touching, the tip of the straw. Make a small mark on the column where the tip of the straw is pointing.

9. After a few hours, check the barometer. If the tip of the straw is pointing higher or lower on the column, make a mark where it is pointing. Check the weather, and make a symbol to indicate it. You might draw a small sun or a cloud, raindrops or snowflakes. Or you might use colored dots or write out the weather in words.

10. Continue to check the barometer every few hours for a couple of days (or longer if the weather stays the same). Each time the tip points to a new place, make a mark and note the weather. Soon you will begin to notice a pattern, and you won't need to make any new marks.

You'll notice that when the tip of the straw is on its way up, a certain kind of weather follows. When the tip is going down, a different kind of weather follows. Use your barometer to predict the weather.

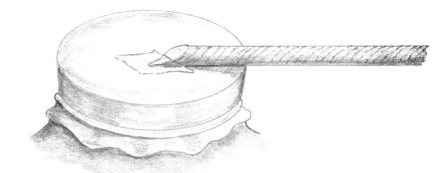

HOW IT WORKS

Air is made up of tiny particles called molecules. There is air inside the jar, held in by the balloon. No air can escape, and no extra air molecules can get inside. The molecules inside the jar press against the balloon, as well as against the sides and bottom of the jar.

There is also air outside the jar, and the outside molecules also press on the balloon. When the pressure inside the jar is less than the pressure outside the jar, then the air outside the jar presses hard enough on the balloon that it pushes in on it. When the balloon is pressed down, the straw tilts upward.

When the pressure inside the jar is greater than the pressure outside the jar, the inside air pushes against the stretchy balloon and causes it to bulge outward. When the balloon bulges outward, the straw tilts down.

Different weather conditions appear with changes in air pressure. Watch your barometer to see which kinds of weather go with high pressure (the straw tip points up) and which kinds of weather go with low pressure (the tip points down).

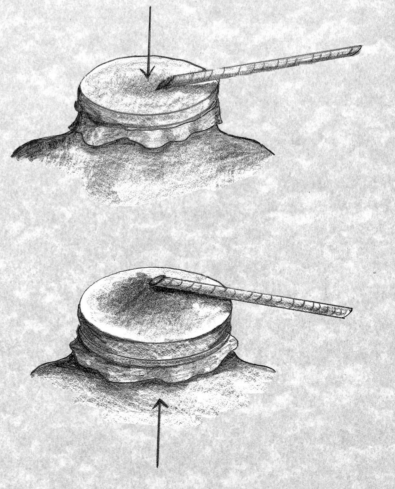

WIND VANE

If you've got a cat, you could use the cat pattern and paint the wind vane to look like your own pet. (All cats are shaped pretty much alike.) If you've got a dog, though, it may not be shaped much like the pattern. You could either use the pattern given, or draw a new one shaped more like your own dog. Then paint it the colors of your pet.

What You'll Need

- Tracing paper
- Pastel crayon or a graphite pencil*
- A piece of 1/4"-thick plywood big enough for the animal. (Our dog measures about 17" x 7", our cat about 12" long and 11" high.)
- A 3/4" x 4" x 26" board
- A saw
- Sandpaper
- Wood sealer
- Acrylic paints
- Paint brushes
- Screw eye and bell (optional)
- A 1-1/4" long piece of brass tubing and a 2" piece of brass rod to fit inside
- A hacksaw
- Carpenter's glue

*These are sold in art supply stores

What to Do

1. Enlarge the pattern to the size you want on a photocopy machine that enlarges. Or draw your own.
2. Trace the pattern onto tracing paper, using a pastel crayon or a graphite pencil—something that rubs off.
3. Lay the pattern on the plywood, crayoned side down, and rub the back of the paper gently, to transfer the pattern to the plywood.
4. Cut out the plywood animal.
5. Sand the cutout, and coat it with wood sealer. (Most kinds are applied with a paint brush.)
6. Paint the animal the colors of your choice. Don't forget to add nose, mouth, whiskers, eyes, and a collar in a contrasting color.
7. If you like, attach a small bell to a tiny screw eye, and screw it into the bottom of the collar.
8. Cut out the three base pieces—the center and both ends of the arrow—from the 3/4" x 4" board.
9. Get an adult to make a 1/4" wide groove 1/2" deep down one 3/4" edge of the board. The bottom of the animal will fit into this slot. This step will take either a power saw or a router.
10. Glue the front and back pieces of the arrow to the base, using carpenter's glue. Slide the animal into its slot, and glue it in place. Let dry.
11. Paint the base the same color as the collar.
12. Drill a hole 1-1/4" deep in the bottom of the weathervane, about 4" back from the wide point of the arrowhead.
13. With a hacksaw, cut a piece of brass tubing 1-1/4" long, and insert it into the hole.
14. Cut a piece of brass rod 2" long. Hammer it 1" into whatever you want the wind vane to sit on—a fencepost, for example. Lower the wind vane onto the brass rod, and allow the wind to do its work.

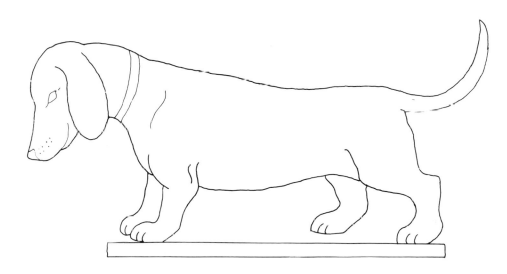

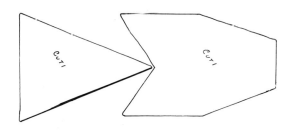

There are lots of different kinds of winds...icy, freeze-your-nose-off winds... sudden gusts that can knock you flat...moist, tropical currents...blasts of hot, sandy, desert air... cool, gentle breezes. People all over the world have given names to the winds. Here are some examples.

HABOOB
In Sudan (a country in Africa) any wind strong enough to create a sand storm.

BRICKFIELDER
Hot, dusty northeast wind that blows during the summer in southeastern Australia.

CHINOOK
Warm, dry, west wind that rushes down the eastern slopes of the Rocky Mountains in the western U.S. and Canada. Chinooks can cause temperatures to rise 20 to 40 degrees in just 15 minutes.

DOLDRUMS
Calm, almost still air near the Equator where northerly and southerly Trade Winds meet. (When people are feeling listless and blue, we sometimes say they're "in the doldrums.")

MISTRAL
Cold, dry, northerly wind that blows off the Mediterranean coasts of Spain and France. Over the centuries, many ships have been lost to mistrals.

WIND POWER

For centuries, the winds moved ships and people and cargo from place to place. Christopher Columbus would never have discovered the New World without wind. Exploring the high seas would have been left to Columbus's great-great-grandchildren, more than 200 years later—after the invention of the steam engine.

But the wind has served more than sailors and explorers. It has been used to grind grain since the 7th century. In fact, we still call almost any machine that's powered by the wind—no matter what job it does—a windmill.

In 15th-century Holland, windmills ran factories that sawed timber, processed wool, and ground spices. Farmers in the United States and Australia have used the wind to pump water to cattle and crops since the mid 1800s. By the early 1900s, there were more than 6 million water-pumping windmills in the U.S.—and there are still thousands operating today.

In the 1920s and 1930s, before electric wires were stretched to almost every community, many farm families in the West and Midwest used small wind generators—windmills that make electricity—to power lights and appliances.

Today, wind power is starting to become popular again. In California, "wind farmers" set up hundreds of wind generators in breezy mountain passes and sell the electricity to the companies that families and businesses get their electricity from. There are now more than 15,000 wind turbines in California, producing enough power to meet the needs of about a million people. California produces 80% of all the world's wind-generated electricity. Denmark produces much of the rest, but Australia, Germany, Spain, the Netherlands, the British Isles, and India also generate large amounts of electricity from the wind.

WHAT MAKES THE WINDS BLOW?

What happens when you blow up a balloon and take your finger off the end? The air whooshes out. That's because when you blew it up you forced air into the balloon under pressure. When you removed your finger, the air did what air does all over the world: move from an area of high pressure (inside the balloon) to an area of lower pressure (the area outside the balloon), in order to even things out.

Now think bigger. Imagine you're ship-wrecked on a tropical

WIND

Without wind, our world would be a completely different place.

Wind spreads the sun's heat around. If breezes didn't blow and air didn't move, more than half of the land on our planet would be too hot for plants to grow. And most of the rest of the earth's surface would be too cold. Nearly two-thirds of the United States would be under ice!

Wind also brings water to plants, animals, and people. Most of the world's moisture comes from the oceans, where it evaporates into the air. The wind blows that moisture in the form of clouds and water vapor to land, where it falls as rain, dew, snow, or ice.

Honeybees usually get the credit for helping plants reproduce by spreading pollen from flower to flower and tree to tree, but wind is really the world's most important pollinator. All evergreens (such as pines, hemlocks, and spruces), and many other trees, including all oaks and birches, rely on the wind to do the job. So do grasses and grains. Without wind, farmers couldn't grow wheat for flour and bread.

And just think of all the seeds you've seen blowing in the wind! Puffy dandelion "parachutes," maple-seed "helicopters," and hundreds of other kinds of seeds are scattered near and far by the wind. In fact, the wind sows more seeds than any other force in nature.

In other words, we have the wind to thank for earth's gentle climate, and for making life possible for most animals and plants—including the ones we humans use for food (such as milk and meat), for clothing (wool and cotton), and for shelter (lumber from trees).

island. As you lie on the beach in the morning, the sun rises higher and higher in the sky. The sand gets hotter and hotter. You get hotter and hotter. The air over the island gets hotter and hotter. And because that hot air weighs less than cold air, it rises—just like the air in a hot-air balloon. Result: There's less air pushing down on the surface of your island.

Meanwhile, out over the ocean, the air is cooler—heavier. It's pushing down more. In other words, the pressure is higher.

So just as you're starting to think, "Whew, it's really hot here," a cool breeze blows steadily in from the ocean—air rushing from a high-pressure area to a low-pressure area, just as it does when you loosen your grip on a balloon. That's why there's almost always a breeze blowing in from the sea when you go to the beach. Ahhh, paradise.

All over the world, wherever there's enough difference in temperature to create a difference in air pressure between two places, the wind blows from high to low trying to keep things equal. And the bigger the difference in pressure, the harder the wind.

FISH KITES

What You'll Need

- Bright colored tissue paper in large sheets*
- Scissors
- A glue stick
- Long pipe cleaners (10 to 12 inches long)
- Sequins, glitter, smaller pieces of colored tissue paper, stick-on dots

*This is available at craft stores and artists' supply stores.

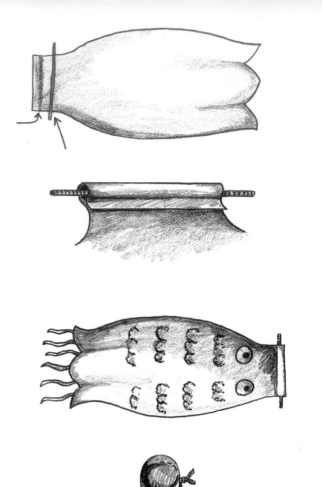

What to Do

1. Fold a piece of tissue paper in half lengthwise. Do *not* crease it.

2. Cut through both layers at one time in the shape shown in the illustration.

3. Unfold the paper.

4. Put a line of glue along the short, straight edge of the paper.

5. Lay a pipe cleaner next to the line of glue (on the side toward the body), then fold the glued paper over the pipe cleaner and press it down.

6. Turn the paper over.

7. Decorate the fish by gluing on some glitter, sequins, or bits of paper, or with stick-on dots sold with office supplies, or with anything you like. Remember that the fish will be folded down the middle, so you'll have to decorate both sides.

8. Holding the kite by the pipe cleaner end, carefully bend the pipe cleaner into a circle, and twist the ends together.

9. Run a line of glue all along one long edge of the fish. Press the other edge of the paper over the glue. Leave the tail end open.

10. Tie kite string to the mouth of the kite to form a bridle.

11. You can tie the bridle to a two-foot-long string and tie the other end of the string to a long pole. Or you can simply use string and run with your fish kite to make it fly.

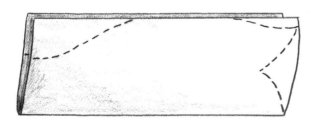

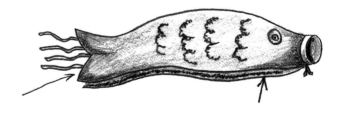

154

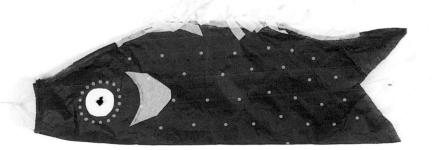

TEXAS NORTHER
Fast-moving, very cold arctic air that sweeps across the Great Plains from Canada into Texas. Texas Northers have been clocked at 70 miles an hour. Temperatures can fall as much as 50 degrees in three hours.

SIROCCO
("SI-ROCK-o")
Stifling hot wind that blows from the Sahara Desert across the north coast of Africa and the Mediterranean Sea to southern Europe, where it is known for making people depressed and irritable. When Italian lawyers defend their clients for doing crazy things, they sometimes "plead the sirocco."

WILLIWAW
In coastal and central Alaska, any brisk wind blowing down off the mountains.

PAMPERA
Extremely cold southerly wind that whips across the prairies (pampas) in Argentina and Uruguay.

SOUTHERLY BUSTER
In Australia, a sudden change from a moderate, relatively warm north wind to a brisk, very cold south wind.

PURGA
In Russia, a fierce northeasterly winter wind that whips snow from the ground into a driving blizzard.

NESTING SHELF

You can attract robins, phoebes, and barn swallows to your home with nesting shelves like this one. It provides a good, safe place for such birds to raise a family. And it's open on two sides, so you get to watch the birds build their nest, lay their eggs, and take care of their young.

What You'll Need

- One 4-foot-long 1 X 12 pine or fir board
- 14 to 18 1-1/2" 4-penny finishing nails
- A saw
- Sandpaper
- A drill
- A hammer
- House paint or wood stain

What to Do

1. Saw the parts of the nesting shelf (top, back, bottom, front, sides, and brace) to the sizes shown in the drawing. Measure carefully before you cut!

2. Drill holes around the bottom, or floor, of the nesting shelf so that rain and moisture can drain away.

3. Sand all the pieces. Make sure the edges are smooth.

4. Paint or stain all the parts using neutral-color house paint or wood stain. Be sure to cover both sides and all four edges of each piece.

5. Nail the front and right side pieces to the bottom. Drill 1/16" holes first to avoid splitting the wood.

6. Now (drilling first each time) attach the left side . . . the back . . . the brace . . . and the top.

7. Hang the nesting shelf six to 10 feet up from the ground on a wall or a tree trunk that faces north or northeast, and wait for a family to move in!

BACK 6 3/4" 10"

BOTTOM 6" 8"

SIDE 10" 8" 9 1/2"

FRONT 1 1/2" 6 3/4"

SIDE 1 1/2" 8"

BRACE 3 1/2" 18"

TOP 10" 10"

EGGS WITH PRESSED FLOWERS AND LEAVES

What You'll Need

■ Hard-boiled eggs
■ Small pressed flowers or leaves
■ Rubber cement

What to Do

1. Make sure the eggs are room temperature—neither hot nor cold. Wipe them with a tissue or soft cloth, to remove dust or smudges.
2. Paint a nice even layer of rubber cement where you want the leaf or flower to be.
3. Lay the leaf or flower on the wet rubber cement, and gently pat it down until it is glued flat to the egg.
4. Glue down all the other leaves and flowers that you want on the egg.
5. After the rubber cement has dried, carefully rub away any extra.

A small ball of rubber cement is good for rubbing other cement away. To make a ball, paint a thick stroke or two of rubber cement on a piece of scrap paper. After it dries, rub it into a ball. Add more cement if it's too small to hold. When you get a ball you can grip between two fingers, use it to clean up your egg.

EGG SHAPES AND COLORS

Between the time that it's laid and the time a baby bird hatches out of it, an egg is an accident waiting to happen. But its own special shape and color help to protect it.

Seabirds that build their nests high up on ledges lay eggs that are round on one end and pointed on the other. If a mother bird accidentally bumps into an egg and it starts to roll, it just goes around in a circle instead of falling off the cliff. Owls, on the other hand, live in hollowed-out trees, where there's practically no danger of an egg tumbling out of the nest.

Owl eggs are almost perfectly round.

Owl eggs are also white—and so are the eggs of most other birds that nest in holes or dark, covered places. That's because, if the eggs were colored, they'd be hard for the mother to see. She might step on them and break them. Birds that nest in the open, on or near the ground, lay eggs that are camouflaged. They're colored, spotted, or dotted so that they blend in with their surroundings and are hard for egg-eating animals (and other birds) to see.

Eggs of a brown-headed cowbird...

a blue jay...

a robin...

and a whippoorwill.

EGG RECORDS

WORLD'S BIGGEST: ostrich eggs, about 5 inches across and 3-1/2 pounds. (It takes 40 minutes to soft-boil one.)

WORLD'S SMALLEST: vervain hummingbird eggs, about 1/3 inch long and1/100 of an ounce.

MOST LAID IN ONE YEAR: 371, by a hard-working chicken.

EGGS DYED
WITH ONION SKINS

What You'll Need

■ Onion skins from yellow or red onions*
■ A pan
■ White eggs
■ Leaves or flowers
■ Old pantyhose or knee-highs
■ Twist ties

*Your local grocery store will probably let you have the loose skins from the onion bin. You'll need enough to fill a large pan.

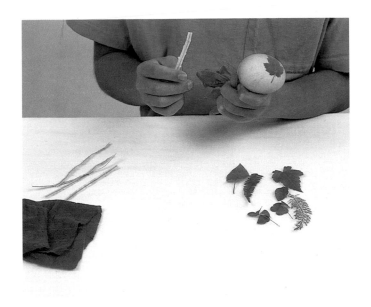

What to Do

1. Put the onion skins in a pan, and add about 3 inches of water (enough to cover the eggs when you add them the next day). Bring the water to a boil, reduce the heat, and simmer the onion skins for about 5 minutes. Remove from the heat and let the pan sit overnight.

2. Cut a piece of old pantyhose about 6 inches square.

3. Now attach a leaf or flower to an egg. To do that, dip the leaf in water and lay it on the egg. (The water helps hold it in position.) Wrap the square of hosiery over the leaf and around the egg, twisting the hose in back and tying it with a twist tie.

4. Put the wrapped eggs in the pan of dye. Dye only one layer of eggs at a time, and use the wet onion skins to keep the eggs apart.

5. Put the pan of eggs and dye on the stove and bring almost to a boil. Quickly reduce the heat (don't let them bang around, or they might break), and simmer about 30 minutes. Remove them from the heat, let them cool, and unwrap the eggs. Dry them off and coat them with a thin layer of vegetable oil, to make them shiny.

6. You can use the dye over and over again. When you're through with it, you can dump it in the garden, to help mulch the plants.

WILD FLOWER CANDLES

What You'll Need

- Paraffin
- Fat white candles
- Pressed wild flowers
- An old tin can with label removed
- An old soft paintbrush
- A pot of water
- Old newspapers

What to Do

1. Collect some wild flowers and press them. Put the flowers between two sheets of paper towel and stack a big book on top, or use a flower press. They'll need to dry for several days.

2. On the day of the project, gather your materials. Be sure the flowers are flat and rather dry.

3. Ask a grownup to help you melt a few chunks of paraffin. To do this, put water in the pot and put the paraffin in the can. Put the can of paraffin in the water. Boil the water in the pot. Watch the paraffin carefully, for it can catch fire easily. *Never melt paraffin directly over the burner. Always use the double boiler method described above.*

4. Hold a candle in one hand so that one side of it is level, and place a wild flower on the candle.

5. Dip the paintbrush in the melted paraffin.

6. Quickly but carefully brush a thin layer of paraffin over the flower to glue it to the side of the candle. If your paintbrush hardens, dip it in the warm paraffin.

7. Continue placing the flowers and painting them down. The paraffin will cool quickly and will harden as it cools.

GIFT TAGS, BOOK MARKS, NOTE CARDS

What You'll Need

- Construction paper
- A pencil
- A ruler
- Pressed leaves and flowers
- A small, pointed paint brush
- White glue
- Crayons, paint pens, or pastel crayons
- Clear self-sticking plastic with removable backing*

*Available at most department stores and discount marts.

What to Do

1. Using the pencil and ruler, draw the outline of your bookmark, tag, or card on the construction paper. If you're making gift tags (as shown in the photo) or note cards, make them big enough to fold in half, and decorate only the front half.

2. Lay your pressed flowers and leaves on the tag, in a pattern you like. Move them carefully, for they are delicate and will break. (A dry paint brush is good for moving them around.)

3. When you get the pressed materials where you want them, pick up one large piece at a time, and use the paint brush to put a *little* white glue on the back. Then put the piece back into position. You only need to glue the large parts, not the stems or tiny leaves.

4. Once everything is glued in place and has had time to dry, look at the design and decide if it needs more decoration. If it does, use your crayons, paint pens, or pastels to add lines or whatever you want. Be careful not to disturb the pressed leaves and flowers.

5. Cut out a piece of contact plastic larger than the outline of the gift tag. Peel off the backing and place the plastic over the tag. Starting at one end, smooth down the plastic and press it firmly against your design.

6. Cut out the gift tag.

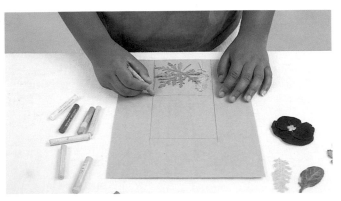

CANDIED VIOLETS

Violets bloom in the early spring, telling us that winter is really over. They grow in damp, shady places and may be white, yellow, or pale lavender, but their best-known color is, of course, "violet." Their heart-shaped leaves and five-petaled flowers are used in soups and salads, and both can be "candied"—although candied leaves are mostly for decoration. Candied flowers look nice on top of cake, fruit, or ice cream.

What You'll Need

■ Violet flowers and leaves
■ An egg white
■ Sugar
■ Brushes

What to Do

1. Wash the violets and leaves, and let them dry.
2. Separate the egg. To do that, hold it over a small, clean bowl, and crack the shell about in the middle. Then pour the egg back and forth between the two shell halves, keeping the yolk in the shell and letting the white run into the bowl. Throw away the shell and the yolk.
3. Dip the small brush in the egg white, and brush it on the violet petals, covering both the front and back sides.
4. Sprinkle sugar on the violets, covering them completely.
5. Put the violets on waxed paper to dry.
6. You can candy the leaves the same way.

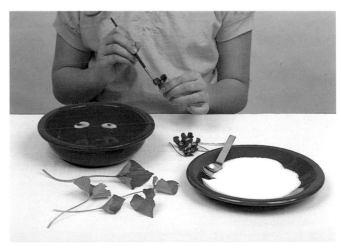

WORMERY

What You'll Need

- A quart-sized glass jar
- Sand
- Dark garden soil
- A trowel
- Worms
- Rotted leaves/compost
- A spray bottle of water
- Black construction paper big enough to wrap around the jar
- Cellophane tape
- Scissors
- Squeeze-on plastic fabric paints

What to Do

1. Place a layer of sand around 1-1/2 inches deep in the jar.

2. Place a layer of soil around the same depth on top of the sand.

3. Continue alternating layers of sand and soil, smoothing each layer as you go.

4. Add 3 or 4 earthworms to the top layer of soil.

5. Cover the top layer with a layer of rotted leaves or compost.

6. Spray the compost or leaves lightly with water.

7. Cut black paper to fit around the jar.

8. Put a strip of tape down one short edge of the paper, about an inch from the end.

9. Decorate the paper with squeeze-on plastic paint.

10. Wrap the paper around the jar end. Make a tab of tape that is attached to the paper on the end that does not have the strip of tape. When the paper is wrapped, you can stick and unstick the tape tab to the shiny cellophane tape strip.

11. Untape the tab after a few days and remove the paper to see what the worms have done to the layers of sand and soil. Make a drawing of their tunnels every few days to record their actions.

EAT DIRT, YOU WORM!

Worms don't just push their way through the soil, they *eat* their way through. In a single day an earthworm gobbles up more than its own weight in dirt, sand, bits of leaves and grass, and almost anything else that happens to be in its way as it burrows from one place to another. By the time the stuff comes out the worm's other end, it has been ground up and mixed with the worm's own body fluids and is a perfect food for plants. (That's why gardeners are always so happy to find earthworms in their garden.)

Sometimes you see worm castings, like little piled-up mud pies, on the ground. But most castings are left behind in the ground, where they become part of the soil.

Earthworms also get food by coming to the surface at night and pulling leaves and other pieces of plants into their burrows. In one study of earthworms in an apple orchard, scientists discovered that, by spring, night crawlers had buried 90% of all the leaves that had fallen the year before—about a ton of leaves per acre!

Worms, in fact, are the reason why Roman ruins

and other ancient buildings seem to "sink" into the ground over the centuries. By constantly churning up the dirt beneath the foundations and adding new soil near the surface, worms gradually bury the buildings.

The reason why earthworms can do so much is that there are so many of them. Researchers have counted as many as two *million* earthworms per acre in some soils in the United States. That's more than 400 worms in every square yard. In fact, the worms in an acre of rich pasture may weigh more than the cows and horses grazing on it—as much as 12 tons!

No wonder earthworms make so much good top-soil. Scientists say that, on the average, the earthworms in an acre of ground add 105,000 pounds of castings to the soil every year!

SUN PRINTS

What You'll Need

You'll need to buy two things at a camera shop:
- A package of photographic paper, either 5 x 7 inches or larger
- A package of fixcr (sodium thiosulfate)

You'll also need:
- A piece of glass slightly larger than the photographic paper
- A piece of heavy cardboard slightly larger than the glass
- A glass dish about 10 x 6 x 2 inches (a glass baking dish would do nicely)
- A sink
- A flat counter top
- Grasses, ferns, feathers, seed heads—whatever you would like to print

What to Do

1. Clean the glass and the glass dish, and dry them both.

2. Put 2 cups of warm water in the glass dish.

3. Slowly add 1/4 cup of fixer crystals to the water, stirring as you add.

4. Take one sheet of photographic paper out of its black, light-proof envelope and lay it on the cardboard, shiny side up.

5. Arrange the items you are printing on the paper. For example, if you're printing a fern, lay it on the paper.

6. Cover the paper and the items with the piece of glass.

7. Put the cardboard with paper and glass in bright sunlight for about 100 seconds. The paper will turn grayish purple.

8. Bring everything inside. (If the paper begins to get pink in places, bring it inside even if the 100 seconds aren't up.)

9. Carefully remove the glass and the items that were printed, and place the paper in the fixer solution. Stir the fixer around and over the print for around 2 minutes. Try not to touch the surface of the print. If it starts to get faded, take it out of the fixer and go on to the next step, even if the two minutes aren't up yet.

10. Rinse the print under cool running water for about 5 minutes.

11. Lay the print on a flat surface to dry. You can use the counter top. The print will change color as it dries.

12. You can punch holes in your prints and tie them together with yarn to make a collection. Or you might want to glue them with rubber cement to colored paper and hang them up for display.

SUN CLOCK

What You'll Need

- A saw
- A piece of wood about 12 inches square
- A piece of plywood or hardboard 1/8 inch thick and about 6 inches by 8 inches
- Two 6-inch strips of wooden molding
- Carpenter's glue
- A watch with hands
- A pencil
- Acrylic paints
- A paintbrush
- Urethane varnish
- A varnish brush

What to Do

1. Cut the wood into the shapes shown in the drawing.

2. Stand the blade up as shown in the picture, exactly in the middle along one edge of the square board. Glue the blade to the board, and glue the pieces of molding on both sides of the blade.

3. Place the sundial in a spot that gets sun all day long. You could put it on the ground, on a tree stump, on a concrete block, or on a few bricks. Wherever it is, place the sundial so that the blade points to the north. Step 4 will tell you how to find north.

4. On a sunny day, hold your watch in your hand and turn it so the hour hand points to the sun. Holding the watch very still, find the spot exactly between the hour hand and the 12. That spot points

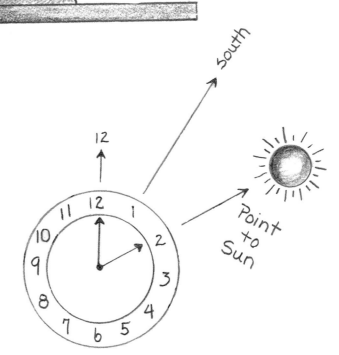

south (if you live in the northern hemisphere). To find north, point exactly opposite.

5. Turn your sun clock so that the blade points north. Mark the position of the clock so you can return it to the same position if you need to move it.

6. This step may take a couple of days. Go outside every hour on the hour, and use a pencil to draw the shadow of the blade on the sundial. Be sure to mark the time on the clock also.

7. After you've marked all the hours of daylight, paint the sun clock. Be sure to include the numerals so you can read them as the shadow of the blade moves across the face of the dial. (We've used Roman numerals, but you can use regular numerals if you'd rather.)

8. With a paint brush, coat the entire sun clock, back and front, with urethane varnish to weatherproof it.

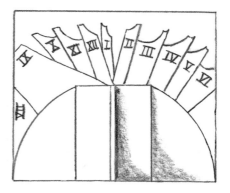

POCKET SUNDIAL

The sundial is the oldest scientific instrument still in use. Long before mechanical clocks and watches were invented, people used sundials to tell time.

As the sun moves across the sky, the shadows it casts change their position. Ancient peoples learned to mark where shadows fell on a sundial to tell the time of day.

This particular sundial is called a cylinder, or shepherd's dial. It was widely used hundreds of years ago because it was inexpensive, simple to make, and easy to carry. Some dials were more elaborate. George Washington carried a silver pocket dial.

What You'll Need

■ A wooded dowel 1 inch thick (a piece of broomstick would do)
■ A nail or an awl
■ A screw eye
■ A wire nail 1 inch long
■ A saw
■ A hammer

What to Do

1. Cut a piece of dowel 4 inches long.
2. With a nail or awl, make a small hole in the top of the dowel, and screw the screw eye into it. The screw eye must be in the center of the dowel end.
3. Hammer the wire nail lightly into the dowel about 1/2 inch from the top (the end with the screw eye). Drive the nail in only far enough to hold it firmly. Be sure the nail sticks straight out.
4. Use a photocopy machine to copy the sundial graph, and carefully cut it out along the dotted lines. Also cut out the small dotted circle. You can color the hour lines if you like.
5. Wrap the graph around the dowel, with the top touching the nail.
6. Overlap the ends of the graph, and tape it with cellophane tape. Don't let the tape touch the dial. Leave the graph a little loose so it can turn freely on the dowel.
7. Push the graph up until it touches the nail, and place a thumbtack at the bottom of the graph to keep it from sliding back down. Don't put the tack through the graph (the graph must turn).
8. Tie a short piece of string to the screw eye.
9. Glue the small circle that you cut out to the bottom end of sundial.

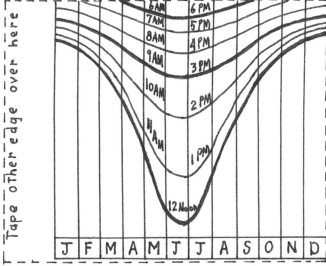

Add 1 Hr. for D.S.T.

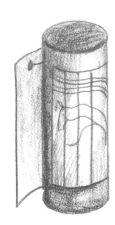
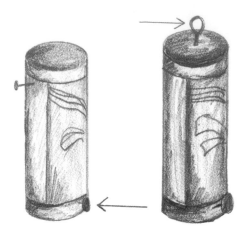

HOW TO USE YOUR SUNDIAL

1. The letters at the bottom of the graph represent the months of the year. Turn the graph on the dowel until the letter for the current month is directly below the nail.

2. Stand with your back to the sun and hold your dial up by the string. (The sun must be shining for the dial to work.)

3. Slowly rotate the entire dial until the shadow of the nail points straight down.

4. The shadow of the head of the nail will indicate the time on the graph. Notice where this nailhead shadow falls on the graph. Each curved line on the graph stands for two different hours. For example, 9 a.m. and 3 p.m. share the same line. If the shadow falls here it is either 9 a.m. or 3 p.m. You must decide which time it really is. Note: During Daylight Savings Time you will have to add one hour to the reading to get the correct time.

5. *Important:* Until you adjust the dial for your location it will not read correctly.

HOW TO ADJUST YOUR SUNDIAL

1. Hold the dial up in the sunlight and see where the nailhead shadow falls. Read the time on the graph.

2. Now, read the time on a normal clock or watch. You must adjust the length of the nail until your dial reads the same time as the clock. You can do this by slowly hammering the nail in until the dial reads correctly, or you may cut the nail off until it is correct.

3. *Important:* If you are doing this during Daylight Savings Time you must adjust the nail to read one hour less than what the clock reads. Later, when using the sundial, you must add one hour to the reading to get the correct time.

LEAF PRINT

What You'll Need

- Paper
- A pencil
- A plate
- Fresh leaves and/or flowers
- A paint brush about 1 inch wide
- Poster or tempera paints
- Box of tissues

What to Do

1. On an extra piece of paper, arrange your leaves and flowers in a circle, to get an idea of what you would like to make with them.

2. Using a pencil, lightly draw a circle on the paper you're going to use for your print. You can make the circle round by tracing around a plate.

3. Make a dot on the circle at the top center and the bottom center.

4. Brush paint on the back of a leaf, and place it carefully on the circle you've drawn. Make sure not to move it around, or the paint will smudge. (If you like, you can practice first on scrap paper.)

5. Cover the leaf with a tissue and smooth it down lightly. After a few seconds, lift the tissue and gently peel off the leaf.

6. Repeat the process with other leaves and flowers, working your way down one side of the circle and then the other.

WHICH LEAF IS WHICH?

There are over 330,000 different kinds of leafy plants in the world—and every one of them has its own special type of leaf!

For instance, some plants have leaves with *saw-toothed edges*, while others have perfectly *smooth* edges.

Saw-toothed vs. smooth.

Some plants' leaves grow directly across the branch from another leaf. Those are known as *opposite-leaved plants*. Other plants have leaves that are never opposite each other. Instead, first there's a leaf on the left, then one on the right, then the next is on the left, and so on. Those are known as *alternate-leaved plants*.

Another clue is the number of leaflets or leaf blades—the flat green part—attached to the stem. *Simple* leaves have just one blade. *Compound* leaves have three or more leaflets on the same stem. *Hand-shaped* compound leaves have leaflets that are arranged like your fingers when you spread out your hand, or like the spokes of a wheel. *Feather-shaped* compound leaves have leaflets arranged up and down both sides of the stem, so the whole thing looks like a big feather.

Opposite vs. alternate.

Of course, leaves aren't just shapes and patterns. Each has its own special beauty. Some leaves are a slightly different color on top than on the bottom. Some reflect the sun's light more intensely than others. And have you noticed that each kind of leaf has its own way of moving in the breeze, depending on its shape, the length or stiffness of its stem, and the way it's attached to the branch? Oak leaves wave up and down, hickory leaves sway and bob, aspen leaves flutter like butterfly wings.

Simple vs. compound.

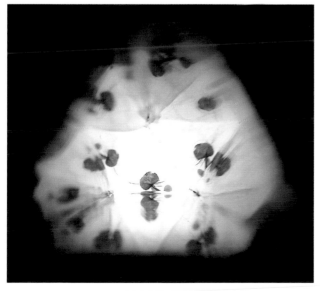

NATURE KALEIDOSCOPE

This project is more complicated than some others in this book, but not as hard as it might look at first. And when you're done, you'll have a kaleidoscope different from anyone else's. Hold it to the light, look through the eyehole, and watch beautiful patterns and colors take shape.

What You'll Need

- A small (4-inch or 10-inch) mailing tube with a lid that slides off and on*
- A sharp craft knife
- A pencil
- A hammer

177

- An awl
- A large screwdriver
- A ruler
- A piece of light cardboard (such as the lid of a shoe box) at least 6 inches wide and as long as your mailing tube
- A sheet of clear acetate**
- A fat permanent black marker that will write on acetate
- Clear contact paper
- Pressed flowers, leaves, and stems

*Look for mailing tubes where stationery and mailing labels are sold.
**Clear acetate is sold in art supply stores.

What to Do

1. Take the cap off the mailing tube. Use the craft knife to cut the metal end off the cap.
2. Cut a 1/2-inch-wide cylinder off the end of the mailing tube. (To make sure your cut is even, mark dots 1/2 inch from the end of the tube in 4 or 5 places, then connect the dots. Use the line to guide you as you cut.)
3. Now make your eyehole. Use the hammer and awl to punch several holes as close together as possible in the metal end of the mailing tube. Then use the screwdriver to ream out the nail holes until you've got one hole about 1/4 inch across.

4. Measure the inside diameter of the mailing tube. Now cut 3 pieces of cardboard. Each one must be a rectangle: as long as the mailing tube and 1/4 inch narrower than the inside diameter of the mailing tube.
5. Cut 3 pieces of acetate the exact size as the 3 pieces of cardboard.
6. Use the marker to completely blacken one side of each piece of acetate.
7. Tape a piece of acetate to each piece of cardboard, with the blackened side against the cardboard. Put the tape only along the short edges of the cardboard, and bend the piece of tape over the end to make it stay.
8. Tape the 3 pieces of cardboard into a 3-sided triangular shape, with the black sides facing inside.
9. Carefully slide the cardboard triangle into the mailing tube, pushing it all the way to the end. The end of the triangle should be even with the rim of the tube. If it sticks out, take it out and trim it to fit. And it should fit tightly into the tube. If it's loose, put tape around the outside to pad it.
10. Next make the endpiece. Use the 1/2-inch cylinder (the one you cut off the mailing tube) to draw one circle on acetate and one on a piece of clear contact paper that has been folded over and stuck together to make a double sheet. Cut out both circles.
11. Tape the acetate circle over one end of the 1/2-inch cylinder.
12. Peel the backing from a piece of clear contact

Mailing tube

Cut metal end off cap

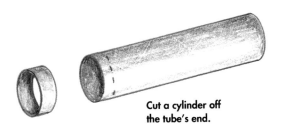

Cut a cylinder off the tube's end.

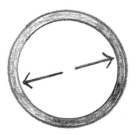

Measure inside diameter.

Cut 3 pieces of cardboard and 3 of acetate.

Tape acetate to cardboard

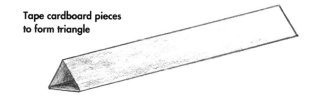

Tape cardboard pieces to form triangle

Insert triangle into mailing tube

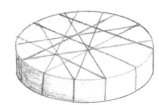

Make endpiece

Insert endpiece into tube

paper that is about 8 inches by 8 inches square. Place it sticky-side-up on the table. Carefully lay pressed flowers, small leaves, and small stems on the contact paper, with about an inch of empty paper around each leaf and flower. Now cover each leaf and flower with clear cellophane tape. Cut out the leaves and flowers and place them in the cylinder. Be sure there are no sticky edges. If the pieces seem to be clumping together, check again for sticky edges.

13. Tape the double-layered contact-paper circle over the open end of the cylinder, just as you taped the acetate circle over the other end. Shake it gently to be sure the pieces inside can move about freely.

14. Carefully slide the endpiece (the taped cylinder) into one end of the cap. Adjust the endpiece until it's even with the edge of the cap.

15. Put the cap (with the endpiece inside) onto the mailing tube. At this point you can test your kaleidoscope by looking toward a window and gently turning the cap while holding the mailing tube up to your eye. Try looking at different sources of light—a window, a light bulb.

16. To decorate the outside of your kaleidoscope, cut a piece of contact paper the same height as the part of the tube you want to decorate, and wide enough to wrap around it. Peel the backing off the paper, and lay pressed leaves or flowers on the sticky paper. Then carefully wrap the paper around the tube, smoothing out any bubbles as you wrap. Or you could draw designs on the tube, or glue cut-out pictures from magazines all over the outside of the tube with rubber cement.

WHAT DO LEAVES DO?

Have you ever leaned back under a shade tree and watched the leaves above you flutter in the breeze? You'd never guess that each one of those leaves is an amazing chemical factory. Leaves manufacture their own food by capturing energy from the sun and using it, in a process called photosynthesis, to change water from the soil and carbon dioxide gas from the air into simple sugar. At the same time, leaves release water vapor and oxygen (the gas we humans need to breathe) into the air.

Fortunately, leaves make much more food than they need for their own growth. They store the leftovers as starches, fats, oils, proteins, and other nutrients. When people or animals or insects eat the plants (or when they eat other creatures that have eaten the plants), they get that stored nourishment. Leaves, in other words, are the planet's basic food factories. Without them, there would be no life on Earth.

The water vapor that leaves give off is also vital. Plants take water in through their roots and draw it up to their leaves for photosynthesis. Most of the water, though, isn't needed, and evaporates into the air through tiny holes, called stomata, in leaf tissue.

Stomata are like the pores in human skin, only much smaller. There are about 161,000 stomata in just one square inch of an apple leaf!

Leaves release so much moisture into the air that they affect humidity and rainfall patterns. An average-size birch tree has about 200,000 leaves and releases more than 4,500 gallons of water in a single summer. The blades of grass in an acre of lawn give off 27,000 gallons of water every week during the growing season! According to some estimates, leaves are responsible for more than half of all the water that falls as rain on the Amazon rain forest!

THE BIGGEST

■ The world's largest leaves are 65 feet long, with stems up to 13 feet. They grow on two kinds of palm trees: the raffia palm, which grows in the Masearene Islands in the Indian Ocean, and the Amazonian bamboo palm, which is native to South America.

■ The world's largest floating leaf is that of the Royal water lily (*Victoria amazonica*). The huge, platelike discs grow up to 8 feet in diameter and will support a 50-pound child.

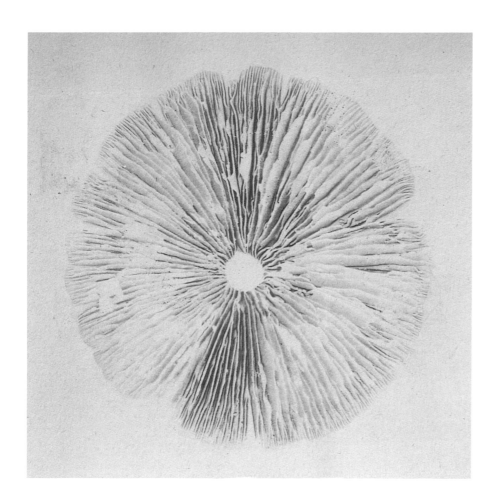

MUSHROOM SPORE PRINTS

Mushrooms come in various colors, and so do the spores they make. By catching the spores on paper before they have a chance to be spread around by the wind, you can make colorful mushroom "fingerprints."

What You'll Need

- Construction paper
- Fresh round-capped mushrooms
- A sharp knife or single-edge razor blade (BE CAREFUL!)
- Bowls or jars big enough to cover the mushroom caps
- A can of hair spray or artist's fixative
- A place to work away from breezes or drafts

MYSTERIOUS MUSHROOMS

Imagine an apple tree that grows entirely under the ground. The trunk and branches are buried. The only time you know the tree is there at all is when the apples pop up out of the soil, one at a time or in little bunches.

Of course, apples don't grow that way. But mushrooms do. A mushroom is the fruit of a plant with "branches" that grow underground, or in any sort of rotting stuff such as old wood or layers of leaves. Next time you find a mushroom, dig around it and you'll discover the "tree": a bunch of fine white threads all tangled together, called mycelium ("my-SEAL-ee-um"). The threads themselves are the "branches," and are called hyphae (HI-fee).

The mushroom's main purpose in life is to make spores. Spores are tiny "seeds" that will grow new mushroom plants. Even big spores are no larger than a speck of dust.

Most mushrooms have a stem and a cap. If you turn the cap over, you'll probably find a circle of thin, fleshy gills or hundreds of little holes. That's where the spores are—millions of them, waiting for a breeze to blow them into the air. Different kinds of mushrooms have different colors of spores. Sometimes, if you run your finger across the gills or holes, you can see a fine powder of spores on your skin. Or, you can take a spore print to see what color the "seeds" are.

What to Do

1. Cut off each mushroom's stem where it's attached to the cap.

2. Put the caps gill-side-down on construction paper. Try using different colors of paper to make the spore prints stand out. If the mushroom's gills are brown, gray, or black, use yellow or white paper. If the gills are white, use green, red, or some other bright color.

3. Put a bowl or jar over each cap to keep drafts out. Leave the mushrooms covered overnight.

4. The next morning, carefully lift the caps straight up off the paper. You'll find an interesting, round spore print under each one. The gills make a circular pattern, like a windmill or the spokes of a wheel.

5. Use hair spray or fixative to keep the spore prints from smudging. Be careful, though, or the spray will blow the spores. Hold the can about one foot away from and above the paper, and aim straight out (not down) at the print, so the spray falls gently on the print. Let the print dry, then spray it one or two more times to make sure it's completely protected.

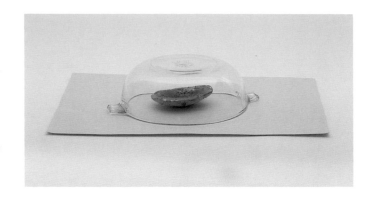

All mushrooms make spores, but not all have a stem, or even a cap. If you see a soft white or gray ball growing on the ground, you've found a puffball mushroom. Give it a gentle poke with your finger. Poof! Out comes a cloud of spores, like a puff of smoke.

In fact, there are thousands of kinds of mushrooms, in all sorts of shapes and colors. No wonder people have always thought mushrooms are magical and mysterious! There are mushrooms that look like icicles, turkey tails, sponges, trumpets, bowls, and pig's ears. There are green, orange, yellow, purple, bright red, and yellow mushrooms. Some ooze a milky liquid when you touch them. Others bruise blue or red. A few even glow in the dark!

Mushrooms have interesting names, too: shaggy mane, black jellydrops, witch's hat, hen of the woods, bear's head, beefsteak, stinkhorn, man-on-a-horse, and prince. Poisonous mushrooms have scary names, like panther cap, death cap, and destroying angel.

Because there are so many different types, and because they're so easy to find, studying mushrooms and collecting spore prints can be a lot of fun. Remember, though: NEVER eat a mushroom that you find outdoors. Eating just a tiny piece of a poisonous kind can make you seriously ill, or even kill you. Only experts can tell the difference between a dangerous mushroom and one that's okay to eat!

PAN PIPES

What You'll Need

- A length of bamboo*
- A small saw or hacksaw
- A piece of wooden stick or dowel
- A sharp penknife
- Glue
- String or twine

*If bamboo does not grow in your area, you can buy a cheap bamboo fishing pole at a sporting goods store.

What to Do

1. Saw off a length of bamboo about 6 or 8 inches long. It must have one end open and one end closed by a joint.

2. With the penknife, cut a sharp notch 1 inch from the open end of the bamboo. The notch must be cut through to the hollow part of the bamboo and must go about 1/3 of the way through the whole piece of bamboo.

3. Whittle out a 1-1/2 inch long wooden plug to go into the open end of the bamboo. It must fit snugly, but not split the bamboo. The plug must have a flat area carved on the top.

4. Put some .glue on the plug and push it into the bamboo until it just gets to the edge of the notch. Be sure the flat area is on top of the plug.

5. Blow into the whistle and move the plug in and out until you get the best sound.

6. Make several whistles of different lengths and get each one adjusted to make a clear whistle sound.

7. Split a piece of bamboo into 4 strips and tie the strips to the whistles, one at a time, as shown in the photo.

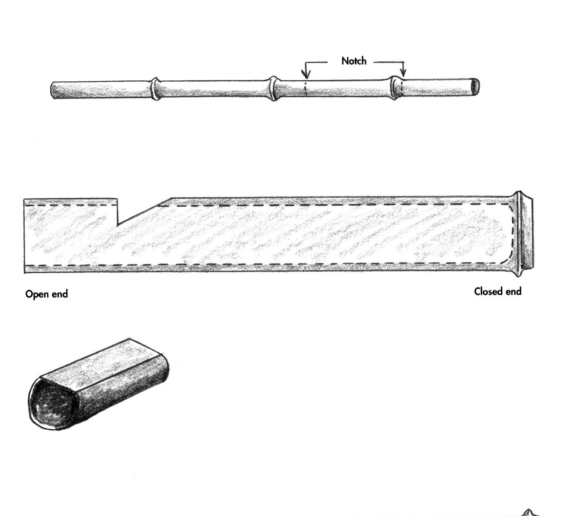

Notch

Open end

Closed end

Insert plug

HERB DOLLS

What You'll Need

- Fresh herbs
- A rubber band
- A piece of ribbon
- A doll's straw hat
- A hat pin

What to Do

1. Form a bunch of fresh herbs, and wrap a rubber band around their stem ends.
2. Tie a ribbon around the doll's "neck."
3. Attach a hat with a hat pin.
4. Hang the doll on the wall, or lean it wherever she's happy.

HERBS

If you asked everyone in your neighborhood to name one herb, chances are that most people would name a cooking herb, such as oregano. Most people don't know that an herb is any plant that has been used for cooking, as a medicine, or for its good smell. So the rose, which has been used for centuries to make teas and creams, is really an herb!

Scientists have found records of herbs dating back to Egypt in 2000 BC, where herb mixtures were used to preserve the bodies of kings and queens buried in the pyramids—in other words, to make mummies. Herbs have been used as medicines for centuries. By medieval times, almost everyone had a large garden of cooking herbs. Rich people used the fragrant herbs to cover up the bad smells of rotten meat (refrigerators had not been invented yet!), while poorer people lived on soups they made from herbs and water.

As time passed, food and housing became easier to find, and now people had time to care about other things, such as smell. Since they did not have toilets, toothbrushes, soaps, or showers, they were always in search of fragrant herbs that would make themselves smell better. When Victorian ladies had friends over to visit, they would carry a small bouquet of sweet-smelling herbs in front of their mouths to cover up their not-so-sweet breath. Victorians also disliked the damp, musky smells that came from the mud walls of their homes, so each home had a room called a stillroom where herbs and spices were made into perfumes to fragrance their clothes, furniture, and walls.

Herbs are still popular today, and they are used for many of the same reasons they were throughout history. We use them for making medicines like the heart drug digitalis, for making sauces, soups, and vinegars, and for making fragrant items such as soaps and candles.

BATH BAGS

If you wrap up some sweet-smelling plants in a loose-weaved fabric and tie it up with a long piece of twine, you can hang the bag from the faucet in your bathtub. Then, while the tub fills, the water will pour through the bag, and you will have scented bath water.

What You'll Need

- Pieces of muslin about 8 or 10 inches square
- Dried herbs and flowers
- Yarn or twine

What to Do

1. Place a handful of dried herbs in the center of each square.
2. Bring the four corners together, and tie the bag up with yarn.

PLANT PERFUMES

What You'll Need

- Grain alcohol*
- Good-smelling flowers or leaves**
- Small glass bottles with tight-fitting caps
- For tags (optional): A pressed leaf or flower from the plant you used to make the perfume, paper, clear self-adhesive paper

* Don't use rubbing alcohol; it has too strong an odor. An adult will have to buy grain alcohol for you. (One well-known brand is Everclear.)
** Examples of good-smelling plants are dried rose petals, lavender leaves or flowers, mint leaves, jasmine flowers, and gardenia petals.

What to Do

1. Chop or cut the plant material into tiny pieces.
2. Put the pieces in a small bottle, and add the grain alcohol. Be sure to fill the bottle completely, so there is very little air in it.

3. Let the perfume sit for two weeks. Then uncap it and strain the perfume to remove the pieces of plant.
4. Smell the perfume. If it smells like the plant, recap the bottle and let it age for another week. If it doesn't smell strong enough, chop up some more of the plant, and let the perfume sit another two weeks.

5. If you like, make a pretty label for your perfume with a pressed leaf or flower. Lay the pressed plant on a small square of paper, then sandwich it between two small squares of clear contact paper. Punch a hole in the corner, thread a small ribbon or string through the hole, and tie it to the bottle.

186

PET COLLARS

Fleas seem to hate the herb pennyroyal, although humans and animals find it very sweet-smelling. A collar stuffed with dried pennyroyal will help keep fleas off your pets. You can make either the loose style, worn by the dog in the pictures, or the tube style, which is more suitable for a cat.

FOR THE LOOSE STYLE:

What You'll Need

- A cotton bandanna or other cotton fabric
- A sewing machine
- Matching thread
- Dried pennyroyal

What to Do

1. Cut the bandanna into a triangle. Make sure one end is long enough to tie comfortably around your dog's neck.
2. Fold over the top edge by about 3 inches. Get an adult to help you sew along the edge, creating a hollow tube. Leave one end open.
3. Stuff dried pennyroyal into the opening.
4. Sew up the opening..

FOR THE TUBE STYLE:

What You'll Need

- A cotton bandanna or other cotton fabric
- A sewing machine
- A piece of Velcro about 3 inches long
- Dried pennyroyal

What to Do

1. Measure your pet's neck. Cut the fabric 3 inches wide and 1/2 inch longer than your pet's neck measurement.

2. Fold the material in half with its right sides together, so you have a long skinny tube. Now sew up the long side and one of the short ends. Turn the tube inside out; the right side of the fabric should now be on the outside.

3. Sew half the Velcro piece on one end. (A piece of Velcro divides into 2 parts.)

4. Using a funnel to make it easier, stuff dried pennyroyal into the tube. Stop stuffing when you've filled the tube up to about 3 inches from the open end.

5. Sew the other half of the Velcro on the other end of the collar. Make sure it's on the opposite side from the first piece, so you can make a circle of the collar and attach it to your pet.

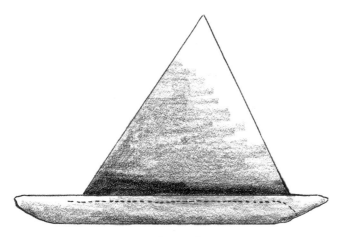

Loose style

Tube style

188

ANT HOUSE

What You'll Need

■ Two glass jars with lids. One must be very narrow—like an olive jar, for example. The other must be slightly taller and wider, so the first jar can fit inside it.
■ A spoon
■ Ants
■ Sand
■ A small piece of wet sponge
■ Honey
■ An awl or nail, and a hammer
■ 2 pieces dark* construction paper
■ Scissors
■ A stapler
■ Tape
■ A rubber band
■ Light colored pencils or crayons

*The paper must be dark to keep the anthouse dark—the way the ants like it.

What to Do

1. Go outside and find some ants.
2. Put the lid on the smaller jar and place it inside the bigger one. Then carefully scoop some ants and the soil around them into the space between the two jars. Fill the jar about halfway with ants and soil.
3. Fill the rest of the bigger jar with sand. Use the stem end of the spoon to mix the sand and soil that are in the space. You do not have to mix it completely.
4. Put the piece of wet sponge and a small spoonful of honey into the jar, on top of the soil-and-sand mix. Then tightly put the lid on the bigger jar.
5. Use the awl or nail and the hammer to punch SMALL holes around the edges of the lid.
6. Cut a circle 8 inches in diameter out of dark construction paper. Make a cut from one edge to the center.
7. Curve the paper circle into a cone shape and staple it where the paper overlaps. Cut another piece of construction paper so that it's as tall as the flat side of the jar, and so that it reaches around the jar once with an inch overlap. Put a piece of clear tape down one short edge.
8. Wrap the paper around the jar. Tape the overlap. (The shiny surface of the edge you've already taped will make it possible for you to untape and retape the paper, so that you can check on your ants from time to time.)
9. Place the rubber band around the edge of the jar lid to help hold the roof of the house on.
10. Decorate the roof and sides of the house with colored pencils or crayons.
11. Set the roof on the house. Check on your ants in a day or so, and watch them tunnel and dig.

POOTER

A pooter is a device that helps you collect small insects without harming them. You'll suck them right into the jar.

What You'll Need

■ A jar
■ A rubber stopper that fits the jar tightly*
■ 2 feet of flexible plastic tubing, about 1/4 inch inside diameter*
■ Scissors
■ A 1-inch square of gauze, cheesecloth, or screening
■ A small rubber band
■ A power drill with a large drill bit (1/4-inch works best)

*Look for the stopper and the plastic tubing in a store that sells wine-making supplies or in a hardware store.

What to Do

1. Get an adult to help you with the first step. With the power drill, drill two holes in the rubber stopper. (If your drill bit is narrower than your plastic tubing, tilt the drill from side to side to widen the hole as you drill.)
2. Cut the plastic tubing in half with scissors. Push each piece through one of the holes in the stopper. If you have trouble forcing the tubing through the holes, put a little dish detergent on the outside of the tubing to lubricate it.
3. Use the rubber band to fasten the gauze square over the end of one piece of tubing. Make sure you put it on an end that will be inside the jar.
4. Put the stopper in the mouth of the jar.

How to Use It

Go outside and look for a small insect. (It must be small enough to fit through the tubing!) Quietly walk up to the insect and place the end of the tube that does NOT have gauze as close as possible to the insect. Put the other tube—the tube with the gauze on it—in your mouth and suck on the other end of it. The insect will be vacuumed into the pooter by the suction. The gauze keeps the insect from being sucked into your mouth.

You can use a magnifying glass to study the insect. When you're finished studying it, unstop the pooter and release the insect into its environment.

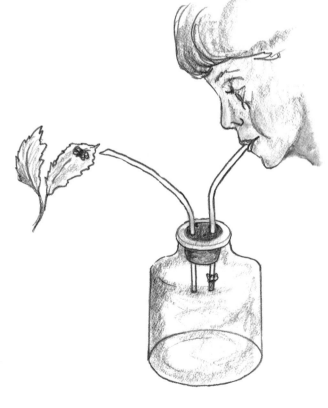

190

BUG BOX

This handy box will hold all the creepy crawlies you catch this summer, as well as any food you need to give them. The screen admits all the air your new "pets" need, and you can watch them go about their business.

What You'll Need

- A board 3/4" by 3-1/2" by 24"
- A piece of 1/4" plywood
- A piece of screening 7-1/2" by 14-1/2"
- A piece of fiber splint 1/2" x 48"*
- A #6 x 3/4" wood screw
- 3/4" finishing nails
- 2 screw eyes
- A saw
- Wood glue
- A coat hanger
- Shears or heavy scissors for cutting screen
- A staple gun

*Fiber splint is used for weaving chair bottoms and is available in many craft stores. Reed for weaving baskets would work fine— or anything else flexible and smooth enough to cover the raw ends of the screening.

What to Do

1. Cut out all the wood pieces to the sizes shown on the drawing.

2. Cut or drill a 1-3/4" hole in one end piece.

3. Screw the door to this piece, using the wood screw. (Drill a hole for the screw first.)

4. Spread wood glue in the cut-out sections of the bottom, and stand the end pieces on top of the cut-out areas. Nail the ends to the bottom with the finishing nails. Let the frame dry.

5. Stretch the screening over the frame and staple it on. Cut off any excess screen.

6. Staple the fiber splint over the edges of the screen, as shown in the picture.

7. Using a nail, start holes at the top of each end, and screw in the screw eyes.

8. Cut and fold a wire coat hanger to make a handle, insert the ends through the screw eyes, and bend the ends so the handle will hold.

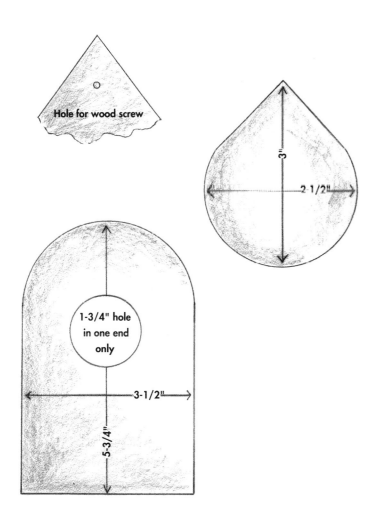

Hole for wood screw

3"

2-1/2"

1-3/4" hole in one end only

3-1/2"

5-3/4"

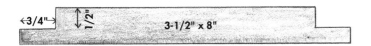

3/4"   1/2"   3-1/2" x 8"

Sand Candles

If you're near a beach, it's fun to make your candles right on the beach by digging holes in the sand. If you aren't near the seashore, you can still make the candles look just as good.

What You'll Need

- A beach; or a plastic dishpan; or a heavy cardboard box lined with a plastic garbage bag
- Sand to fill the container*
- A spray bottle filled with water
- Seashells
- Paraffin or beeswax**
  1 pound will make 3 or 4 small candles or 1 large one.
- Old crayons
- A tin can
- A pan
- A hot pad or oven mit
- Candle wicking**
- A big paper clip
- A soft paint brush

*Sand can be found in discount marts and lumberyards.

**Paraffin can be found in grocery stores and discount marts, alongside the canning supplies. Beeswax and candle wicking are sold in craft stores.

What to Do

1. Fill the dishpan or box with damp sand, and pat it smooth and level.
2. Dig a hole the size and shape you want your candle to be. Spray the sand with water if it crumbles.
3. Press seashells into the sides of the hole, with the shells' right sides facing the sand.
4. Ask an adult to help you melt the paraffin or wax. Place the paraffin or wax in the tin can, and add a

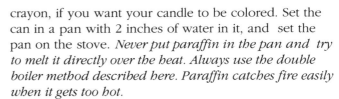

crayon, if you want your candle to be colored. Set the can in a pan with 2 inches of water in it, and set the pan on the stove. *Never put paraffin in the pan and try to melt it directly over the heat. Always use the double boiler method described here. Paraffin catches fire easily when it gets too hot.*

5. Dip a piece of wicking 4 inches longer than your candle in melted wax. Let it cool for 5 minutes, until it's stiff.

6. Place the dried wick in the middle of the sand hole. If the bottom of the hole will be the top of the candle, stick the wick an inch or so into the bottom of the hole. Hold onto the wick while you go onto the next step.

7. Using a hot pad or oven mitt, carefully pour the melted wax into the hole, filling it to the top.

8. As the wax cools, an air pocket may form beneath the surface. Use a straightened out paper clip to poke a hole in the wax skin. The skin may then collapse, and you will need to add more wax. You may need to repeat this step several times.

9. Let the candle cool for a couple of hours, or longer if it's a big one. Don't move the pan of sand.

10. When the candle is hard, gently dig the sand away from the edge with your finger. Soon you'll be able to grasp the candle and wiggle it like a loose tooth. Wiggle it out of the sand.

11. Stand the candle on the sand and gently brush the loose sand off, using a soft paint brush. Damp sand will stick to the candle, but it will dry quickly and you'll be able to brush it off. The finished candle will look sandy, and your seashells will peek through like shells on the beach at low tide.

THE AMAZING OCEAN

The ocean covers more than 70% of the Earth, or about 140 million square miles. It contains 97% of all the water in the world.

Although the ocean is actually one huge body of water, geographers divide it into four major oceans: the Pacific, Atlantic, Indian, and Arctic. The largest is the Pacific, which stretches across 64 million square miles, or about one-third of the planet. You could fit all the world's continents (North and South America, Europe, Asia, Africa, Australia and Antarctica) into the Pacific, and there'd still be over 7,000 square miles of sea left.

The deepest place in the ocean is in the Mariana Trench, in the western Pacific. The water there is over 6-1/2 miles (about 36,000 feet) deep. If you put the world's tallest mountain, Mt. Everest, into the Mariana Trench, the mountain's peak would be more than a mile beneath the water's surface!

The land under the sea has plains, hills, mountains, and valleys much like the land we live on. In some places, there are huge gorges and canyons at least as big as America's Grand Canyon. The highest underwater mountain, in the Pacific Ocean between New Zealand and the island of Samoa, is 28,500 feet tall. It's actually the second biggest mountain in the world.

FISH PRINT

What You'll Need

- A whole fish, cleaned but with the head on*
- Old newspapers
- Tempera paint
- A large, soft paint brush, about 1 inch wide
- Paper for the print**

*One way to get a whole fish is to catch your own. If you don't fish, the next easiest is a fish market or the meat department in the grocery store. If you don't see any whole fish on display, ask the person behind the counter to get a whole fish for you. Tell him or her that you want the fish cleaned but not scaled and that you want the head left on. Fish that are rather flat work best.
**The best kind of paper to use is Japanese block printing paper, which you can get in an art supply store. You can also use tissue paper or white shelf paper or soft drawing paper. The paper should be strong enough to stand up under wet paint. Shiny paper won't hold paint well.

What to Do

1. Lay the fish on a piece of old newspaper, and paint the entire fish with tempera paint.
2. Carefully lift the fish, trying not to touch the painted surfaces, and place it, painted side up, on a clean piece of newspaper.
3. Lay the piece of print paper over the fish, being careful not to move the paper once it touches the fish.

4. Gently rub the paper where it lies over the fish. Be sure not to move the paper.

5. Carefully peel the paper back from the fish and lay it flat to dry.

6. Use the fish print to make a simple banner, to decorate carp kite (see page 154), to wrap a present or to cover a book.

BANNER

What You'll Need

■ A fish print
■ Rubber cement
■ Scissors
■ 2 pieces of bamboo, each as long as the paper is wide. (If you don't have any of your own to cut, you can buy slender bamboo in a garden supply store where sticks are sold as tomato stakes.)
■ Yarn

What to Do

1. Turn the print right side down, and fold down 1 inch along both the top and bottom edges of the paper.

2. Brush a thin line of rubber cement along the very edge of each fold, and press the fold to the paper. Remember, you're creating a "tunnel" for the bamboo stick, so don't glue down the whole flap.

3. Cut tabs about an inch apart all along the two edges

4. Thread the bamboo poles through the tabs.

5. Cut a long piece of yarn and tie its ends to the ends of the top piece of bamboo, so that you can hang the banner.

SAND PAINTING

What You'll Need

- Powdered tempera paints*
- Sand—the whiter and finer, the better
- Small containers to mix colored sand in
- A spoon for each color
- A clean, dry glass jar or bottle
- Improvised tools for moving sand around, such as an opened-out paperclip, small, flat plastic sticks, etc.

*Look for them at a school supply store or craft store. If you can find only liquid tempera paints, you can use them too. But after you color the sand, you'll have to let it dry for a few days before you paint with it.

What to Do

1. Put about 1 cup of sand in each container. Add some paint, and stir until the color is even. Try mixing different colors together until you get a color you like.
2. Spoon the first layer of colored sand into the jar.

WHAT IS SAND?

If you take a rock and pound it with a hammer hard enough and long enough, you'll make sand. Nature does the same thing, but instead of a hammer it uses water, wind, and weather to crush rocks into tiny pieces.

All over the world, from the highest mountains to the ocean shores, nature is battering away at rocks to create the gritty material we call sand. Rain washes it into the soil and into streams and rivers, where it rolls along downstream. Eventually, much of the sand is washed out to sea.

Meanwhile, ocean waves constantly churn up rocks in the water and smash them together with other rocks, rock fragments, and sand. Gradually big pieces become small pieces, small pieces become tiny fragments, coarse sand becomes fine sand. Storms, tides, waves, and currents move the sand around. Some of it ends up on shore to make beaches and dunes. Some is buried at the bottom of the sea in huge piles.

There are many kinds of rocks, so there are many kinds of sand. Quartz, which is usually white or clear, is the most common mineral in sand. It comes from granite, a type of rock found almost everywhere in the world. Some beaches in Hawaii and other Pacific islands are made of black sand, which is actually grains of worn-down hardened lava, from volcanoes. Most beach sand also contains tiny bits of seashells and coral. Some beaches, such as Florida's famous white sand beaches, are made almost entirely of shell sand!

Make it as deep as you want, and smooth the top.

3. Carefully add the second color of sand right on top of the first. When it's as deep as you want and smooth on top, slide one of your flat tools down the side of the jar to move the sand into shapes.

This takes some practice, but soon you'll be able to push shapes into the bottom layer and then push the second layer to fill in the spaces that were left.

4. Smooth the second layer, adding more sand if you need to.

5. Add the other layers the same way. For variety, you can make a small section of a layer a different color from the rest. You can also push a shape into a layer and fill just that shape with a small amount of a different color.

How to Use It

Your sand painting makes a good candle holder. Or set a small potted plant on top. Or make a colorful terrarium in a large container, such as a gallon jar. Do the sand painting on the bottom 2 or 3 inches. Then top the sand painting with 4 inches of soil, add small plants, spray them with water, and cover the jar.

198

BEACH BASKET

What You'll Need

- Long grasses and sedges gathered from wetlands and dunes near the beach
- Vines, such as honeysuckle and grape
- Hand snippers or pruners
- A garbage bag
- An empty 1-gallon plastic milk jug with the top cut off

What to Do

1. Check with an adult before you go out to gather materials. Some grasses, such as sea oats, are endangered species and should never be picked. Be sure the grasses you want to gather are okay to pick. Take along a garbage bag to carry your grasses in and a pair of garden snippers or pruners for cutting.

Look at the back of the beach along the dunes or at a salt marsh near the beach for the longest grasses and sedges you can find. (Grasses have hollow, round stems. Sedges have solid, triangular-shaped stems.)

It's best to gather vines in fall or winter because they don't have so much juice in them then, and they are tougher and stronger. If you have to gather in spring or summer, pick the older part of the vine rather than the tender, new growth. The best vines for this basket are about as big around as a pencil—no bigger. Remove all leaves as you cut vines, but leave the curly tendrils on grapevines if you like the way they look.

2. You can store basketry materials for as long as you want. Be sure to keep them out of the sun in a cool, dry place. It's better NOT to store them in plastic bags, as they will mildew. Hang them up or stand them loosely in a trash can or small garbage can until you're ready to use them.

When you are ready to work, soak the materials for at least an hour in a tub full of water. If the materials are newly picked, you may not need to soak them at all. To see if they need soaking or if they have soaked long enough, wind an end of a vine or piece of grass around your finger. It should go around your finger

without breaking. Some vines have light bark on them that might crack when you wind the vine around your finger. If the inside of the vine doesn't break, you can go ahead and use the material.

3. To make the basket, first cut 8 *stakes* out of vines. Cut the stakes about 3 feet long, all the same length.

4. Lay 4 of the stakes side by side crossways on top of the other 4 stakes, as in Figure 1.

5. Select a long piece of grass or sedge or a slender vine to be the first *weaver*. Holding the tail of the weaver in place, wrap the weaver over 4 of the stakes that are ON TOP OF the cross, under the next 4 stakes, over the next 4, and under the last 4. Continue going over 4/under 4 for 3 more rounds. The bottom of your basket should now look like Figure 2.

6. At the end of the 4th round, bend the weaver around the 4 stakes it has just gone over, and go UNDER those 4 stakes, headed in the opposite direction (look at Figure 3). Go 4 rounds of over 4/under 4, just as you did before. The bottom of the basket should now look like Figure 4.

7. You will now begin BREAKING DOWN the groups of

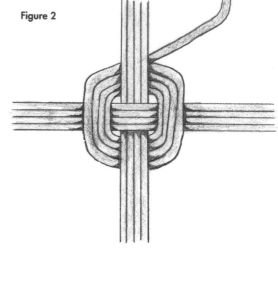

Figure 2

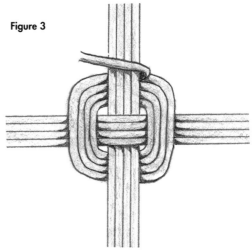

Figure 3

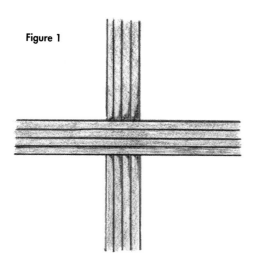

Figure 1

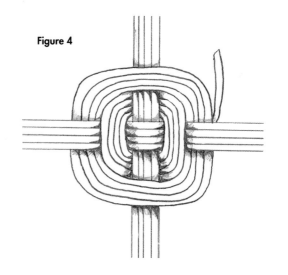

Figure 4

Figure 5

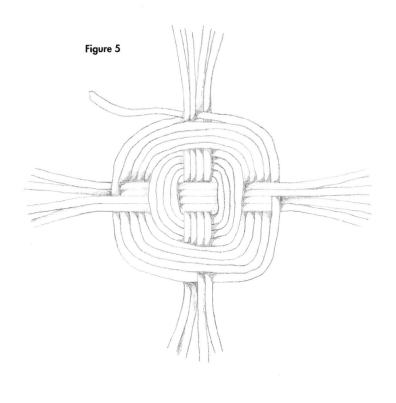

4 into groups of 2. Continue going over and under in the same direction, but this round go over 2/under 2. Pull the groups of 4 stakes apart as you weave, as in Figure 5.

8. When you get back to pair #1, you will notice something: if you went OVER pair #2 as you would if you kept going over 2/under 2, you would find that you would be placing your weaver exactly as it was on the last round, giving you two "overs" on the same pair of stakes. To avoid this problem, when you get back to #1, go UNDER it, even though you just went under #8. Then continue as usual, going OVER the next 2, under the next 2, etc. Each time you get back to #1 you will have to make this same adjustment and go the opposite way that you would expect to go. Just remember that your stakes, as well as your weavers, should look like Figure 6 (over-under-over-under).

9. Weave a few rounds with pairs of stakes, and then break down to single stakes. That is, go over 1/under 1.

10. As you weave, you'll need to add new weavers every round or so. To do that, simply hold the first few inches of the new weaver with the last few inches of the old weaver and use them together. As the old

Figure 6

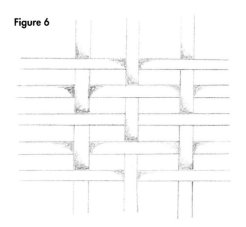

Figure 7

Figure 8

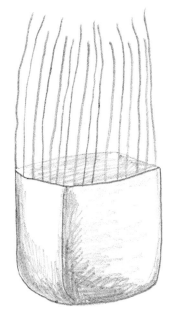

weaver ends, the new one will already be attached and can take over. See Figure 7.

11. After you have made the bottom of the basket the size you want it to be, you will need to curve the walls upward and inward. An easy way to do this is to gather all the stakes in the center, and then push the bottom down into the empty milk carton, as in Figure 8.

Let the basket sit for an hour or so. When you take it out, the stakes will be curved up into the shape of the walls of the basket.

12. Continue weaving until you are about 4 inches from the ends of the stakes (Figure 9). You can stop sooner if you want a smaller basket, but don't let the ends of the stakes get any shorter than about 4 inches or it will be very difficult to make a border on the basket.

13. To make a border, soak the stake ends until they are flexible. Then bend each stake over in front of the stake just after itself. As you go around the rim bending the stakes, a simple braid will form and the stakes will hold each other down and in place. Poke the end of the last stake under the first folded-over stake, as in Figure 10.

14. Trim any long ends with garden pruners.

Figure 10

Figure 9

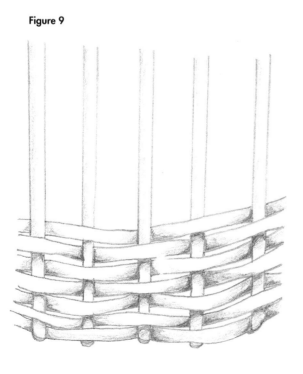

202

LEAF STAINED GLASS

What You'll Need

- Waxed paper
- Pressed leaves*
- Scissors
- An iron
- Old newspapers.

*See page 73 for directions for pressing flowers and leaves.

What to Do

1. Tear off two pieces of waxed paper a little larger than you want your finished stained glass to be.

2. Lay one piece of waxed paper on top of several sections of old newspaper.

3. Arrange the leaves on the waxed paper.

4. Put the second piece of waxed paper on top of the leaves.

5. With the iron set on "low," gently press the waxed paper sandwich. You will see the pieces of paper joining together. Keep moving the iron in circles until the whole top piece of paper is fused to the leaves and to the bottom paper

6. Trim the edges of the waxed paper to make them straight.

7. Hang your stained glass in a window using cellophane tape

WHY DO LEAVES TURN COLORS IN AUTUMN?

Nature really shows off in autumn, when the leaves on trees and shrubs in most parts of the top half of the world burst into colors. It's almost as though someone painted them. But actually, the secret of nature's artistry is inside the leaves. That's where, during the spring and summer, a substance called chlorophyll (pronounced klor-o-fill) uses energy from the sun to help make food for the plant. Chlorophyll is also what makes leaves green.

But there are other colors in leaves, too. It's just that, during the growing season, there's so much bold green chlorophyll you can't see the others. In the fall, though, the chlorophyll slowly fades, and the "shy" colors pop out, as if to say, "See? We're here, too!" The hidden colors are yellows, oranges, reds, browns, and even purple.

Some plants have mostly just one color in them. Poplar leaves, for instance, are strictly bright yellow, and sugar maple leaves are fiery red. Other leaves are a mixture of colors. Oak leaves, for example, have yellow, orange, and brown in them. Depending on how much of each color is mixed in, oak leaves can be anything from bright gold to dull bronze.

Some autumns are more colorful than others. Weather is the reason why. Usually, cool temperatures and lots of sunshine make an especially bright and beautiful fall leaf show. But if there was little rain during the summer, there will be more brown or dull-colored leaves and fewer bright red ones.

LEAF COLLECTION BOX

If you like to gather leaves, it's fun to save your collection. Just press the leaves, glue each one to an index card, and cover it with clear self-adhesive shelf paper. Then file it in a box you've decorated. For example, the leaves in the picture are all from scented geraniums, so they're filed under "G."

What You'll Need

- A wooden file box, the kind that holds index cards*
- Extra-fine sandpaper or steel wool
- Petroleum jelly
- A household sponge, cut into pieces about 2 inches by 1 inch
- Green acrylic paint**
- A paper plate
- A red paint pen
- A spray can of clear acrylic sealer**

 *Wooden file boxes are sold in craft stores and office supply stores.
**Acrylic paints and acrylic sealer are sold in craft stores and art supply stores.

What to Do

1. With the sandpaper or steel wool, lightly sand the sides of the box you're going to paint on.
2. It's best to work on one side of the box at a time. Put a dab of petroleum jelly in the center of each leaf and then position it on the box, jelly side down, smoothing it out. The jelly will hold the leaf in place temporarily.
3. When you've put all the leaves where you want them on one side of the box, put a little green paint on a paper plate. Dampen a piece of sponge, and dip it into the paint. Dab paint over and around the leaves on the box. Be careful not to move the leaves.
4. When the paint has dried, remove the leaves and wipe off any jelly that's left with a tissue.
5. Then do the other sides of the box the same way.
6. Use the red paint pen to add red dots where the box looks a little blank. The dots will look like little red berries.
7. When the paint is very dry, spray the painted sides with clear acrylic sealer, to protect it.

WHY DO TREES DROP THEIR LEAVES?

Animals get ready for the winter by adding more fat and growing thicker fur to keep warm. Trees get ready by dropping their leaves to keep from dying of thirst.

Leaves use up huge amounts of water. That's no problem most of the year, but in the winter, when the ground is frozen, a tree can't draw water in through its roots. It has to survive mostly on just the water stored in its trunk and branches. A leafy tree would quickly use up all the water and die. But a leafless tree can live on stored water for months.

So, as the weather gets colder and the leaves turn colors, a thin, soft layer forms between each leaf's stem and the twig or branch. All it takes to break the layer is a gust of wind, and the leaf comes tumbling down.

That's not the end of the story, though. On the ground beneath the tree, all the leaves gradually soften and fall apart. Before long they become part of the soil. Their nutrients are drawn up through the roots, into the tree itself, and eventually up to the leaves again.

In a way, then, leaves never really die. They just recycle themselves.

NEEDLE KNOWLEDGE

Most evergreens have leaves that look like needles. Many people think that evergreen trees never lose their leaves, but they do. Most types actually do shed their needles, but not all at once the way oaks and maples do. Instead, they drop their leaves gradually, continually replacing the ones that are lost with new needles.

What really sets evergreen leaves apart is their ability to survive winter. Their tough, thick skin and waxy coating protect them from freezing or drying out during cold, windy weather.

If you look closely at an evergreen's leaves, you can tell what kind of tree it is.

■ *If the needles are pointed and are growing in bunches,* with each group stuck together at the bottom by a little papery strip, you're looking at a pine tree. Only pine trees grow needles in clusters.

■ *If the needles are stiff and sharp and are growing all around the branch,* it's a spruce tree. Spruce needles actually have four sides.

■ *If the needles are flat and short with rounded ends and* are growing opposite each other on the branch, it's either a fir tree or a hemlock tree. But now look at the tree's top. If it's straight and pointed like a big spear, you've found a fir tree. If the top is sort of droopy-looking, the tree is c hemlock.

■ *If the "needles" are actually branches or twigs covered by tiny flat, green triangular leaves,* the tree is probably a cedar or cypress.

EVERGREEN GARLAND

What You'll Need

■ Fresh evergreen branches. (You can use all one kind or mix in several different kinds.)
■ Dried flowers, if you like
■ Flexible wire
■ Heavy cord or wire, for the spine*
■ Scissors

*Jute cord, the kind used for macrame craft projects, works well. So does a heavy-gauge wire, available in hardware stores.

What to Do

1. Cut the evergreens into small branches, about 6 to 8 inches long. If you're using dried flowers to add color, cut their stems about the same length or shorter.
2. Take a handful of branches and wire them together by their stems, using the flexible wire.
3. Make a whole series of these bunches, using your greenery and flowers any way you want. You can make a bunch of all one thing—all greens, all flowers—or combine different things in each bunch.
4. Cut the heavy cord or wire—the spine of the garland—as long as you want the garland to be.
5. Using the flexible wire, attach one of the bunches you've made to the spine. Just wrap the wire around the stems and the spine. Start at one end of the spine.
6. Then wire a second bunch onto the spine. Point the bunches in the same direction, and make sure the greenery from the second bunch overlaps the stems of the first.
7. Keep wiring on bunches of greenery and flowers until you've covered the spine. Then tie a knot in each end of the cord.
8. If you want, you can attach other decorations. Just glue these to it with tacky glue.

PAPER WITH INLAID LEAVES

What You'll Need

■ A blender
■ Scraps of old paper torn into small pieces*
■ Water
■ A plain wooden picture frame, 8 x 10 inches or larger
■ A piece of window screen material, 12 x 14 inches or larger
■ A staple gun or some waterproof glue
■ Pressed leaves or flower petals
■ A large plastic dishpan or baby bathtub
■ Some clean rags, at least 15 x 15 inches square
■ Old newspapers
■ A rolling pin
■ Metal shears or scissors to cut the screen
■ A bottle of chlorine bleach (optional)

*Soft, thick paper is best. You can also use lint from a dryer.

What to Do

1. Put the torn scraps of paper and water in the blender to soak.

2. Meanwhile, stretch the screen over the picture frame and staple it into place.

3. Blend the paper and water until it's smooth mush. If you're using dryer lint or any colored paper scraps and you want your paper to be white, add 1/4 cup of chlorine bleach to the blender.

4. Pour batches of mush into the tub, adding a little water if the mush is too thick, until you have around 5 inches of mushy water in the dishpan or baby bathtub.

5. Place the pressed leaves in a handy spot near the pan of mush.

6. Dip the frame under the mush; then, holding it level, shift it back and forth until a layer of mush settles evenly over the surface. This layer should be around 1/2 inch thick.

7. Without tilting the frame, lift frame and mush layer out of the dishpan. Hold the frame over the pan to let water drain out. If the mush clumps together or if there are holes, put the frame back under the mush layer and try again.

8. As soon as you have drained most of the water from the mush on the frame, press flattened leaves or flower petals into the layer of mush in a pleasing arrangement. They need not be completely covered, but must be at least partially covered or they won't stay on the paper

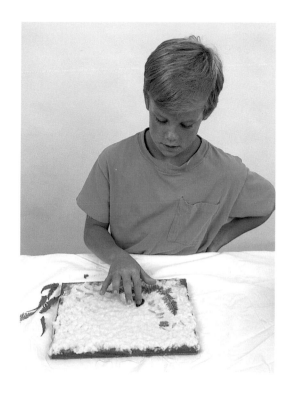

when it dries. You can gently push some mush over the leaves to help bury them.

9. Place a clean rag over the top of the drained mush layer. Press down gently, squeezing out more water.

10. Lay a few pieces of old newspaper down on a table. Carefully turn the frame, wet paper, and rag upside down onto the newspaper, and lift off the frame. Cover the wet paper with another rag. You now have a sandwich of two rags with a layer of wet paper in the middle.

11. Roll the sandwich with the rolling pin to press out even more water.

12. Carefully peel off the top rag. Turn the wet paper and bottom rag over onto either a smooth counter top or a piece of glass (you can use a window for this), paper side down, and then carefully peel off the remaining rag.

13. Let the paper dry overnight or longer.

14. If you want very smooth paper, spray the dry paper with spray laundry starch, put a clean smooth rag over the damp paper, and iron it with a slightly warm iron until the paper is dry. The starch will make the paper better for writing on, too.

15. You can use your inlaid paper to make cards, to wrap presents, for a cover for a handmade book, to write notes on, or in a window as a decorative window covering.

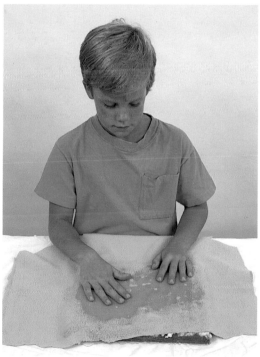

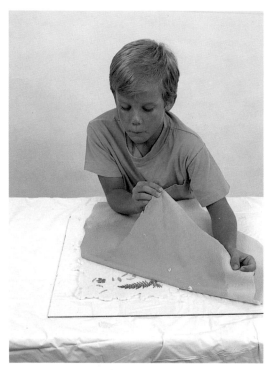

SEED MOSAIC

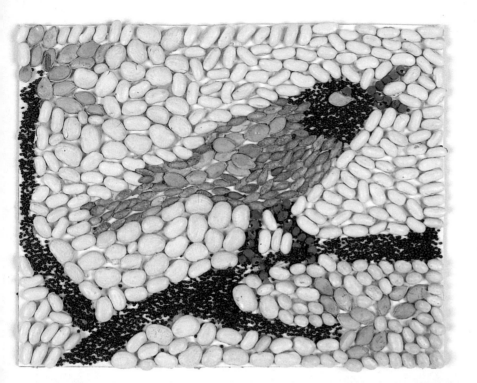

What You'll Need

■ A piece of heavy cardboard
■ A pencil
■ White glue
■ A variety of seeds

What to Do

1. Sketch your design lightly on the cardboard. You can draw real things, like animals, or just sketch in shapes that please you.
2. Glue the seeds on the cardboard to fill in your design.
3. For very tiny seeds, use a paintbrush to paint glue on the cardboard, then sprinkle the seeds onto the glue. Use your fingers to push the seeds in place. After a few minutes, turn the cardboard over and lightly tap the back, so that the extra seeds can fall off,

TRAVELING SEEDS

Seeds are nature's way of spreading plants around. If a seed falls straight to the ground beneath the mother plant and starts to grow, it has to compete with the bigger plant for sunlight, food, and water. Seeds get a much better start in life if they travel to new ground.

Many seeds, like the puffy "parachute" seeds of the dandelion, ride the wind. A dandelion flower launches hundreds of tiny seed travelers, each with its own cluster of silky hairs to keep it in the air as long as possible. Poplar and willow trees have very light seeds with a little balloon of cottony fluff that catches the breeze and can sail for miles.

Maple, elm, and ash trees send out winged seeds that twirl and spin like helicopter blades. The seeds are quite heavy, but they grow high up among the branches, where winds are strong enough to blow the "whirlybirds" to new soil.

Pinecones and the cones from other evergreens are full of "flying" seeds. Young cones are green and their scales are closed tight. But gradually the cones become dry and brown, and the seeds inside ripen. The cones open up and the papery seeds flutter away in the breeze. Most cones on the ground have already let their seeds go. If you can find a ripe cone still on the tree, peel it apart and toss the seeds into the air to see how they fly.

The seeds in fruits and berries get to their new location in a different way: They ride inside the stomachs of the birds and animals that eat them. Most seeds can't be digested, so they come out with their own little pile of manure fertilizer to help them grow.

Other seeds ride on animals—and on people, too. If you've ever taken a

A jewelweed flower

walk in some weeds and found your pants and socks covered with stickers and prickly burrs, you know how. Burdock, tickseed, and lots of other wild plants have seed cases covered with little hooks or spines that cling to fur and clothing. That's how some plants got from the New World to Europe (and vice-versa)—the seeds hitched a ride on the clothes of early explorers!

Ground squirrels and blue jays are the world's best planters of oak tree seeds. Both like to bury acorns, one at a time in its own hole, to be eaten later. But they don't always come back to get the nuts. Wildlife biologists say that's why oak trees often outnumber others types in forests.

Some plants literally throw their seeds to new soil! Jewelweed plants are called "touch-me-nots" because, if you touch a seed pod, it bursts open with a pop and hurls a shower of seeds in every direction. Witch hazel pods explode with so much force they toss their brown, shiny seeds as far as 40 feet!

Another clever traveler is the seed from alder trees, which grow along streams and rivers. Each little seed, dropped from small cones on the alder's branches, has tiny pockets of air that keep it afloat as it cruises downstream to a muddy growing place.

TWIG AND CONE WREATH

What You'll Need

- A wire coat hanger
- Lots of twigs
- Flexible wire
- Shears or heavy scissors
- Cones
- Berries
- Tacky glue

What to Do

1. Untwist the handle of the coat hanger, bend the coat hanger into a circle, and retwist it closed.

2. Cut several pieces of wire about 6 inches long. Green floral wire, available in craft stores, is excellent, but any fine-gauge wire will work.

3. Take a handful of twigs and form them into a bunch. Wrap a piece of wire around the bunch at one end, and twist the ends of the wire together so the twigs stay together.

4. When you have several bunches made, start the wreath. Hold a bunch against the coat hanger circle, and wire it on with another piece of wire.

5. Wire on a second bunch of twigs, overlapping the wired ends of the first. Keep adding bunches of twigs until the coat hanger is covered.

6. With tacky glue, glue on small or medium-size cones wherever they look good. For extra color, glue on some bright berries.

7. Let the glue dry, then hang the wreath on a door, on a mantle, or on the wall.

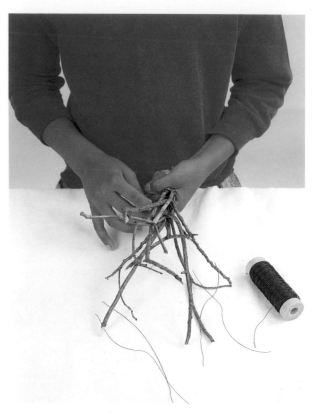

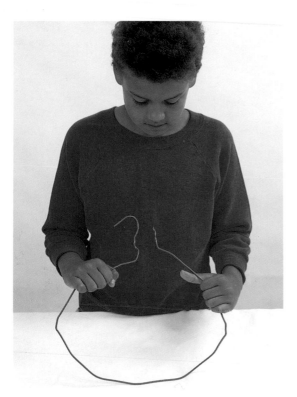

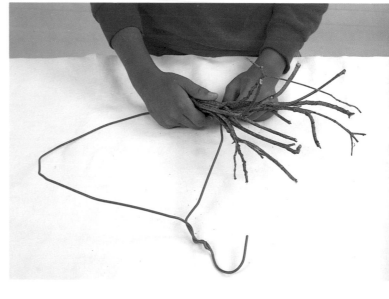

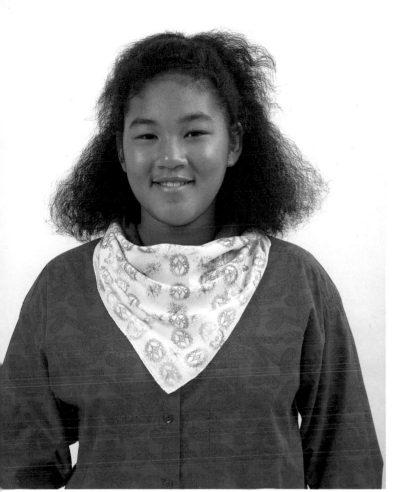

BANDANNA

What You'll Need

- A walnut or other nut
- A white or solid-colored handkerchief about 18 inches square
- An iron
- Newspaper
- Old rags or a piece of foam
- An ink pad

What to Do

1. Get an adult to help you cut the walnut across the middle—opposite to the way it would normally split. (A hammer and chisel will work.) Cut one of the halves in half again. Get all the meat out of the inside and make sure the outside is clean. You may need a toothpick and an old toothbrush to get all the meat out.

2. Fold the handkerchief in half several times, until it's about 3 inches square. Iron the folded handkerchief well, and when you unfold it, the crease marks will form squares. Use this grid to help keep your design symmetrical over the whole hanky.

3. Place newspapers over a layer of old rags or a piece of foam rubber, to create a soft surface. Open the handkerchief and lay it out on the newspaper.

4. Using the creases as guidelines, begin making your design. Press the nutshell firmly into the stamp pad and then onto the handkerchief. (You may want to practice a few times on scratch paper first.) Work out from the center. Use all sides of the shell—the half, the quarter, and the outside.

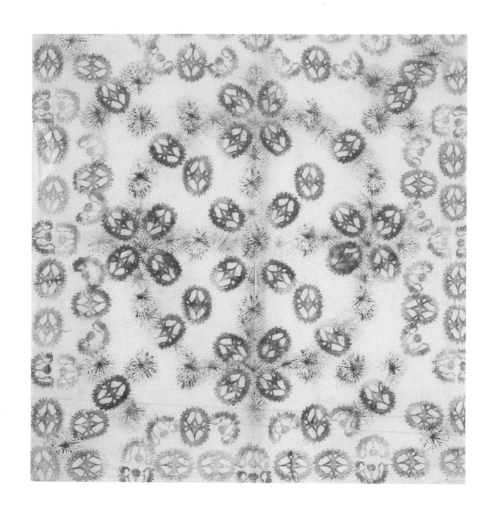

APPLE MONSTERS

What You'll Need

- A large apple
- A paring knife
- A wooden craft stick (like the ones found in Popsicles)
- Two cloves
- A few grains of uncooked rice
- A sock
- Scissors
- White glue

What to Do

1. Carefully peel the skin off the apple, leaving a small circle of skin at the stem end. Push a craft stick into the bottom.

2. Carve a dent for each eye, and a nose.

3. Carve a slit for the mouth.

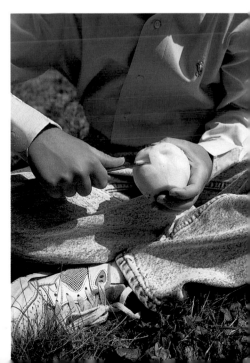

4. Push a clove into each eye socket. Push grains of rice into the area on top of and below the mouth slit for teeth.

5. Set the apple in a warm, dry place for a couple of weeks. Check it OFTEN to be sure it doesn't rot.

If the place is too damp, the apple will begin to get green spots. If this happens, try putting the apple in a warm oven (200 degrees F.) with the door slightly open for an hour. That will hasten the drying.

6. As the apple dries, you can squeeze it and mold it into a face that you like. The apple will get harder and harder and smaller and smaller as it dries.

7. When the apple is dry, make a body for it, using a sock. Cut a small hole in the toe for the craft stick to go through, and a hole on either side of the toe for your fingers to stick out and be the puppet's arms. Decorate the sock with fabric paint, or glue on decorations. You can also add yarn hair, or make a hat from a ring cut from the ankle end of the sock.

You can hold onto the craft stick with three fingers and stick the other two out of the holes.

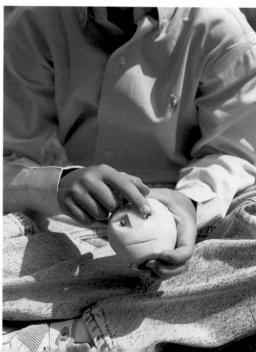

CORN HUSK FLOWERS

What You'll Need

- Corn husks
- Fabric dye (optional)
- Flexible wire (the spool kind)
- Scissors
- Stiff, heavy wire for the stem
- Floral tape

What to Do

1. Corn husks are sold in some craft stores. Or you can shuck your own. Just peel the husks off several ears of

corn and spread the husks in the sun to dry, turning them every few hours.

2. Husks look good left their natural color, but you can also dye them bright colors. Get an adult to help you with this step. Dissolve about half a package of fabric dye (available in most grocery stores) in half a gallon of water, and heat to boiling. Put the dry husks in the hot dye, remove the dye from the heat, and let the husks soak overnight, or until they are the color you want.

2. Tear your husks lengthwise into strips. You'll need 5 good strips about 1-3/4 inches wide for the petals.

3. Use your less attractive husks to make the center of the flower. Roll the husks into a roll about 3/4 inch wide, and wrap flexible wire around them about an inch from one end. Cut off the wire ends and the extra husk.

4. Fold a petal in half, and position it against the center. Wrap a piece of wire around the center and the petal, twist the ends together, and trim off the wire ends. Then add the other petals around the center in the same way.

5. Cut off the extra husks on the bottom of the flower, cutting the bottom into a point.

6. Cut a piece of heavy wire about 18 inches long, and bend a "fish hook" into one end. Insert the other end into the center of the flower and pull it all the way in, until the fish hook disappears into the flower.

7. Wrap floral tape around the base of the flower and all the way down the stem. Green floral tape is sold in craft stores. It sticks to itself (or anything else) when it's stretched, so pull on it as you wrap.

a

TURNIP LANTERNS

What You'll Need

■ The largest turnip you can find
■ A sharp paring knife
■ A teaspoon
■ String
■ Scissors
■ A small tea candle or a very short (1–2 inch) end of a regular sized candle
■ An awl or large nail

What to Do

1. Carving a turnip is something like carving a pumpkin except that the skin is softer and there are no seeds in the inside. The inside can be tough, however. To start out, cut a slice off of the top (stem end) of the turnip; then make a series of cuts about an inch deep into the meat of the turnip.

2. When you have made a number of cuts, try wiggling some of the pieces out with the knife or scooping them

b

d

c

e

out with the spoon. If you are still having trouble getting any pieces out, make more and perhaps deeper cuts. Eventually you should be able to scoop out a shallow hole.

3. Now take the knife and cut a circle around the inside edge, and continue to make deep, short cuts to loosen the next layer of meat. Again, when you have made a number of cuts, scoop out the meat. Continue with this process until the inside is hollowed out. Be careful not to cut too close to the wall or the bottom.

4. Select the side that you want to put the face on, and carve the face. Stick the paring knife into the turnip at an angle aiming away from the hole you are cutting.

Continue making cuts like this one all around the eyes, nose, and mouth. You can get fancy and add eyebrows if you have a big enough turnip.

5. With the awl or nail, poke three holes for the strings, on either side of the eyes and directly in back of the face. Tie a piece of string 12 inches long in each hole; then tie the 3 ends together.

6. Place the little candle inside the turnip. Hang the turnip in a window with the candle lit and watch the spooky shadows dance!

f

224

CASTS OF ANIMAL TRACKS

What You'll Need

- Quick-drying plaster of Paris
- A plastic container for mixing
- A spoon
- A container of water
- Petroleum jelly
- A strip of posterboard about 18 inches long and 2 inches wide
- 2 paper clips
- A trowel
- A plastic dishpan, or some other container

What to Do

1. Find an animal track.

2. Carefully clear away any leaves, sticks, or stones around the track. Be careful not to touch it.

3. Put some plaster of Paris in the plastic container and slowly add water, stirring as you pour. Add water and stir until the plaster is the consistency of thick cream.

4. Cover one side of the posterboard strip with petroleum jelly. Bend the strip into a ring, with the jelly on the inside. Make the ring the size you want your finished cast to be. Clip the ring together with the paper clip, and put the ring on top of the animal track.

5. Pour the plaster of Paris into the ring until the track is covered by at least an inch of plaster. Bend the second paper clip in half and set it on top of the plaster, to use as a hook for hanging the cast on the wall.

6. Leave the cast for at least 30 minutes to set up. Then use the trowel to carefully dig around the cast. Don't try to clean it off yet. Dig up some soil with the cast so you don't gouge the plaster, which won't be quite hard yet. Place it in the dishpan to carry home.

7. Let the cast set up overnight. Then remove the paper ring and brush off the loose soil. Hang it up by the paper clip hook.

ANIMAL TRACKS

Most wild animals are shy and afraid of people. Many come out only at night or in the very early morning when humans are sleeping. You may never see them, but you know they're around by the tracks they leave behind. Figuring out what kind of animal made the tracks can be a lot of fun.

A good first step is to count the number of toes and claws in a footprint. That's usually enough to tell you the general type of animal.

Members of the dog family (dogs, foxes, wolves, and coyotes) leave tracks that have four toes in the front footprint and four in the rear footprint, and you can usually see claw marks.

Members of the cat family (bobcat, lynx, mountain lion, and ordinary house cat) also have four toes front and rear. But cats pull their claws in when they walk, so they don't leave claw marks.

Rabbits, too, have four toes up front and in back, and sometimes you can see claws. But the real giveaway is the size of their feet: The back feet are two to three times bigger than the front!

Most mice, rats and other rodents (chipmunks, squirrels, woodchucks, beavers, and muskrats) have four toes in front and five in back. The toes are usually spread out like a fan or hand.

Animals that make tracks with five toes front and rear, with claw marks, are usually members of the weasel family (skunks, otters, badgers, minks, weasels, and wolverines).

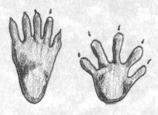

But if those clawed, five-toed tracks remind you a little of a human foot or hand, they were probably made by a bear, raccoon, or opossum.

All hoofed animals (deer, cows, moose, sheep, mountain goats) make prints with two large "toes" side by side. An exception is the horse, which leaves upside-down, U-shaped prints: the outline of the horseshoes nailed to its hooves.

227

THE TRACKER

When Tom Brown, Jr. was eight years old, he began to learn tracking from an 83-year-old Apache Indian named Stalking Wolf. The more time Tom spent in the woods learning the traditional Native American ways to read animal signs, the more drawn into tracking he became. He would spend hours on his belly studying tracks. In fact, he spent so much time crawling on the ground that he developed a callus—an extra layer of tough skin—across his lower chest!

Stalking Wolf taught Tom that each track tells a story, and helped him learn how to see tracks even on bare rock! Today, Tom Brown, Jr. is known far and wide as "The Tracker." Police departments call on him often to help them find criminals or lost hikers. He is considered the best tracker in the country. From a single footprint, he can tell not only whether a person is a man or woman, boy or girl, but also the person's weight and height, whether they're left-handed or right-handed, and even whether they've eaten recently.

Tom has written many books about tracking, and runs a tracking and wilderness survival school in which he has taught thousands of people. "Every mark is a track," Tom teaches. "Every dent, scrape, every rolling hill, every scratch is a track. The Grand Canyon is a water track. A fallen tree is a track of the disease that killed it and the wind that knocked it over. The ground is an open book. It is littered with tracks, from the largest to the smallest, and each one tells you something."

Most of all, Tom wants people to understand that learning how to track animals is a way to become closer to all of nature. "You don't have to follow an animal very far," he says, "before you realize that its tracks are connected to the tracks of everything else, including your own tracks. You begin to see the web of life."

WALK LIKE A BEAR

One way to "read" animal tracks is to study how different animals walk. Each walking style makes a particular pattern of tracks on the ground.

The best way to learn the patterns is to practice how different animals move. Get down on all fours and pretend you're an animal. Your hands are front feet and your knees are rear feet. (It's best to do this on soft ground or sand, so you can see the track patterns you make.)

Now "walk" by moving your right front foot and your left rear foot at the same time . . . then your left front foot and your right rear foot . . . and so on. That's how all cats, dogs, and hoofed animals (such as deer) move when they travel at normal speed. They're known as diagonal or perfect walkers. They make a nearly straight, left-foot, right-foot pattern of tracks.

Now try another one. Move your right front and right rear feet at the same time, then your left front and left rear feet, and so on. Now you're walking like a bear. Bears and other wide-bodied animals (such as porcupines, raccoons, opossums, and beavers) are pacers, or imperfect walkers. They sort of waddle when they walk and leave a close, zigzag pattern. Often, one side's

DIAGONAL WALKERS   **PACERS**   **BOUNDERS**   **HOPPERS**

front print is almost directly across from the other side's rear print.

Bounders include most members of the weasel family. They more or less bounce from one place to another. To imitate a bounder, move both your front feet forward at the same time with a kind of lunging motion, then quickly bring your rear feet up just behind the front feet. Then move the front feet forward again, then the rear, etc. Bounders make an evenly spaced, boxlike pattern, with right and left paw prints pretty much side by side.

Rabbits and most rodents, including squirrels, are hoppers. They move by jumping ahead with their rear feet, coming down on their front feet, and then pulling their rear feet in front of and to either side of the forefeet to push off again. Few people are nimble enough to do this as gracefully as a rabbit, but you can try. Ready? Reach out with your front "feet," then bring your knees up ahead of and to the outside of your arms. You probably won't be able to push off with your rear feet (actually, your knees), but you'll get the idea.

BIGFOOT TRACKS?

Tom Steenburg tracks bigger game than cats and squirrels. A Canadian who lives in Water Valley, Alberta, Steenburg searches for the footprints of a huge, furry, manlike creature known as the Sasquatch, or Bigfoot. No one, including Steenburg, is sure that such a creature exists. In fact, most scientists laugh at the whole idea of an eight-foot-tall giant roaming around Canada and the American Northwest.

But hundreds of people claim to have caught a glimpse of Bigfoot, and people have been finding huge, human-like footprints for over a hundred years. Whenever Steenburg finds a huge footprint, he makes a plaster cast of it. And while many people laugh, no one can explain how those footprints got there.

SNOW CANDLES

What You'll Need

- Snow
- Paraffin or beeswax
- A tin can
- A pan
- Old crayons or old colored candles
- Candle wicking*
- Waxed paper
- A stick
- An oven mitt

*Candle wicking is sold in craft stores.

What to Do

1. Get an adult to help you with this step. Place the paraffin or beeswax in the tin can. Pour 2 inches of water into the pan, and add the can of paraffin. Heat the pan on the stove until the water boils, then turn the burner down so that the water simmers but doesn't boil. Carefully watch the paraffin as it melts. Stir in old crayons or old pieces of colored candles if you want your snow candles to have color.

Never put paraffin directly in a pan over the burner. The paraffin may catch fire if you do. Always use the double boiler method described here.

2. As soon as the wax melts, turn off the stove. Dip the candle wicking in the melted wax, so that it is fairly stiff. Lay it out straight on a piece of waxed paper to dry.

3. Go outside to prepare the snow mold. Find a spot where the snow is at least a foot deep and cold and dry enough to hold its shape when you poke a hole in it.

4. Use a stick to poke a hole a few inches deep in the snow. This will be your candle mold. Experiment with different shapes of holes. When you are satisfied with the shape, go back inside and turn the stove on again. It won't take long for the water to get hot again and for the wax to melt if it has hardened a bit.

5. Using an oven mitt or hot pad, carry the can of melted wax and the piece of candle wicking outside to the snow mold. Dangle the wick down the center of the mold, and carefully pour the melted wax around the wick into the hole. Hold onto the wick for a few minutes until the wax cools and hardens enough to hold the wick straight.

6. Let the candle cool for about an hour.

SNOW

A snowflake is actually a bunch of ice crystals stuck together. The life of an ice crystal begins two to six miles up in the sky, when a tiny droplet of water freezes around a speck of dust, bacteria, or another ice crystal. Then the new crystal starts to fall.

The crystal's shape depends on the temperature and the amount of water in the air. As it falls through the sky, it changes shape constantly—with every slight change in air temperature or moisture, every little breeze. Sometimes it changes completely, other times only a little. A flat, straight-sided crystal may suddenly sprout "arms." A beautiful snow "star" may lose its points, and then grow spiny needles at one end.

Even the slight differences in temperature and moisture from one side of a crystal to the other make the two sides different.

That's why most scientists believe that the chances of two snow crystals being exactly alike are slim. Each one is created by its own special miniature "climate," by the exact conditions it falls through from one second to the next—and even by the way it falls.

7. Carefully dig the candle out of the hole by digging around it with your hands. Bring the candle inside and rinse it off under cool water.

8. Trim the wick to about an inch. Carefully trim or scrape off any bumps on the bottom of the candle so it will stand up.

9. Make an arrangement for a table or mantle by cutting a few evergreen branches and using them to surround the base of the candle. Try nestling several candles in some evergreen branches.

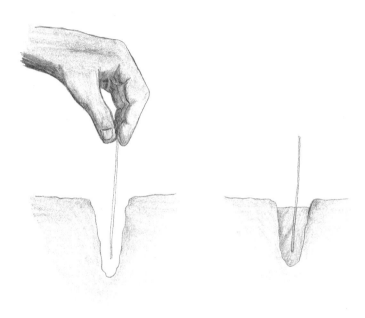

Every time it flutters, turns over, or bumps into another crystal, it changes shape.

Before it reaches the ground, an ice crystal may fall for as long as two hours and may travel hundreds of miles. Usually, somewhere along the way it catches onto a little puff of other crystals joined together—a snowflake. Finally, it floats to earth, along with trillions of other snowflakes.

KINDS OF SNOW
Generally, there are three types of fresh snow. There's dry, fluffy snow—the kind that floats down from the sky like big feathers. It's made mostly of snow "stars" from low, cold clouds.

There's wet snow, the sort that's extra good for making snowballs and snow people. Its crystals look like flat, six-sided plates, and come from low, fairly warm clouds.

Also, there's fine, dry, powdery snow—the kind that looks like sugar and blows in the wind with a soft, hissing sound. It's made up of tiny crystals shaped like discs or pegs from high, very cold clouds.

Snow Sculpture

What You'll Need

- Snow (slushy snow works best, like the snow on a warmish day after a snowfall)
- Heavy, waterproof gloves
- A small hatchet
- A hammer
- A wide chisel

What to Do

1. Decide what to make and where you want it to be. Remember that white snow shows up better against a dark background, such as some evergreen bushes or trees, or against a brick wall or in a dark building.

2. Decide how big you want your sculpture to be— probably no taller than you are. Start with simple shapes, such as a snow person, an elephant, a bear, a house, a whale, etc.

3. Begin by making large snow boulders. To do this, roll hard-packed snowballs along the snowy ground until the boulder is as large as you can lift. It helps to roll in the direction of your building site, so you won't have to carry the boulder as far.

4. When your boulders are next to each other, stack them in the general shape of the finished figure—a pyramid, for example, a rectangle, or a square.

5. When your boulders are arranged, start smoothing them into the shape of the figure. Add smaller boulders and snowballs to fill out the figure. Scoop away snow that you don't need. If the snow gets hard, use the hatchet to hack away unwanted snow.

6. Keep in mind that the bottom is the weakest part of the sculpture, and shore it up with more snow if it seems to weaken or begins to cave in while you are working.

7. After you've built the general shape, begin to add details. You can use the end of a twig to add fine lines. If the snow has gotten hard, use the hammer and chisel carefully to chip way small areas. Some people like to use objects in their sculptures, such as pine cones, twigs, carrots, etc.

8. Be sure to photograph your sculpture if you want to keep it!

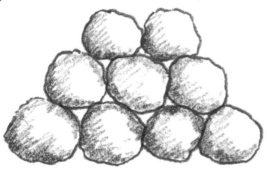

SNOW FACTS

■ One inch of rain would make about 10 inches of snow.

■ There are about one million ice crystals in a patch of snow two feet wide, two feet long, and 10 inches deep.

■ The odds of two ice crystals being exactly alike: one in 105,000,000 (that's 10 to the five millionth power) .

■ The greatest snowfall in one day (24 hours): 76 inches—over six feet—on April 14 to 15, 1921, in Silver Lake, Colorado.

■ The greatest snowfall in one year: 1,224 inches—that's 102 feet— at the Paradise Ranger Station, Mt. Rainier, Washington, between February 19, 1971 and February 18, 1972.

SNOW FOLKLORE

■ When hornets build their nests higher than usual, expect a snowy winter.

■ When a dog howls at the moon in winter it is a sign of snow.

■ If snow begins in mid of day,
Expect a foot of it to lay.

■ The day of the month of the season's first snowfall is the number of days it will snow that winter.

■ Put a pint of snow from the season's first snowfall on a stove and slowly melt it. The number of bubbles that rise to the surface is the number of snowfalls to expect.

■ Large flakes at first, the storm will last.
Small flakes at first, it'll be over fast.

THE SNOWFLAKE MAN

In 1880, when Wilson Bentley was 15 years old, his mother showed him a microscope. It changed his life forever.

The Vermont farm boy became fascinated with looking at things under the microscope. Most interesting of all were snowflakes. He spent hours gazing through his microscope at snowflakes he collected as they fell. At first, he tried to draw the shapes. But he couldn't capture the true beauty of the delicate crystals.

Then he read that it was possible to take photographs through a microscope. Wilson knew nothing about photography, but he convinced his father to buy him a camera. It took him months to learn how, but on January 15, 1885, when he was 20 years old, Wilson Bentley did it: He took the first successful "photo-micrograph" of an ice crystal.

For the next 48 years, Bentley spent his winters in a cold, open shed catching snowflakes on a velvet-lined tray and quickly photographing them. Soon he became known far and wide as the "Snowflake Man."

All together, Wilson Bentley took more than 4,500 separate ice crystal photomicrographs. In 1931, almost half of his photos were published in a now-famous book, Snow Crystals. Scientists still use it to help them study the wonder of snow.

BIRDS' MIDWINTER TREE

What You'll Need

■ A bag of whole cranberries or other red edible berries
■ A bag of peanuts in their shells
■ An apple
■ A kiwi fruit
■ 2 oranges
■ Some whole cloves
■ Some heavy cotton thread
■ A needle
■ Raffia* or heavy string or cord

*Raffia is available in craft stores.

What to Do

1. Make a garland of the cranberries by stringing them on a doubled length of thread. (If you want, string some popped corn with the cranberries. It will show up well if you don't have snow, and the birds like it.)

2. Push the needle through the middle of the peanuts to make a peanut garland.

3. Slice the apple, the kiwi, and one of the oranges crosswise, so that each slice has a pretty pattern. Make the slices rather thin (about 1/4 inch thick).

Put a loop of raffia or cord through the edge of each slice. Use a pointed stick or a small screwdriver to poke a hole to put the cord or raffia through.

4. Make pomanders for the birds. (They won't eat the cloves, but the pomanders will look nice on the tree.) Poke holes all over an orange with an awl or a small screwdriver, and insert small cloves.

Cut four pieces of raffia about a foot long, and tie them together about 3 inches from their ends. Put the pomander in the center, and tie the raffia together at the other end. Hang from a branch.

GUESS WHO'S COMING TO DINNER

Lots of birds like fruit, including catbirds, orioles, redwings, robins, and tanagers.

BIRD FEEDER

This simple feeder attaches to the outside of a window, so you can watch the birds when they drop in for dinner. Filling the feeder is a snap, too: Just open your window and pour in some seed!

The feeder looks good just painted a neutral color. If you want to make it even fancier, you can paint a design on the roof, like the ivy shown in the photograph.

If you're not used to shopping for boards or screws, ask the sales person at the hardware store to help you find the things on this list. See page 349 for a bird feeder made from recycled material!

What You'll Need

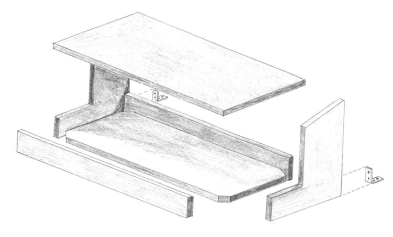

- An 8-foot-long 1 X 12 pine or fir board (to make the top, bottom, sides, and back)
- A 2-foot-long 1 X 3 pine or fir board (for the front)

239

- 16 to 20 #6 1-1/4" brass or galvanized wood screws
- Two 1-1/2" corner brackets with screws
- A saw
- Sandpaper
- A drill
- A screwdriver
- Boiled linseed oil
- House paint

What to Do

1. Saw the top, bottom, side, and back parts of the feeder to the sizes shown in the drawings. (Remember the carpenter's Golden Rule: Measure twice, cut once!)

2. Sand all edges smooth.

3. Paint the top, sides, back, and front with a neutral-color latex or oil house paint. Be sure that all surfaces—both sides and the edges—of each piece are covered. *Don't* paint the feeder bottom; if you do, birds might eat bits of paint as they peck at their food.

4. Pour linseed oil onto the feeder bottom and rub it in thoroughly with a rag to protect the wood.

5. Attach the feeder back to the bottom with wood screws. Drill holes first to avoid splitting the wood.

6. Now (drilling first each time) screw on the sides . . . the front . . . and the top.

7. Give the feeder a final coat of paint, and you're done!

8. Mount the feeder to the window sill with corner brackets, as shown.

To Paint the Roof:

What You'll Need

- A pencil
- Ivy leaves
- Green and brown paint pens
- Yellow and green paint, suitable for outdoor use. (Hobby enamel or exterior latex would both work.)
- Paint brushes, pointed
- A narrow dowel (about 1/4 inch thick) sharpened in a pencil sharpener

What to Do

1. Find some ivy and study how it grows. Then, using a

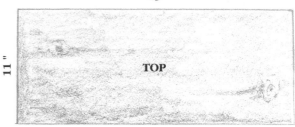

25"

11"

TOP

22-1/2"

2-1/2"

BACK

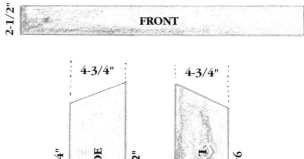

22-1/2"

8"

BOTTOM

1/2" CUT AT EACH CORNER

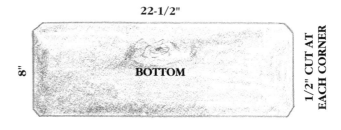

24"

2-1/2"

FRONT

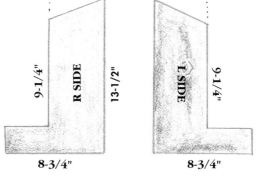

4-3/4"

4-3/4"

9-1/4"

R SIDE

13-1/2"

L SIDE

9-1/4"

2-1/4"

8-3/4"

8-3/4"

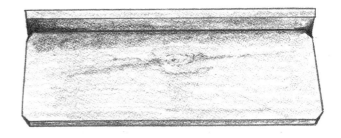

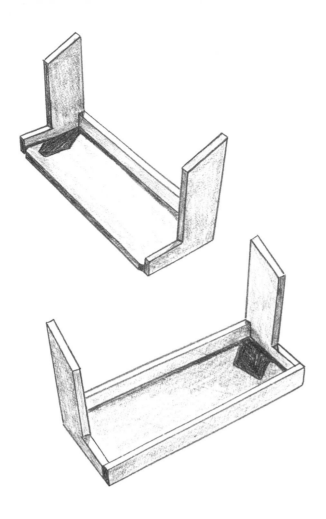

pencil, lightly sketch just a branch (no leaves) on the roof. Start with the main branch and then add the smaller branches.

2. Lay an ivy leaf a little ways away from the branch, and trace around the leaf with a pencil. Trace as many different leaves as you want, using different sizes. Use small ones at the ends of branches.

3. Sketch in the stems with a pencil.

4. With a green paint pen, go over the pencil tracings of your leaves, stems, and branches. Let dry.

5. Paint in the leaves, using green paint and a paint brush. Start at the left. Fill in one leaf, and before it's dry, use the sharpened dowel to draw in the leaf veins. (Look at the real ivy again.) If you make a mistake, just re-paint the leaf and try again.

6. Do the same for each of the leaves. As you get toward the end of the branch, mix a little yellow paint into your green paint, to make the leaves look smaller and younger.

7. Using the brown paint pen, go over the branches again. Put the brown line right underneath the green one, to look like a shadow.

WHO EATS WHAT?

Have you noticed that some birds—cardinals, for instance—spend most of their time in trees or shrubs, but others, such as robins and towhees, are usually on the ground? That's because different birds like different kinds of food. You wouldn't go to a seafood restaurant if you were hungry for pizza, right? The same is true for birds: They head for the places that serve the meals they want.

Cardinals, blue jays, and other birds with strong beaks like large berries and seeds, so they forage in holly trees, juniper bushes, and other types of vegetation that produce that sort of food. Robins are fond of earthworms, and towhees dine on crawling insects, so they peck and scratch at ground level. Sparrows and mourning doves eat small to medium seeds from tall grasses and low shrubs.

By watching where and what different birds eat in the wild, you can figure out which kinds of bird seed are most likely to attract those birds to your feeders. Just choose seeds that are similar in size and shape to the ones the birds eat from nature's menu. (Of course, some birds—such as house wrens—eat only insects. They won't come to a feeder no matter what sort of seed you offer them!)

Nearly all birds that feed in trees and bushes favor black oil-type sunflower, while seed-eating birds that forage on or near the ground are especially fond of white proso millet. Some birds are fussy about their food. The American goldfinch rejects virtually all bird foods except niger thistle and hulled sunflower seeds. Others, such as the white-throated sparrow, will try almost any seed you offer.

On the next page is a list of who eats what.

Millet: doves, sparrows.

Thistle: finches.

Safflower: cardinals, doves, sparrows.

Corn: sparrows, jays, doves.

Hulled sunflower: finches, jays, cardinals, chickadees.

Black oil sunflower: cardinals, chickadees, titmice, grosbeaks, finches.

Striped sunflower: titmice, cardinals, jays, grosbeaks.

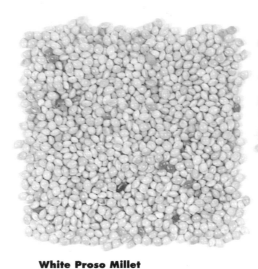

White Proso Millet

Mixed Seeds

Niger Thistle

Safflower

Finely Cracked Corn

Hulled Sunflower

Black Oil Sunflower

Striped Sunflower

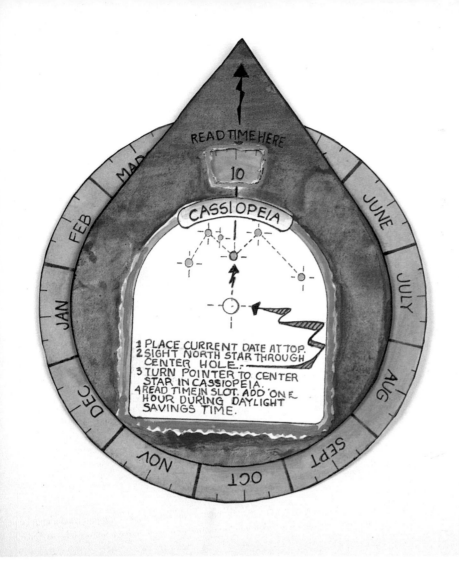

On the dial illustration:

READ TIME HERE

10

CASSIOPEIA

1 PLACE CURRENT DATE AT TOP.
2 SIGHT NORTH STAR THROUGH
  CENTER HOLE.
3 TURN POINTER TO CENTER
  STAR IN CASSIOPEIA.
4 READ TIME IN SLOT. ADD ONE
  HOUR DURING DAYLIGHT
  SAVINGS TIME.

Months around the outer dial: JAN, FEB, MAR, JUNE, JULY, AUG, SEPT, OCT, NOV, DEC

NOCTURNE NIGHT DIAL

With this colorful dial, you can tell time by the stars. Just turn the large outer dial so the current date is at the top, and look through the center hole at the north star. Turn the pointer to the center star in Cassiopeia, and read the time in the slot. (During Daylight Savings Time, you'll have to add one hour to the time that appears in the slot.)

What You'll Need

- Scissors
- White glue
- Posterboard
- A grommet

What to Do

1. Copy the drawings of both dials— the round one and the pointed one—on a photocopy machine.

2. Cut out the photocopied dials, and glue each one onto a piece of posterboard. Trim the posterboard to fit.

3. Color both dials with anything you like—crayons, watercolors, magic markers.

4. Cut out the slot at the top of the pointed dial.

5. Lay the pointed dial on top of the round one, so that the cut-out slot is over the circle of times. Cut a hole through the center of both dials.

6. Attach the two dials in the center with a grommet. Grommets have two important characteristics: they're hollow in the center, so you can sight through the center of the dial; and they'll allow the pointed dial to rotate. A grommet is installed with an inexpensive metal tool.

If you don't want to use a grommet, look for something else that might do the same job. For example, an audio intake valve—the kind used to attach an electric guitar to an amplifier—would also work.

HOW TO FIND THE NORTH STAR AND CASSIOPEIA

To locate the constellation Cassiopeia, you must look into the northern section of the night sky. If you don't know someone who can point this area out to you, use a compass to find true north.

Next, try to find the Big Dipper in this part of the sky. It will be near the northern horizon and is quite large. On winter evenings it will be standing on its handle, just to the right of due north. During summer evenings the Big Dipper will be to the left of due north and standing on the dipper part.

Regardless of the position of the Big Dipper, you can use it to find the North Star and Cassiopeia. The two stars that make the front edge of the dipper part are called the "pointers," and point to the North Star, which is about four times as far away from the Dipper as the pointers are apart.

Don't stop after locating the North Star. Continue along in the same direction, going an equal distance on the other side of the star until you see a group of stars that form a large zigzag W. This is the constellation Cassiopeia. It may not be right side up and may look more like an M.

You will not be able to find Cassiopeia in the evening sky from May through August, because it will be below the northern horizon. However, on clear evenings during the winter months, you will be able to see this constellation as it arcs across the northern sky.

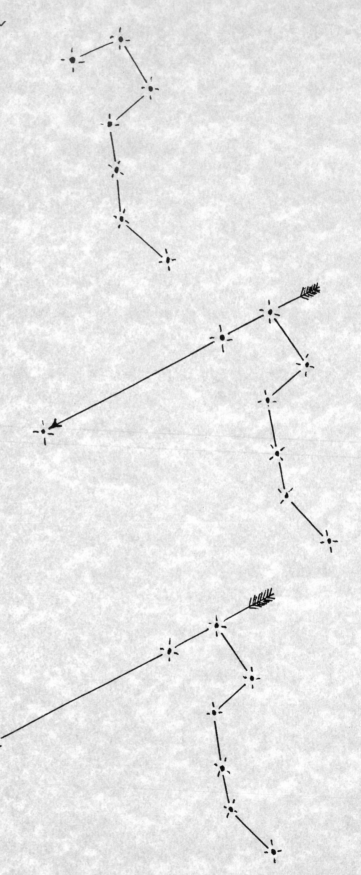

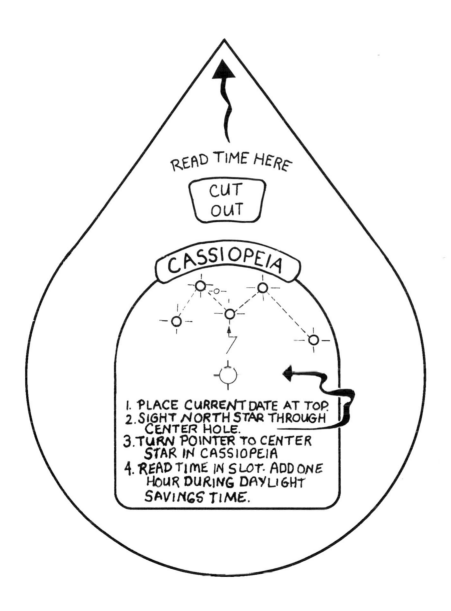

READ TIME HERE

CUT OUT

CASSIOPEIA

1. PLACE CURRENT DATE AT TOP.
2. SIGHT NORTH STAR THROUGH CENTER HOLE.
3. TURN POINTER TO CENTER STAR IN CASSIOPEIA
4. READ TIME IN SLOT. ADD ONE HOUR DURING DAYLIGHT SAVINGS TIME.

Pointed dial for Nocturne Night Dial. This one goes on top.

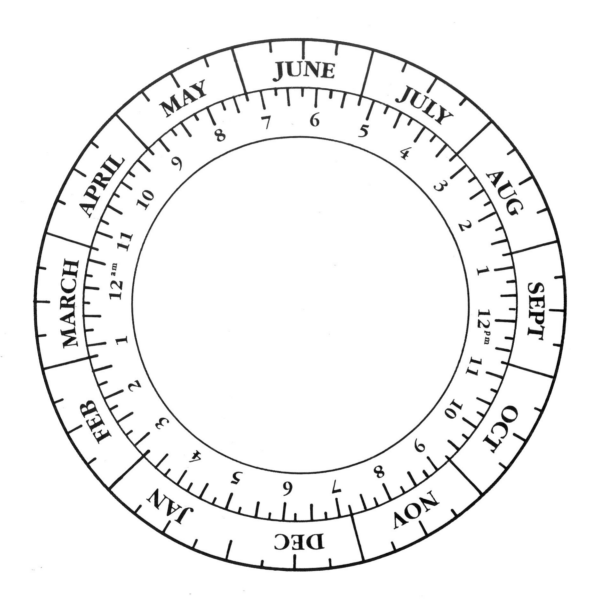

Round dial for Nocturne Night Dial. This one goes on the bottom.

CONSTELLATION VIEWERS

What You'll Need

- An empty can from potato chips, soup, or canned vegetables; or an empty oatmeal box; or a mailing tube
- Tracing paper
- A pencil
- Scissors
- An awl or a large nail and a hammer
- A sky map or other guide to the constellations
- Paper, glue, tape, sequins, plastic fabric paint, and other materials to cover and decorate the outside of the viewer
- A large permanent marker

What to Do

1. Remove one lid from the can or box.

2. Trace around the outside of the closed end of the can with the pencil and tracing paper.

3. Find a diagram of the constellation you want to make, and draw the dots representing stars inside the circle you have drawn on the tracing paper.

4. Turn the tracing paper over so that you can see the reverse of the constellation, and place it over the closed end of the can or box. Using the awl or large nail, hammer holes in the end of the can or box in the places where the dots representing stars are on your diagram. (If you are using an oatmeal box, you can poke the holes with the awl or nail without the hammer.)

5. Reach down into the can or box with the permanent marker, and color the entire inside of the end black. If you are using a can, you should be able to reach the end

easily. (If you are using a potato chip can, you may not be able to reach the end and will have to skip this step.)

6. Now color the outside of the end of the can or box black.

7. Use paper to cover the outside of the can. Then decorate it with sequins, fabric paint, markers, or anything else that strikes your fancy.

8. To view your constellation, face a window or a light source, and hold the viewer up to your eye.

Above: The constellation Orion, from inside a constellation viewer. Opposite page: This photograph is called a star trail. The photographer pointed his camera at the night sky and left the shutter open for 12 hours. As the stars moved across the sky, they left trails of light on the film. The bright semicircle in the center is the North Star.

BARK RUBBING

What You'll Need

- A tree
- A piece of construction paper
- A piece of screening 7-1/2" by 14-1/2"
- Masking tape
- A crayon

What to Do

1. Find an interesting patch of bark, and tape the construction paper over it.
2. Holding the crayon flat side against the tree, rub up and down over the paper, pressing firmly. Keep coloring until you get an interesting pattern.
3. Remove the tape and inspect your bark rubbing. Try different trees, and look at the different patterns you get.

BARK

When most people think of trees, they think of leaves and branches. But when you're out walking in the woods, what part of the tree is closest to you? What part do you see most clearly? Not the leaves and branches. You see the trunks—and particularly the bark covering them.

Tree bark comes in all sorts of colors and textures, depending on the kind of tree. Paper birch trees are famous for their satiny, light-colored bark that peels off in strips. Some North American Indian tribes used the bark to make canoes. Maple trees have gray, shaggy bark.

Left: Maple
Right: Sycamore

249

Beech trees have very smooth, sleek bark. That's why beech branches look like strong, muscled arms. Sourwood bark comes in huge square blocks.

Sometimes the bark on a tree's branches looks different from the bark on its trunk. That's because the trunk is the oldest part of the tree, so its bark tends to be thicker, darker, or more deeply furrowed.

You can identify some trees just by the color of their bark. For instance, you can tell a sycamore tree from a long way off by its crazy-quilt patches of light and dark. Sweet cherry trees have deep red

bark with thin black stripes circling the trunk. And the bark of a young striped maple is bright green with white up-and-down stripes!

A tree's bark is its protective outer "skin." Just beneath is the inner bark, which carries nourishing sap to feed the tree and supply energy to its roots. The bark of some trees, such as birches, really is as thin as skin. Redwood

Left: Mountain Laurel
Right: Sourwood

trees, though, have bark as much as a foot thick. And the bark of a giant sequoia tree can be two feet thick!

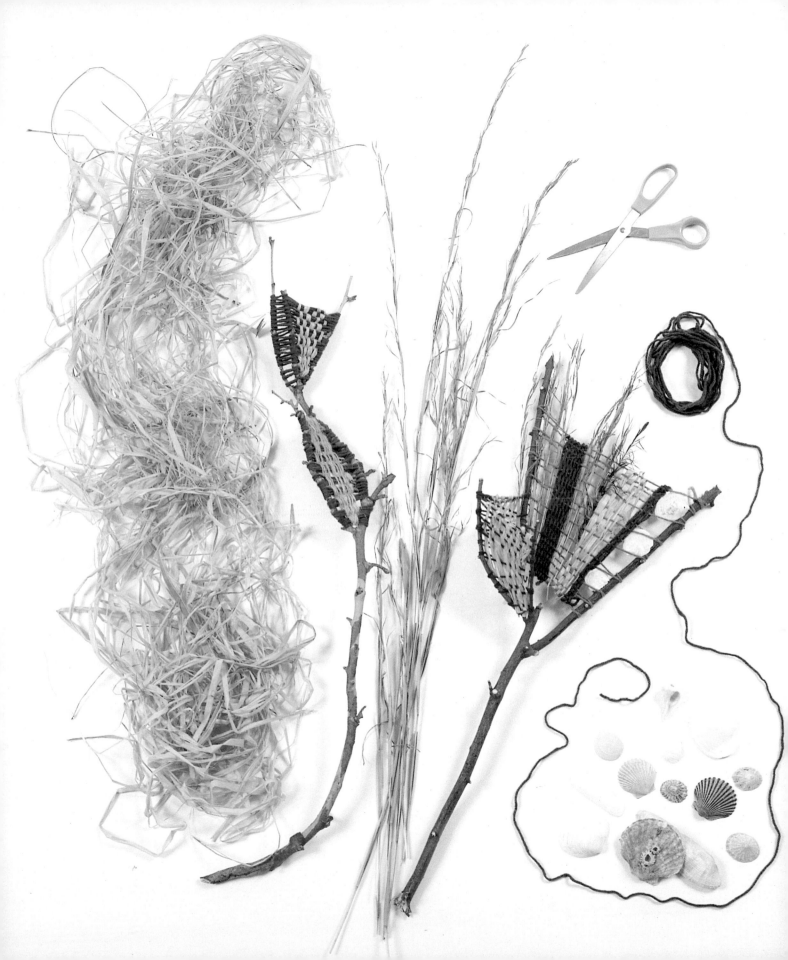

TWIG WEAVING

What You'll Need

- A forked tree branch
- Yarn or string
- Raffia,* long grasses, or more string
- Any of these: feathers, seedpods, long strips of bark, moss, seashells

*Raffia is sold in craft stores.

What to Do

1. Tie one end of the yarn to the top of one of the forks of the branch.

2. Stretch the yarn across to the other fork, and wrap it around once.

3. Stretch the yarn back across to the first fork, about 1/4 inch below the first wrap (where the knot is). Wrap the yarn around.

4. Continue taking the yarn back and forth between the forks, wrapping it each time, until you reach the bottom of the fork.

5. Now weave the other materials up and down through the yarn. Go over one strand of yarn, then under the next, then over, and so on.

6. Between the strands of yarn place seashells, mosses, or other things too short to weave.

Another idea: Try using a branch with more than one fork. The large weaving pictured has three forks—and is shaped sort of like a baseball mitt.

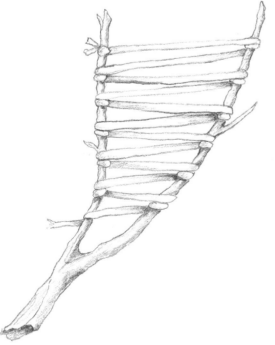

252

GEE-HAW WHIMMY DIDDLE

What You'll Need

- A dead branch with several forks
- Hand clippers
- A pocket knife
- An awl
- A very small drill (also known as a pin vise)
- An 18-gauge wire brad or escutcheon pin 3/4 inch long*

*Brads and nails come in various "gauges," or widths.

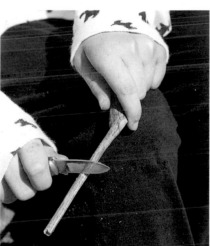

253

What to Do

1. With your hand clippers, cut a off a piece of the branch, so that you have a short piece for the handle and a longer piece about 1/4 inch in diameter. (A handle isn't essential; a whimmy diddle can be a perfectly straight twig. But the handle makes it easier to work.)

2. Scrape the bark off the twig with your pocket knife.

3. Trim off the ragged edges of the twig with your knife.

4. Cut off the whimmy diddle so it's about 5 or 6 inches long, and round off the end a little.

5. Cut 7 to 9 shallow notches.

6. With the awl or a nail, make a dent in the center of the end. Then use the pin vise to drill a hole about 3/4 inch deep into the end.

7. Now make the propeller. Cut a small piece of twig about 1-1/2 inches long (the end you cut off the whimmy diddle will be perfect). Scrape the bark off the propeller.

8. About 1/4 inch from each end, cut a ring around the propeller.

9. Carve the wood out between the rings, to make the propeller flat.

10. With a ruler, find the center of the propeller, and drill a hole that's just slightly bigger than the brad you're going to attach the propeller with.

11. Attach the propeller by nailing the brad into the hole.

12. Go back to the branch, cut yourself a rubbing stick, and scrape the bark off it.

How to Whimmy Diddle

1. To make the whimmy diddle *gee* (spin to the right), hold the rubbing stick in your right hand and crook your forefinger over it. As you rub the stick up and down the notches, let your forefinger rub down the far side of the whimmy.

2. To make it *haw* (spin to the left), move your hand forward so that your forefinger doesn't touch the notched stick but your thumb rubs against the near side of the whimmy diddle as you rub up and down the notches.

3. These directions are for a right-handed person. A lefty would do just the opposite.

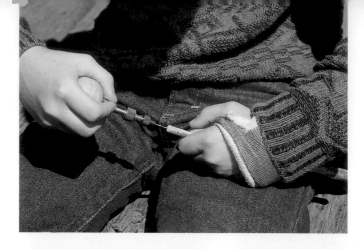

POMANDER

Hundreds of years ago, people made pomanders and carried them when they visited sick people. They believed that the smell of a pomander would protect them from disease. Today we use pomanders because their delicious scent will make our closets and drawers smell good.

What You'll Need

- An orange
- Tape
- A knitting needle, a nail, or an awl
- About 1 ounce of whole cloves
- 2 feet of ribbon, cut in half

What to Do

1. Starting at the stem end, put a piece of tape around the orange. The add a second piece, so that you divide the orange into quarters. The ribbon will go over the tape path.

2. Starting next to the tape, poke holes in the orange with the knitting needle, nail, or awl, and put a clove into each hole. Put the holes as close together as possible.

3. Remove the tape and roll the pomander in powdered cinnamon, nutmeg, and ginger, to make it extra spicy. If you can find some powdered orris root—available at some natural food stores and craft stores—add it to the mixture. The orris root helps preserve the pomander.

4. Lay the ribbon in the paths you left for it, and tie up the pomander.

5. Place it in a cool, dark closet until it is hard and dry. It will shrink as it dries and will smell spicy and wonderful for years.

SCENTED SOAP

FOR CLEAR SOAP:

What You'll Need

- 2 pans, one small enough to sit inside the other
- A bar of clear, unscented glycerin soap
- 1/4 teaspoon essential oil fragrance*
- Food coloring
- Dried mint leaves, rose petals, or lavender leaves or blossoms
- Plastic cups or other small plastic containers, for molds. (The brown cups in the photo are drinking cups for camping trips.)
- Nonstick cooking spray or mineral oil

*Available at craft stores, discount marts, and health food stores.

What to Do

1. Cut the soap into small pieces, and put them in the smaller pan.
2. Get a grown-up to help you melt the soap. Fill the larger pan half full of water, bring it to a boil, and put the smaller pan with the soap inside the larger one. Stir the soap as it melts.
3. Add fragrance and color. For a very mild-smelling bar of soap, chop up some mint leaves into tiny pieces, bruise them with a mortar and pestle, and add them to the melted soap. Or crumble up dried rose petals and add them to a different bar. For a stronger scent, you'll have to use an essential oil.
4. Spray the inside of your mold with nonstick cooking spray, or grease it with mineral oil. Pour in the melted soap.
5. Place the mold in the refrigerator for a few hours. When the soap is firm, set the bottom of the mold in hot tap water for a few seconds, flex the mold, and pop out the soap.

FOR SEMISOFT SOAP:

What You'll Need

■ A small glass custard cup or dish

■ A blender

■ A bar of Ivory soap or other unscented, white, floating soap

■ 12 ounces of water or scented water

■ 1 teaspoon essential oil (optional)

■ Food coloring

■ Mint leaves, lavender leaves, rose petals

■ Uncooked oatmeal (if you want oatmeal scrub soap)

■ Nonstick cooking spray or mineral oil

What to Do

1. Make scented water by boiling 12 ounces of water, then pouring it over mint leaves, lavender leaves, or rose petals. Cover the water and let it steep for 15 minutes or so. (People who specialize in herbs call this water an "infusion.")

2. Cut the bar of soap into small pieces.

3. Put the soap and the water in the blender. If you want an oatmeal scrub soap, add 2 tablespoons of uncooked oatmeal.

4. Add a few drops of food coloring.

5. If you want stronger-smelling soap, add a few drops of essential oil.

6. Blend the mixture for about 15 seconds.

7. Pour the soft soap into greased dishes and let cool. When the soap is cool and somewhat solid, scoop it up in your hands and mold it into balls. It will stay semisoft, so you can pinch off pieces as you need it.

258

Ecology
Crafts

Introduction
to Ecology Crafts

Maybe your first question is, What's **ECOLOGY?** You can figure it out yourself.

- ☛ **ECO** *means environment or habitat, the place where a plant or animal usually lives or grows.*

- ☛ **LOGY** *means the science of, or the study of.*

It can't just be the study of habitat, because that would leave out what lives there. So **ECOLOGY** is the study of how plants and animals (including people) interact with where they live...and with each other.

All the plants and animals that live together in one environment form a natural community, called an ecosystem. A lake is an ecosystem. So is a city park. And an ocean. And a desert. And your yard. And a flowerpot.

Does that mean this section is about how to make homes for plants and animals? Not quite. It's about how you can interact in friendly ways with all the living things around you...and with their habitats. About how you can respect everyone's home—Planet Earth—and at the same time have fun making things.

Of course you don't ever mean to harm any creature. You don't go around kicking anthills or pulling down birds' nests. But there are lots of things you can do every day to *help* Planet Earth and all living things. Ecology is a truly awesome adventure.

Do you ever feel like just one person doesn't make much difference in the world? Did you ever want to do something wonderful for the world?

Well, *you're* just one person. And you can make a BIG difference. You are probably already doing wonderful things for the world. You just don't know it.

This section shows you lots of terrific things you can do to be even more of a friend to Planet Earth . . . and to all the amazing plants and animals who live here with you.

The Projects in This Section

All the projects you can make from this section try to:

- *Use materials that are recycled or reused, or*

- *Use art materials you can find in nature, without harming any habitat or living thing.*

Some things just aren't reusable—you can't reuse glue or paint, for instance. (But you can save leftover paint and use it for something else.) Sometimes you need a certain size of wood, and you don't have scraps that size. But every project tries not to use brand new materials as much as possible.

Reduce. Reuse. Recycle.

You'll see these words a lot in this part. Because they describe what people who want to be friends of Planet Earth do. People like you.

TALKING TRASH

Did you know we are running out of space to put all the stuff we throw away? Three ways to help keep Planet Earth from turning into Planet Trash are **reducing, reusing, and recycling.**

REDUCING

This kind of **reducing** *doesn't mean going on a diet. It means creating less garbage by buying less stuff.*

- I don't know about you, but I buy lots of things I don't really need—like books I could get from the library or birthday cards or gift wrap I could make myself. (And people like homemade things better!)

- An easy way to reduce is to take cloth or net bags with me to the store, instead of using the store's plastic bags—but I often forget!

- Sometimes I buy things I don't even use— I have shirts I've never worn, an electric screwdriver that doesn't work very well, a little tape recorder I've used one time. When I can remember, before I buy something I try to ask myself, Do I really need this? Could I borrow it from a friend? Or could I make it myself?

REUSING

Reusing means saving something I might usually throw away, and using it over again or giving it to someone else to use.

- When I'm finished reading a magazine, I put it in the box at the library for someone to read. I try to reuse plastic bags and glass jars and the blank side of paper. Sometimes I have garage sales—so can you!

- Secondhand stores and charity and church groups always want secondhand clothes and toys. Also notebooks, radios, tape players— almost anything. They give them away to people who need them—like homeless people or people whose homes have burned down or been flooded. Or they sell them very cheaply.

- I also buy things at secondhand stores— that's another way of reusing. Check out these stores yourself—you'll find lots of things there for the projects in this book. Also check out flea markets...and garage sales.

- Lots of projects in this book show you great ways to reuse bottles, jars, paper, cans, newspaper, packing material, magazines, paper bags, even old clothes. (You can turn really old clothes into rags.)

Reducing, reusing, and recycling *are all easy to do—but sometimes hard to remember to do. A book full of great ideas for you is 50 Simple Things Kids Can Do to Recycle, by the Earthworks Group. Meanwhile, I'm going to write myself a big sign and stick it on my bathroom mirror:* **Reduce! Reuse! Recycle!**

RECYCLING

Of course you know about **recycling** *and why it's so important—mainly so we won't be buried under tons of garbage and make the air so polluted we can't breathe. And also because not recycling wastes trees and energy and metal and oil and raccoons.*

- Raccoons? Yes. And robins, rabbits, rhinoceroses—every wild animal you've ever heard of. Because when we have to bury garbage...or when we cut down trees...or pollute the air by burning trash...we're messing around with the places wild animals live—their habitats.

- Instead of throwing out glass bottles, aluminum cans, paper, corrugated cardboard, soda bottles, and old phone books, I try to remember to put them in my recycling box and take them to the recycling center. If you're lucky, your city picks up your recycled stuff, just like the trash trucks come for your trash.

- If you have a garden or a yard, you can recycle lots of your garbage and yard waste like grass and leaves into plant food, called compost (see page 311). This lets it become part of the life cycle again, instead of buried in a trash heap.

Excellent
Eco-EXTRAVAGANZAS

ECOLOGY CRAFTS

CLAY PINCH POTS AND ANIMALS

ALMOST NOTHING IS MORE FUN THAN MESSING AROUND WITH CLAY. YOU CAN MAKE SOMETHING FAMILIAR, LIKE THESE BOWLS AND ANIMALS, OR A SHAPE TOTALLY YOUR OWN. YOU MAY BE ABLE TO FIND CLAY IN THE BANK OF A CREEK OR NEAR A PLACE WHERE BRICKS ARE MADE, OR YOU CAN GET IT AT A CRAFT STORE. TO CLEAN YOUR OWN CLAY, SEE PAGE 268.

WHAT YOU NEED

- A ball of clay as big as your two fists
- A stick or other tool to make designs
- Water

WHAT TO DO

1· Slam the clay down on a big rock or, if you're indoors, on a table covered with newspaper. Pound it, slam it, turn it, pound it, slam it. Keep doing this for about ten minutes—you're getting the air bubbles out of the clay so it won't burst when you fire it in the kiln. This is called *wedging*.

2· Make a ball of clay that you can hold comfortably in your hand. As you hold the clay in one hand, push your other thumb into the middle of the ball almost to the bottom. Keep your thumb there, and very gently and very slowly turn the ball and squeeze the sides between your thumb and fingers as you begin to make a pot.

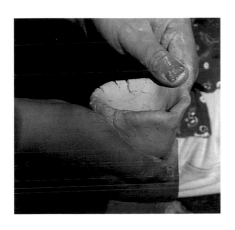

3· Keep turning the pot, and move your thumb up a little at a time toward the top edge, gently pressing as you go to keep the sides of the pot the same thickness. If you see a crack in the clay, rub it gently with a wet finger.

4· Put your pot in a cool place to dry for a day, not out in the sun, which might crack it by drying it too fast. Cover it with a plastic bag.

5· When your pot has dried for one day, you can make designs on it with a stick or other sharp tool.

6· For a special look, when your pot is as hard as leather—not completely dry but not wet—you can burnish it, that is, make it shiny. Rub the surface with a smooth stone or the back of a spoon. After your pot is fired in the kiln, it will be shiny black or brown, like the darkest one in the picture.

TO MAKE ANIMALS

1· Turn a small pinch pot upside down and model it into a frog, an owl, a bear, or any animal you can imagine. Try pushing the top sides up with your thumbs to make frog eyes or owl eyes or bear ears.

2· You can use a sharpened stick, a popsicle stick, or a pencil to press and form legs and feet, eyes, a mouth, or a beak. You might want to make lines for feathers or fur with your stick or pencil.

FIND AND CLEAN YOUR OWN CLAY

You can buy clay in craft stores, but it's more fun to hunt for it. If you decide to go clay hunting, you need to plan ahead. The clay needs to sit for about two weeks after you find it and clean it before you use it. If you're in a big hurry to make something, you'll probably want to buy your clay.

Two good ways to find clay are to explore around creeks and to follow brick trucks. Unless you're unusually speedy, to follow brick trucks you'll need an adult helper to drive you.

Bricks are made from clay, so trucks that leave brickyards empty are often headed for a big clay deposit to load up. If you ask either at the brickyard or one of the truck drivers, they will usually be glad to tell you where their clay is and let you take some. The white clay pots and animals in this book are made from clay found by following a brick truck (see page 267.)

Around creeks, look along the banks for slippery soil that has nothing growing on it. You can tell it's clay by the feel, and it's usually a different color from the soil around it.

Try to take only as much clay as you will use, so you don't disturb the creek environment any more than you need to.

Cleaning Clay

YOU'LL NEED
- dry clay
- a large sieve or a piece of old window screen nailed to a frame
- a bucket or large pan

First, dry your clay in chunks like those in the photo. Then break the dry clay into small pieces and rub and shake them through the sieve or screen, into the bucket. Throw away any pebbles and sticks—whatever's left in the screen.

Next, add lots of water to your clay and let it sit for a day and a night. It's better to add more water than you think you'll need—it won't hurt the clay. When you can make a long worm with the clay that sticks together well, it's just right. Take the clay out of the water and wrap it in rags to keep it damp.

Cool Tool

MAKE YOUR OWN SAWDUST KILN

You can fire your own clay pots, beads, and animals with this kiln—fired clay is much harder and tougher than clay that dries by itself. Your pots will be black or brown or speckled—part of the fun is not knowing exactly what color you'll find. Clay you fire in this kiln will not hold liquid well, so you can use your pots for just about anything but mugs and vases.

Smart Safety Tip:
Have an adult and a bucket of water close by whenever you're working with fire.

Making a Kiln

YOU'LL NEED

- A metal garbage can with a lid
- A hammer
- A big nail or an awl
- A screwdriver
- A bucketful of dry sawdust (from a lumberyard)
- Matches
- Some newspaper
- A bucket of water
- A spray bottle of water
- 12 to 16 bricks
- 4 small chunks of wet clay

1. Find a safe place to build your kiln, outside and away from trees or dry leaves. Bare ground or cement is perfect.

2. Next you punch holes with the hammer and nail. You need four holes about 3" from the bottom of the can, four holes in the middle, and four holes about 3" from the top of the can. Try to make them an equal distance apart around the can. Now twist a screwdriver in the holes to make them about ½" across.

3. Make a circle with four stacks of bricks to go under the can. When you put the can on top, be sure it's steady, not tippy.

4. Now make a sawdust layer 3" or 4" deep in the bottom of the can. Place your pots or other clay you want to fire on top. They should be 2" apart and 4" from the side of the can. Add another 3" of sawdust to cover the pots—be sure to fill the insides of the pots with sawdust too.

5. If you can't fit all your pots in one layer, you can add more sawdust and more layers of pots until the last layer of sawdust is 6" from the top of the can. Now tightly twist about eight sheets of newspaper and place them side by side on top of your last layer of sawdust.

6. Put four chunks of wet clay around the top rim of the can, equal distances apart. These will keep the top from being too tight and will let enough oxygen in to keep your fire burning well.

Smart Safety Tip:
Do not add anymore sawdust to the fire. Sawdust burns very quickly and you could be burned.

7. Light the newspaper carefully. Wait until the fire is burning well and you can see the top of the sawdust before you put on the lid.

8. Gently rest the lid on the chunks of clay. If you put the lid on tight, the fire will go out. If the fire does go out, twist more sheets of newspaper and start the fire over. If the sawdust is burning too fast, spray on a little water to calm it down.

9. Wait for eight to fifteen hours! The time depends on how many things you fired. Check your pots when there is no more smoke coming from the can and when the can is cool to the touch. Carefully lift the lid. All of the sawdust should be gone. In the ashes you'll find your amazing pots or jewelry—who knows what color!

TWIG FRAME

A NYWHERE TREES GROW, YOU CAN FIND TWIGS ON THE GROUND—IN THE PARK, IN YOUR YARD, ON VACATION (MAYBE NOT IF YOU GO TO THE BEACH). YOU CAN MAKE FRAMES FOR YOUR OWN FAVORITE PICTURES AND FRAMES FOR SPECIAL PICTURES TO GIVE TO FRIENDS. YOU CAN FRAME OTHER THINGS BESIDES PICTURES, OF COURSE— ANYTHING YOU CAN GLUE TO THE CARDBOARD.

WHAT YOU NEED
- Twigs collected from the ground
- Cardboard
- White glue
- Twine, raffia, or string
- Scissors
- A pencil
- A ruler
- A picture

WHAT TO DO

1· To make the back of your frame, figure out how big you want your frame to be and draw the outline on your cardboard with a ruler, then cut it out.

2· Break twigs to the sizes you need for all four sides. You probably want 3 or 4 twigs on each side.

3· Make a bundle of sticks for one side. Wrap twine around each end. Do this for all four sides.

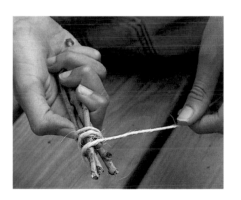

4· Glue your picture on the cardboard. Put plenty of glue on one bundle of sticks and glue it along one side of the picture. Glue the other three sides of the frame.

COLLECTING BAG

HERE'S A GREAT REUSABLE CANVAS BAG TO TAKE ON NATURE WALKS, WHEN YOU'RE OUT COLLECTING SUPPLIES FOR YOUR PROJECTS. AND IT'S PERFECT FOR SHOPPING (TO AVOID USING PLASTIC BAGS)...OR ON CAMPING TRIPS...OR OVERNIGHTS. YOUR DESIGN MAKES IT THE ONLY ONE OF ITS KIND IN THE WORLD.

WHAT YOU NEED
- A canvas tote bag
- A black paint pen
- Acrylic tube paints
- A small, round paintbrush
- Matte medium to thin paints (from craft or art supply stores)
- Masking tape
- Paper and pencil
- A piece of cardboard as big as the bag

WHAT TO DO

1. Tape the cardboard firmly inside your bag. Sketch your design idea on paper, then sketch it on your bag.

2. Paint your design and let it dry.

3. Outline the shapes with the black paint pen.

BIRCH BARK BASKET

YOU CAN MAKE NEAT BASKETS OUT OF NATURAL MATERIALS LIKE VINES, TWIGS, AND BARK. THE MAIN THING TO REMEMBER ABOUT MAKING ANYTHING WITH BARK IS TO GET THE BARK FROM THE GROUND, NOT FROM A TREE. PULLING BARK OFF A LIVE TREE CAN KILL THE TREE, BECAUSE IT LETS INSECTS IN.

WHAT YOU NEED

- Pieces of birch bark and small twigs gathered from the ground
- Bits of moss
- Acorns
- A soup can
- 2 clothespins
- Sharp scissors
- A ruler
- A hot glue gun and glue

WHAT TO DO

1· Cut out pieces of birch bark:

- A piece about 4" wide and 12" long—wide enough and long enough to wrap around your soup can
- A circle about 2½" across for the bottom
- A handle piece about 9½" long and 1" wide

2· Wrap the large piece around the soup can, overlapping the edges at least 1½". Ask an adult to help you with the hot glue gun. Hot glue the edges together. Wrap a few rubber bands around the bark to hold it together while the glue dries.

3· Slide the can out of the basket and glue the bottom on. Press firmly on a table for a few minutes until the glue dries completely.

4· Gently fold the handle and fit it inside the edges of the basket. Hold it in place with clothespins. Remove the clothespins one at a time to hot glue the handle in place. Put the clothespins back on and leave them until the glue dries.

5· Decorate your basket with moss, acorns, and twigs or other natural materials. Hot glue them on.

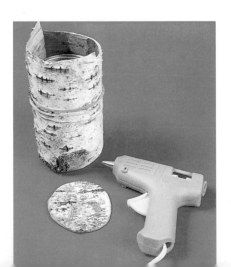

You Can Do It

When Melissa Poe was nine years old, a TV show got her worrying about the environment. She wrote a letter to the president then, George Bush:

Dear Mr. President,

Please will you do something about pollution. I want to live till I am 100 years old. Mr. President, if you ignore this letter we will all die of pollution and the ozone layer.

Please help.

Melissa Poe, Age 9

She also wrote suggestions to newspapers, TV stations, and local politicians. She says that then "I decided to do some of the ideas I had put in the letter, like putting up signs. I first thought about cardboard signs, but then my mom told me about billboards."

Over the next months, Melissa Poe's letter showed up on 250 billboards around the country, including one on Pennsylvania Avenue near the White House where the president couldn't miss it.

EARTH FLAG: *In this photo taken in 1995, the Earth Flag had 20,000 squares handmade by kids, showing their concerns and hopes for the future of the earth. Here it's on display on the Mall in Washington, D.C., to celebrate the 25th anniversary of Earth Day. Kids F.A.C.E. began the flag project—and kept the flag growing.*

Kids F.A.C.E. Gets Going

People began writing to Melissa Poe asking if they could help, or if there was a club kids could join. She started a club called Kids F.A.C.E.—Kids For a Clean Environment. "In the beginning it was just six of my friends," she said. "We did whatever we could, like recycling, planting trees, little things to help."

Then Melissa Poe went on the *Today* show on TV. Kids F.A.C.E. went up to 30 members, then to hundreds, then to thousands.

That was 8 years ago. Melissa Poe is now seventeen. Her club has a budget of $52,000 a year. Kids F.A.C.E. sends out two million copies of their newsletter every two months...gets more than 200 letters a day...has more than 3,000 club chapters in 15 countries...and more than 300,000 members. Membership is free to kids and teachers.

Melissa expects to leave Kids F.A.C.E. soon—it's a kids' club, for kids, by kids. "I want another kid to come along to be the president of the club," she says. "Perhaps someone about 12 who can go and speak in public like I do."

Kids F.A.C.E. members have planted more than 4,000 trees to improve wildlife habitat. They teach other kids and adults about recycling, rainforests, and other environmental issues. They raise money to save the rain forest, help save wildlife...and do whatever they can to help Planet Earth.

SEAL PUP: *Some Kids F.A.C.E. members join the club's Animal Care Team and help out at places like the Marine Mammal Care Center in San Pedro, California. There they might help feed northern elephant seal pups by hand and train them how to catch fish in their natural environment. Or they might help clean tar off baby seals with a mixture of mayonnaise and dishwashing detergent.*

You Can Make a Difference

Melissa Poe says some kids at her school made fun of her at first. "When I was younger, kids would not talk to me at basketball games or they would gang up on me and say, 'Let's get her.' Even today, kids come up to me and say, in a snide way, 'Aren't you that save-the-world girl?'" Maybe they're jealous.

"You can't always think about what other people are going to think of you when you do something," she says. "You have to follow what you think and want to do. When someone says, 'You're just a kid, you can't do that,' I want to prove them wrong. I tell kids that they can do something, that they can get involved and start a club or do something at their school. Don't let anyone tell you that you can't do what you want. As long as you believe that you can make a difference, you can do it."

WANT TO KNOW MORE?
Write to:
Kids F.A.C.E.
P.O. Box 158254
Nashville, TN 37215

TREE-SAVER CHAIR

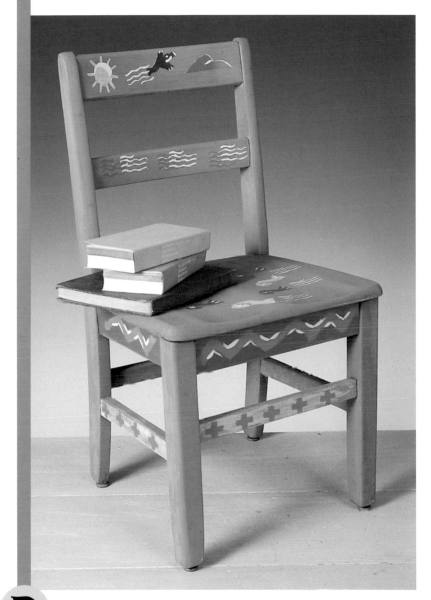

WHAT YOU NEED
- An old wooden chair
- Sandpaper
- Clean rags
- Leftover latex or acrylic paints
- Used manila folders or thin cardboard
- Paper and a pencil or marking pen
- Rubber glue or double-sided tape
- A small paintbrush or stencil brush
- Urethane sealer or varnish from a hardware department
- A larger brush for the varnish

WHAT TO DO

1· Sand all the old varnish or paint off your chair.

DESIGNING AND PAINTING YOUR OWN CHAIR IS SO MUCH FUN YOU'LL WANT TO MAKE A TABLE TO MATCH...AND A DESK...AND A STOOL. YOU CAN FIND GOOD STRONG OLD CHAIRS AT FLEA MARKETS AND SECONDHAND STORES. YOU MIGHT NOT SAVE A WHOLE TREE BY MAKING OVER AN OLD CHAIR INSTEAD OF BUYING A NEW ONE, BUT YOU'LL SAVE PART OF A TREE. IT ALL ADDS UP...TO A FOREST.

2. Dip a rag into the paint you want to use for your main color and rub it on the chair. Keep rubbing to let the paint sink into the wood. You can add more paint for a darker color, or use just a little on your rag for a lighter color. Let the chair dry completely. This should take about 14 hours, or overnight.

3. On a piece of paper, draw the designs you want to put on your chair. Plan where each design will go. Copy the designs onto paper the thickness of manila folders. To make stencils, you cut out the part of the design that you want to paint onto the chair. If you want to paint a cross, you cut out the cross. You will paint on top of the paper, and the paint will go through the cross-shaped opening.

4. Stick the first stencil you want to paint tightly to the chair with rubber glue or double-sided tape. You don't want any paint to slide under the paper and mess up your design.

If you have never painted stencils before, you might want to practice a few times on some scrap wood or another piece of paper. Dab on paint with your brush—not too much or it will smear under the stencil. Continue painting stencils on the chair until it looks the way you want it to.

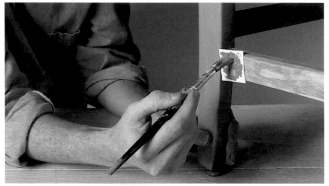

5. When all your stencils are completely dry, you can paint on a coat of urethane sealer or varnish to protect your new paint job.

**Evening came,
and the old fir trees
behind the cottage
began to rustle more loudly
as a strong wind swept along,
roaring among the branches.
Heidi's heart beat faster.
She thought she had never
heard anything so beautiful
and went skipping and running
for sheer joy under the trees.**

—JOHANNA SPYRI, *Heidi*

We'd Be up a Tree without Trees

Trees look like they're just standing around doing nothing most of the time, but they're as important to our ecosystem as humans. Here are some things about trees most people don't know—or don't think about.

In the summertime, one young tree keeps the air as cool as 10 air conditioners going 20 hours a day.

Young trees are our best air purifiers. One acre of young trees uses 5 to 6 tons of carbon dioxide a year—that's 10,000 to 12,000 pounds of the gas that animals and people breathe out. That same acre gives us 4 tons of fresh oxygen to breathe (8,000 pounds).

Around the world, forests provide homes for almost half of all living things.

Maybe your house is built at least partly from trees. Most of the world's buildings are.

This book used to be part of a tree. Trees give us paper, furniture, and lots of other things we use every day.

Trees give us food—apples, peaches, pears, mangos, oranges (you can list lots more fruits)...walnuts, pecans, coconuts, and all kinds of nuts (not peanuts...or doughnuts).

LET'S ROOT FOR TREES! *The average American uses seven trees a year, in paper, wood, and other tree products. These kids are planting cypress trees to make shade, oxygen, and a healthier environment in Asheville, North Carolina. The project sponsor is Quality Forward.*

SPECIAL PRINTS GIFT WRAP

THE GREAT THING ABOUT STAMP PRINTING IS YOU CAN USE THE SAME STAMPS TO DECORATE ALL KINDS OF THINGS—WRAPPING PAPER, BIRTHDAY CARDS, PLACE MATS, WRITING PAPER, T-SHIRTS. TRY DIFFERENT COLORS AND DIFFERENT COMBINATIONS... HAVE FRIENDS OVER AND STAMP IT ON OUT!

WHAT YOU NEED
- Reused paper from mailed packages or paper bags and tissue paper
- Any items with interesting shapes that you can paint
- Idaho potatoes
- A bunch of celery
- Acrylic paints
- Paintbrushes
- A knife (a butter knife is okay)
- Cookie cutters

WHAT TO DO
TO MAKE CABBAGE ROSE PAPER

Cut off the bottom of a bunch of celery. (Store the rest of the celery in the refrigerator to eat.) Paint the bottom of the stalk with acrylic paint and stamp it on tissue paper. If you want to use more than one color, wash off the celery and start over.

TO MAKE HANDS PAPER

Have an old saucer or plastic top for each paint color. Add some water to your acrylic paints, then dip your palm in the paint or paint your hand, then slap your hand onto the paper

TO MAKE VEGETABLE PAPER

1· Cut a potato in half lengthwise. Cut out shapes with a cookie cutter or make up your own shapes. For this vegetable paper, the shapes are a green pea, an eggplant, and a chili pepper.

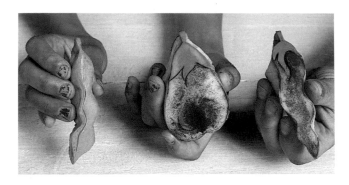

2· Paint your potato stamps and stamp your paper.

Oh, Christmas Tree!

Did you know that

▲ Every year for Christmas we cut down enough trees in the United States and Canada to make a forest big enough to cover Rhode Island?

▲ You can save a tree if you don't buy a cut tree but decorate a live Christmas tree growing in a pot instead?

▲ You can plant your live Christmas tree in the ground after the holidays and decorate it with food for the birds...or keep it in the pot and use it again next year?

If you don't have a place to plant your living Christmas tree, maybe you can plant it at school or in a friend's yard. Or maybe your city would help you to plant it in a city park.

THE LIVINGEST CHRISTMAS TREE: *A living Christmas tree looks as joyful as a chopped-down tree—maybe more—and you help protect the planet at the same time.*

Bag Bonnets

WHAT YOU NEED

- 2 brown paper grocery bags for each hat
- Paper mache mix in a dishpan or other large pan (see page 321). Wallpaper paste mix works best for these hats.
- Aluminum foil
- Cooking oil
- A bowl that fits your head, for the daisy hat
- A flower pot that fits your head, for the Darth Vader hat
- Scissors
- A flat, smooth surface you can wipe clean

REUSE PAPER GROCERY BAGS AND NEWSPAPER BY CREATING GREAT HATS FOR COSTUMES, PARTIES, AND DRESS-UP. BE A PIRATE...A FASHION MODEL...A COWPOKE...A SPACE INVADER... AN ALIEN. WHATEVER YOU CAN IMAGINE, YOU CAN MAKE. INVITE A FRIEND OVER FOR A HAT-MAKING PARTY!

WHAT TO DO

1. Mix up plenty of paper mache mix. It will be lumpy and kind of slimy.

2. Cut open the bags at the seams and flatten them out. Then slide one bag into the pan. Make sure to cover all of the paper with mix.

ECO EXTRA: Americans use 50 million tons of paper every year...more than a billion trees' worth.

3· Slide it very slowly out of the pan. It's heavy! Hold it over the pan and gently squeeze the extra mix back into the pan. Then lay the bag carefully on a flat surface and flatten it out. Slide extra mix off with the side of your hand. Repeat this with the second bag.

4· Turn the bowl upside down and smear the outside with plenty of cooking oil. Cover the bowl with a piece of aluminum foil. Then carefully drape the wet bags over the bowl, one at a time.

5· Shape the bags onto the bowl. Fold one side up for the daisy hat. Repeat all of these steps with two other bags for the Darth Vader flower pot hat (except don't turn up the side).

6· When the bags are completely dry, lift the hat forms off the bowl and flower pot.

7· Cut around the edges to make your hats. Decorate with flowers, paint, feathers, or whatever belongs on your hat.

FLY-AWAY-HOME GOURD BIRDHOUSE

EARLY NATIVE AMERICAN INDIANS HUNG GOURDS ON BRANCHES FOR THE BIRDS. THINK ABOUT THAT WHEN YOU HANG UP YOUR GOURD BIRDHOUSE IN THE EARLY SPRING. MAYBE THE BIRDS THAT COME TO YOUR GOURD ARE THE GREAT-GREAT-GREAT-GREAT-GRANDCHILDREN OF THE BIRDS WHO ONCE LIVED IN AMERICAN INDIAN GOURDS. YOU CAN EXPECT TREE SWALLOWS, VIOLET-GREEN SWALLOWS, WRENS, AND CHICKADEES IN THIS BIRDHOUSE.

Smart Safety Tip:
Before you start, ask an adult to help you get the gourd ready for its new owners. The directions are on page 287.

WHAT YOU NEED

- Cleaned gourd with entry hole and drainage holes
- Piece of sponge
- Leftover exterior house paints or acrylic paint—dark green, white, yellow, red
- Old dishes or reused plastic containers to mix paint in
- Small artist's paintbrushes
- String, wire, or leather thong
- Newspaper

WHAT TO DO

1· Tie a piece of string through the top holes so you can hang your gourd up to dry after you've painted it. With the sponge, pat the gourd all over with dark green paint. Cover the whole gourd. Hang it up to dry.

2· Rinse out the sponge. Mix a little white or yellow paint into some dark green paint to make light green. Dip in the sponge and test out some light green patterns on a piece of paper to see what looks good. When the dark green paint is dry, lightly pat the light green paint on the gourd. Let some of the dark green show through. Hang the gourd up to dry.

3· If you want your ladybugs marching in lines, when the light green paint is dry, draw pencil lines for your bugs to march along. Then paint the ladybug bodies on the gourd with red paint. Hang it up to dry.

4· When the red paint is dry, paint on the black ladybug heads. With the tip of a brush, paint a black line down all the ladybugs' backs. Give each bug two black antennae and six black legs. You can make the black ladybug dots with the wooden end of the brush—try this on paper first. Hang the gourd up to dry.

5· When your gourd is dry, hang it up with your string, wire, or leather thong.

CLEANING HOUSE FOR YOUR BIRDS

Before you decorate your gourd, you need to get it in good shape for the birds to move into. For all of these steps, ask an adult to help you.

WHAT YOU NEED
- A dried gourd, about 9" across
- A drill or sharp knife
- Household bleach
- Rubber gloves
- A pot scrubber or brush
- A pencil
- A ruler
- A long-handled spoon
- String or wire for hanging

WHAT TO DO

1· Soak the gourd in a solution of ¼ cup bleach to a gallon of water for half an hour. Put on rubber gloves and scrub the gourd with a pot scrubber. Get it really clean. Then rinse it, dry it, and let it dry in the air for half an hour.

2· Drill or carve small holes about an inch down from the top for hanging.

3· Hang the gourd up to mark the entry hole. The hole needs to be along the outer-most curve of the gourd, 4" to 6" above the bottom, pointing straight out—not slanted up or down. Draw a hole 1½" across and 2⅜" high for tree swallows. If you have more chickadees and wrens around your house, draw a hole 1⅛" in diameter. Drill or carve the entry hole.

4· Drill or carve 3 or 4 small drainage holes in the bottom of the gourd, at the lowest point when it is hanging up.

5· Completely clean out the insides of the gourd with the long-handled spoon.

HANGING UP YOUR GOURD HOUSE

Once you have decorated your gourd bird-house, you want birds to build a nest in it, right? Lots of birdhouses never have birds in them, because someone hangs them up in the wrong place or at the wrong time.

Here are some things you can do so birds will want to build their nest in your birdhouse.

IF YOUR HOUSE IS FOR WRENS, HANG IT:
- 5 to 10 feet off the ground in a tree or under an overhanging roof.
- In early April if you live in the South, in early May in the North.
- Near a brush pile or near lots of bushes, if you can.
- Where it will get some sun.

IF YOUR HOUSE IS FOR CHICKADEES, HANG IT:
- 5 to 15 feet off the ground in a tree. Hardwood trees are best—oak, hickory, maple, beech, walnut, elm, willow.
- In early April in the South, early May in the North.
- Where it gets sun for about half the day.
- With the entrance facing away from the wind, if you can.

IF YOUR HOUSE IS FOR SWALLOWS, HANG IT:
- FOR TREE SWALLOWS, 4 to 5 feet off the ground near a pond, river, or other large water if you can.
- FOR VIOLET-GREEN SWALLOWS, 10 to 15 feet off the ground and under an overhanging roof
- In late February in the South, in late April in the North.
- With the entrance facing away from the wind.

What's a Bald Eagle? What's a Grizzly Bear?

Some day there might not be any more grizzlies or American crocodiles. Or any sea turtles, giant pandas, brown pelicans, or whooping cranes. All of these species, or kinds, of animals and birds are endangered. They are in danger of disappearing from the earth. Not one brown pelican or sea turtle anywhere in the world.

BALD EAGLES, *America's national birds, aren't bald...but they are endangered in every state they live in, from Florida to Maine, New York to California.*

BLUEBIRDS: *Twenty years ago, eastern bluebirds were vanishing fast from the United States. Then people began building special bluebird nest boxes, and hanging them in places bluebirds like to live. They stopped the bluebirds from disappearing. Every person who hung up a bluebird house helped.*

BROWN PELICANS *(whose beaks can hold more than their belly can) hang out on the fishing pier in Cedar Key, Florida, waiting for handouts. The birds are endangered in most of the places they live, including California, Louisiana, Mississippi, Oregon, Texas, and Washington.*

HEDGEHOG CACTUS *is one of many endangered U.S. wildflowers. You probably wouldn't pick these—they're too much like porcupines! But it's a good idea not to pick any wildflowers unless you know their species is not in danger of disappearing.*

THE MANATEE STAMP (AND OTHERS TOO!):

For three years, third graders at Westfield Area Elementary in Pennsylvania got people to write letters to convince the U.S. Postal Service to create a manatee stamp. In 1996 the U.S. Post Office issued endangered species stamps to remind everyone about endangered wildlife. One of them was a Florida manatee! The other species on the stamps are the black-footed ferret, thick-billed parrot, Hawaiian monk seal, American crocodile, ocelot, Schaus swallowtail butterfly, Wyoming toad, brown pelican, California condor, Gila trout, San Francisco garter snake, Woodland caribou, Florida panther, and piping plover.

- Many kinds of animals, wildflowers, and birds have already disappeared—more than 100 just in the United States. We say they are *extinct*, just like dinosaurs.

- Without help, another 400 species will soon disappear.

- Every week, about 20 species of plants and animals disappear from the world. Don't you wish you could have seen a passenger pigeon or a duck-billed platypus?

The good news is that there are at least 100,000 species of plants and animals left in the United States...and about 14 million in the world. You and I and other people who care can help save endangered species and others that are at risk—about 20,000 in the United States right now.

Humans are the reason most species become extinct. People destroy the places they live, or change those places so much the species die. People cut down forests. They build towns and neighborhoods where plants and animals used to live. They move rivers or dam them up.

What can we do? How can we help save the manatees? How about the Hawaiian monk seals? And the hedgehog cactus?

GRIZZLY BEARS *and gulls fish together in Alaska. Grizzlies are endangered in every other state where they live—Colorado, Idaho, Washington, and Wyoming.*

LITTER puts many animals and birds in danger. This sea turtle has swallowed a plastic bag it thought was a jellyfish. Sea turtles are endangered everywhere they live, not just because of litter. Many people still eat sea turtles or catch them just for their shells. People have built houses and condos on many of the beaches where sea turtles used to lay their eggs.

WHOOPING CRANES are almost extinct. In 1941, only 15 were left in the entire United States. Today about 150 are alive, including those in captivity. They live in wilderness wetlands, marshes, and wet prairies.

What Kids Can Do

TAKE CARE OF YOUR ENVIRONMENTS. Every time you reduce, reuse, and recycle, you're helping save the planet for all living things.. Every time you go outside, you're visiting many creatures' homes. When you walk in a park or the woods, leave flowers and insects and animals where you find them. Leave nests where they are. Respect other living things and their homes.

PICK UP LITTER. Some people remember to take a bag with them when they go for walks, so they can pick up litter. They are wonderful earth-savers. Anytime you're outside and you see litter, pick it up if you can and throw it in the trash or recycle bin. Litter often harms animals and birds.

ADOPT A PIECE OF ENDANGERED LAND. See page 390.

ADOPT A RARE ANIMAL IN A ZOO. Some zoos are trying to save rare animals by making homes for them like their natural habitats. Most zoos let you pick the kind of animal you want to adopt. You send in money to take care of the animal, and the zoo sends you a photo and news of your animal. It could cost as much as $25. You could get friends to help you or have a garage sale or a car wash to make the money.

ADOPT AN ENDANGERED ANIMAL. You can adopt a bison through the Nature Conservancy...a manatee through Save the Manatee...a whale through the International Wildlife Coalition...a dolphin through the EPI Group Limited...an eagle through Conservation International... and many other animals through other environmental groups. Usually you need to send the group some money, and you get a picture and a newsletter and news of your animal. You can find out about these groups at the library or on the Internet. Before you send any money, ask your parents or the librarian to be sure the group is a good one for you to join.

2

Awesome Eco-Adventures

ECOLOGY CRAFTS

BACKYARD WETLAND

YOU CAN BUILD YOUR OWN SMALL ECOLOGICAL SYSTEM IN YOUR BACKYARD BY PUTTING IN A POND. IF YOU PLACE ROCKS JUST ABOVE THE WATER LINE, BIRDS CAN DRINK FROM IT, AND YOU'RE SURE TO HAVE VISITS FROM RACCOONS, SQUIRRELS, AND FROGS WHO LIVE NEARBY.

After visiting Philadelphia, Louis would fly south with his wife and children so they could see the great savannas where alligators dozed in the swamp water and Turkey Buzzards soared in the sky. And then they would return home to spend the winter in the Red Rock Lakes of Montana, in the lovely, serene Centennial Valley, where all Trumpeter Swans feels safe and unafraid.

—E.B. White, *The Trumpet of the Swan*

WHAT YOU NEED

- A 32-gallon plastic garbage can— green, black, or brown blends in best
- Strong scissors
- A tape measure or ruler
- A shovel
- Large rocks
- Floating pond plants
- Small landscape plants or moss
- Water

WHAT TO DO

1· Trim off the top of the garbage can, so what you have left is 20" high.

2· Find a flat spot and dig a hole that the can will fit in, with about 2" of the top sticking out of the ground.

3· Put the can in the hole, fill it with water, and pack dirt around it if there are any spaces to fill in.

4· Place stones around the rim, and some plants or moss between the stones. Pack dirt tightly around the stones and plants.

5· To take care of your wetland and the wildlife who visit it, scoop out leaves and twigs that fall into it. Keep the water level high, so your visitors can get a drink easily.

The Wet, Wet World of Water

DID YOU KNOW THAT...

- More than half of your body is water?
- Water covers more than three quarters of our planet? (That means for every square mile of land, there are three square miles of water.)
- Only a tiny bit of all water on earth is fresh water...and most of that is frozen at the north and south poles?

So everyone is being careful about taking care of water, right? Wrong. Some kids in New Jersey made a list of all the trash they found along a river near their school. They found tires, socks, a flowerpot, newspaper, cardboard, soda cans, a blanket, lawn chairs, a shopping cart, oil cans, golf bags, shopping bags, roof shingles, and a kitchen sink...and that's not all.

ALLIGATORS *find a safe home in this protected wetland in Gainesville, Florida.*

WHAT ABOUT THE OCEAN?

You might think something as big as the ocean can take care of itself. Nope. No matter where you live, the water around you ends up in the ocean...or sometimes in a lake. Creeks and streams run through wetlands and into rivers, and rivers run into the ocean.

So when you hear about endangered species in the wetlands or in the ocean, you can help, even if you've never seen the ocean and live hundreds of miles away.

HOW CAN YOU HELP?

- *Learn about marine creatures (animals and fish that live in the water)...talk to people about how special they are.*
- *Cut up plastic six-pack carriers before you throw them away— snip each circle with scissors. For some reason, many six-pack carriers end up in the ocean. Sea creatures can get tangled in the rings and strangle or starve.*
- *Use only the water you need for brushing your teeth or washing dishes. Don't let the water just run.*
- *Take short showers instead of baths—it saves water.*
- *If you go fishing, don't throw any trash in the water.*
- *Tell your parents you know how to save up to 5,000 gallons of water a year (this saves money too)! Just fill a gallon plastic bottle with water and put it in your toilet tank.*
- *Collect rainwater for watering your plants and trees. Put a bucket or a barrel outside with a screen over the top.*

A SEA BIRD *confuses ocean trash with food.*

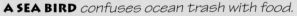

WANT TO KNOW MORE?

A good place to find out more about protecting the ocean and its wildlife is:

**Center for Marine Conservation
1725 DeSales Street, NW
Washington, D.C. 20036**

WHEN YOU BRING HOME THAT GREAT STUFF FROM A CAMPING TRIP OR NATURE WALK, YOU NEED A SAFE PLACE TO KEEP IT ALL...LIKE BLUE JAY AND GOLDFINCH FEATHERS, ROCKS WITH MICA IN THEM, SHARKS' TEETH FROM THE CREEK, ACORNS, SEED PODS, AND ARROWHEADS. YOU NEED A PLACE OF YOUR OWN, WHERE YOU CAN TAKE THEM OUT AND LOOK AT THEM, AND WHEN YOU NEED THEM FOR A PROJECT, YOU KNOW RIGHT WHERE THEY ARE. YOU COULD USE A SPECIAL DRAWER OR SHELF...OR YOU COULD MAKE THIS NIFTY COLLECTIONS BOX BY RECYCLING A CARDBOARD BOX AND MAGAZINES.

ECO EXTRA
King Phillip Came Over for Ginger Snaps

The next time you're feeling dumb, remind yourself that you know a lot more than Aristotle did. He classified all living things into only three groups: human beings, plants, and animals. As you immediately see, he forgot insects, fish, birds, and several other kinds of creatures. Today scientists classify every living thing—including you—into a **K**ingdom, then a **P**hylum, then a **C**lass, an **O**rder, a **F**amily, a **G**enus, and a **S**pecies. *King Phillip Came Over For Ginger Snaps*. (Remember it—you'll need it for biology.)

COLLECTIONS BOX

WHAT YOU NEED
- 9 large matchboxes (If you need bigger boxes, use shoe boxes. You can use as many boxes as you want to, as long as you have the same number in each layer.)
- A large corrugated cardboard box
- Old magazines, calendars, catalogues, etc.
- Acrylic paints
- A paintbrush
- A sharp knife
- Scissors
- 9 brass paper fasteners or small nuts and bolts
- A glue stick
- Masking tape or cellophane tape
- Some cotton
- A piece of paper with one blank side for labels

WHAT TO DO

1· You can either wait for years, saving up empty matchboxes, or you can empty out nine matchboxes right now. Give the matches to an adult to store in a coffee can or other container with a top.

2· For the front of your drawers, paint one end of each matchbox. Or cut out pictures from magazines and glue them on.

3· For the drawer knobs, ask an adult to help you make a hole in the center of each drawer front with an awl or sharp knife. If you're using brass fasteners for the knobs, stick a fastener in each drawer, and flatten out the legs on the inside to hold it. If you're using nuts and bolts, stick a bolt through each hole and screw on a nut from the inside to hold it.

4· Glue a label on each drawer.

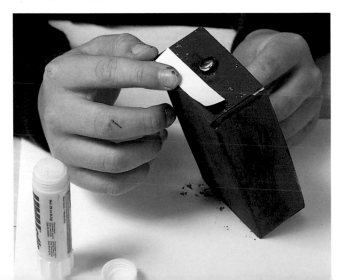

5· Stack your drawers with the same number of drawers in each stack—here we have three stacks of three drawers. Tape each stack together with masking tape or cellophane tape, then tape all the drawers together with the stacks beside each other.

6· Make a cardboard box to fit your drawers. You'll probably need to cut up a bigger box to fit, and tape the sides together. You want your stack of drawers to fit tight in your box. If the whole stack of drawers pulls out of the box when you try to open a drawer, you can glue or tape the stack to the inside of the box.

7· Decorate your box however you want to. You can glue on magazine pictures, like the box here, or glue on any kind of paper, or paint it. You may want to put cotton in some or all of the drawers, if some of your collections are fragile.

BIRCH BARK CANOE

Tired though he was, he climbed a spruce tree and found some spruce gum. With this he plugged the seam and stopped the leak. Even so, the canoe turned out to be a cranky little craft. If Stuart had not had plenty of experience on the water, he would have got into serious trouble with it.

—E.B. White, *Stuart Little*

FIRST, YOU NEED A BIRCH TREE THAT HAS SHED SOME OF ITS BARK. ONCE YOU'VE SEWED UP YOUR CANOE, IT WILL REALLY FLOAT, BUT IT'S NOT WATERTIGHT. NATIVE AMERICAN INDIANS OFTEN SEALED THE SEAMS OF THEIR BIRCH BARK CANOES WITH A MIXTURE OF SPRUCE GUM AND ANIMAL FAT. YOU CAN TRY THAT IF YOU WANT TO, BUT IT'S HARD TO GET THE MIX RIGHT.

WHAT YOU NEED

- A piece of birch bark collected from the ground, large enough to fit the canoe pattern
- Some thin, bendable twigs or vine
- Raffia or fishing line
- A tapestry needle with a large eye
- An awl
- Sharp, strong scissors
- 2 spring-type clothespins
- A hot glue gun and glue
- Paper and pencil
- A bowl of warm water

WHAT TO DO

1· Trace over the canoe pattern on page 46 on another sheet of paper and cut out the pattern. If you want a bigger canoe, you can enlarge the pattern on a copy machine.

2· Trace the pattern onto your bark and cut out the canoe shape.

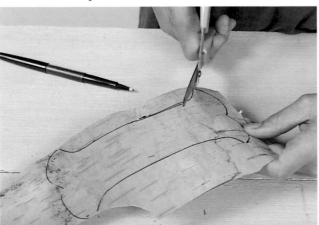

3· Soak your bark in warm water for a moment until you can bend it.

4· Gently bend the sides together and use clothespins to hold the canoe until it dries.

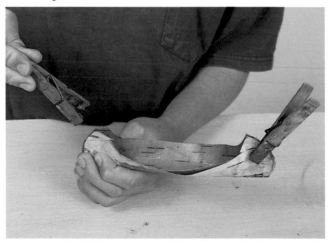

5· Ask an adult to help you hot glue the sides together. Press the glued sides together with clothespins until the glue dries.

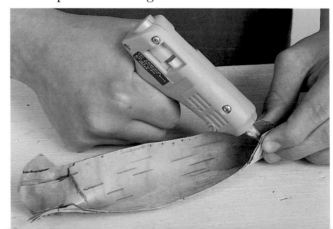

6· Ask an adult to help you make holes with the awl for lacing, along the top sides of the canoe.

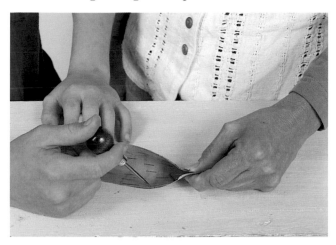

7· Thread your needle with the raffia or fishing line. Lay a piece of twig as long as your canoe along the top, so you can lace it to the canoe. Begin lacing at one end and sew up the side at an angle. Then sew back down the same side to create a crisscross pattern. Repeat on the other side.

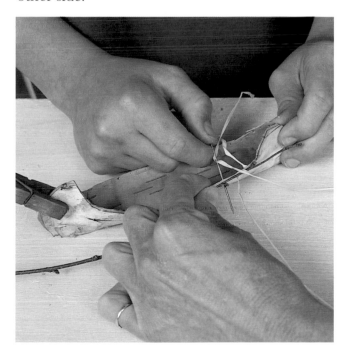

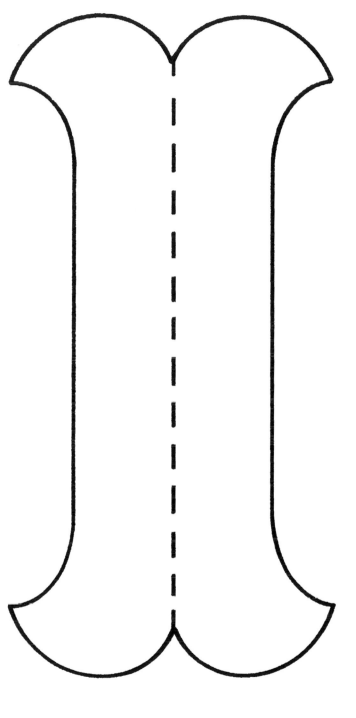

Happy Earth Day! April 22

The first Earth Day was April 22, 1970—more than 25 years ago. Since then, kids like you all across the United States have worked hard to help protect the earth. They plant trees, recycle trash, and raise money to preserve endangered habitats and species.

• In Hawaii, a Girl Scout troop made an overgrown pond into a wildlife sanctuary. They cleared a path, hauled away trash, and planted native grasses and plants. Now native water birds use the pond again, and volunteer groups keep the habitat safe for wildlife.

• One boy, an Eagle Scout in Illinois, actually created three acres of wetland, a safe home for many birds and plants. He designed the wetland by computer. Then he collected more than 600 plants, and organized other Scouts to help him plant them. He worked with an architect to design and build a boardwalk through the area, with signs explaining wetlands for visitors.

• Elementary school students in Virginia raised money to build a nature trail, with a bridge, benches, and a picnic area. They also included a compost bin and a recycling center.

• Students at a Massachusetts school started a program to recycle lunch waste. They have turned more than four tons of food and paper trash into compost. Students spread the compost in gardens, and they plant flowers all over town.

• A fourth-grade class in Michigan raised money to save a stand of white pine that was about to be cut down. They collected money in their school to "Save a Pine Tree." Then they got other schools involved. They had enough money to save 20 trees. Finally the entire town got interested, and bought the whole 80 acres the trees were growing on...and saved all the white pine trees.

KIDS LIKE YOU *help keep creeks, rivers, and lakes clean. In many cities, kids help on "Clean Streams Day" by picking up litter, like these boys cleaning up a section of creek in Asheville, North Carolina.*

CANADA GEESE *and many other birds need clean water and safe wetlands to survive.*

LOG CABIN PLANTER

OF COURSE, IF A REAL LOG CABIN HAD THESE SPACES BETWEEN THE LOGS, THE WIND WOULD BLOW RIGHT THROUGH. BUT THE DESIGN WORKS FINE FOR HOLDING FLOWERPOTS. TO STACK THE LOGS CLOSER TOGETHER, YOU COULD CARVE OUT NICHES IN EACH LOG FOR THE ONES ON TOP OF IT TO LIE IN. YOU CAN ALSO MAKE A FLOOR FOR YOUR PLANTER BY NAILING STICKS ALL THE WAY ACROSS THE BOTTOM.

WHAT YOU NEED

- Twigs collected from the ground, 1/2" to 3/4" across
- Small flat-headed nails
- Pruning shears
- A hammer
- Sandpaper

WHAT TO DO

1· Decide how big you want your planter. If you know what flowerpot you want to put in it, measure that to see how long your sticks need to be. Cut as many twigs as you need, all the same length. (The planter in the photo has 14 twigs.)

2· Choose two twigs with flat sides for the bottom twigs. If they don't lie flat, sand them until they do. You want your planter to be steady when it's finished. Your nails go about 1" in from the ends of the twigs. Hammer nails partway through both ends of both bottom twigs.

3· Hammer nails through the ends of 2 more twigs for the next layer. With the nail points of the bottom twigs pointing up, lay the third twig across the nails (with its nail points pointing up), and hammer it down. Then add the fourth twig, and so on.

4· Keep adding layers of twigs until you have the planter as tall as you want it. Make the top layer extra stable by hammering nails down through the sticks into the layer below, as well as up from the layer below. Put a potted plant on a saucer inside your planter.

BAT HOUSE

HUMANS HAVE TAKEN OVER OR DESTROYED LOTS OF PLACES WHERE BATS USED TO LIVE, LIKE ABANDONED BUILDINGS, DEAD TREES, BARNS, AND CLIFFS. SO BATS ARE HAPPY TO FIND WARM, DARK PLACES TO HANG, LIKE THIS BAT HOUSE. THIS IS THE MOST CHALLENGING PROJECT IN THE BOOK— TEAM UP WITH AN ADULT OR TWO WHO HAVE HAD LOTS OF PRACTICE WITH A SAW AND DRILL. WHAT MAKES THIS HOUSE INTERESTING—AND PLANET FRIENDLY—IS THAT IT'S MADE OF OLD BARN WOOD.

ECO EXTRA!
Natural Bug Zappers

One little brown bat eats about 500 insects every hour! The more bats we have flying around chomping on mosquitoes, moths, beetles, stinkbugs, and leafhoppers, the less poisonous insecticides farmers and gardeners will need to use.

TOOLS AND WOOD YOU NEED

- A handsaw
- A 3/8" electric drill
- 1/8" and 1/4" drill bits
- A #8 countersink
- A hammer
- Clamps
- A Phillips screwdriver
- A tape measure
- Roots or curly branches for decoration
- Old wood
  - Roof: 6" x 18"
  - Sides: each 2" x 21½"
  - Top frame: 2" x 11½"
  - Bottom frame: 1" x 11½"
  - Front and back: each 15½" x 21½" (as many boards as you need to make the front and back the right length and width)

SUPPLIES YOU NEED

- 2¼" decking screws, #8
- ½" staples
- A 15 x 23" piece of old fiberglass window screening or ¼" hardware cloth
- ½" wood screws, #4
- Exterior wood glue

WHAT TO DO

1· Cut all the pieces of wood to the right size.

2· Make a box by clamping the sides against the top frame and the bottom frame. The lower edge of the frame should be about ½" above the end of each side. Ask an adult to help you drill. First drill holes at the corners for the decking screws. Fasten the box together with glue and decking screws.

☞ **To see if bats have moved into your bat house, check it twice a month in the summer, once in fall and winter. When they have lived there awhile, it won't bother them if you take a quick peek with a flashlight.**

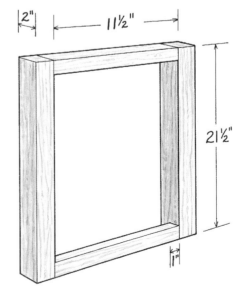

3. Drill ¼" mounting holes through the center of the back pieces that will go at the top and bottom of the frame. Then clamp the back pieces on the frame, centered and even with the ends of each side. Leave a ¾" entrance gap between the back and the bottom frame. Drill 2 holes per board with a #8 drill bit. Fasten with decking screws.

4. On the inside of the house, staple the piece of screen to the back, top frame, and sides. Trim it to fit. The screen helps the bats cling to the inside.

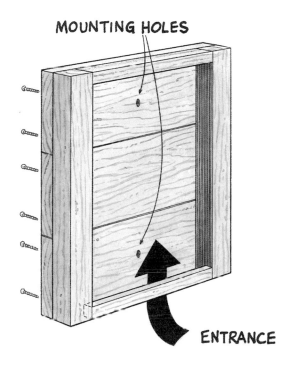

MOUNTING HOLES

ENTRANCE

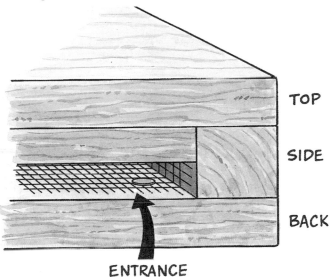

TOP

SIDE

BACK

ENTRANCE

BAT HOUSE HINTS

In many states, bat species are now endangered, like this Indiana bat. Putting up bat houses in safe places helps bats survive.

- The house needs to get at least 4 hours of sun a day. More sun is even better.

- The higher up the better—at least 12 to 15 feet up on a tree, the side of a building, or a pole.

- If you put your house within a quarter mile of water, like a stream, river, or lake, where there are lots of insects, you are more likely to find bats living in it.

- If you live in a cool or cold climate, paint your bat house a dark color or cover it with tar paper, to absorb and hold heat.

5. Center the front pieces on the frame, even with the upper ends of each side and with the bottom frame.

6. Center the roof on top of the house with its rear edge even with the back. Drill 6 holes with a #8 drill bit. Fasten the roof using glue and decking screws. If you plan to add a flag, use a ¼" bit to drill a ½"-deep hole in the center of the roof.

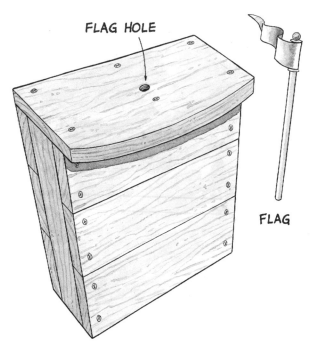

FLAG HOLE

FLAG

7. Add your own ornaments and natural objects to the face of the box, like the curly roots here or bits of found metal.

8. Bats don't like drafts. If the boards of your house don't fit together snugly, seal the spaces with silicone caulk.

Up with Bats!

People have a lot of wrong ideas about bats. For instance... Bats are blind. Bats like to fly into people's hair. Bats have rabies. Vampire bats will suck your blood (yum).

Some facts about bats are:

- Bats can see just fine. But they get around by *echolocation*—they send out squeaks, clicks, and buzzes and listen for the echoes when those sounds bounce off objects in their path, and then they fly around them... so they *locate* things by their *echoes*.

- By echolocation, an ordinary brown bat can detect a human hair three feet away. But like anyone else, bats would rather stay out of people's hair. There's nothing batty about bats.

- Bats do not usually have rabies. But it is important to know that no wild animals like to be caught. If you can catch one, it is probably sick. So it is best not to touch any wild animals, including bats.

- Vampire bats don't attack humans—mostly horses, pigs, and cows, and only in Latin America. They don't suck blood. They bite, then deposit a substance that keeps blood flowing, then lap up the blood. Scientists have just found that the substance in vampire bat saliva that keeps blood flowing is twenty times stronger than anything else like it. Someday this substance may help with serious human problems like heart attacks and strokes.

Up with bats! Be a Batkid!

Help stamp out the silly things people say about bats... spread these important bat truths!

BIG BROWN BATS: *If you live in the United States, you are most likely to have big brown bats come to your bat house— even though there are 40 species of U.S. bats. Big brown bats are about*

4½ inches long, with wings that open to about 12 inches. Baby bats are born in late May and early June, when big brown bats form nursery colonies of 20 to 300 bats. It takes the young bats only a month to learn to fly.

NEXT TIME SOMEONE AT YOUR HOUSE BREAKS A PLATE, SAY THANKS, SAVE THE PIECES (CALLED SHARDS), AND MAKE ONE OF THESE FANCY FLOWER POTS. OR RECYCLE A PLATE FROM A GARAGE SALE OR SECONDHAND STORE. ANYONE WITH A GARDEN HAS OLD CLAY POTS AROUND. ADD A PLANT, AND YOU'VE CREATED A COOL GIFT.

Smart Safety Tip:
Always wear safety glasses when you use tile nippers. In this project, bits of the plate might fly up into your eyes when you're cutting.

WHAT YOU NEED

- Plates (one or two dinner plates will cover the rim of at least one 6" pot)
- Clay pots—scrub dirt off with soap and water and allow to dry
- Ceramic tile adhesive and ceramic tile grout from a hardware department. (You can also use floor or wall grout. Floor grout works best if you're leaving large spaces between the plate bits. With wall grout you must place the plate bits close together.)
- Tile nippers
- A plastic knife or old kitchen knife
- Rags
- An old container for mixing grout
- Newspaper
- Latex gloves
- Safety glasses

307

WHAT TO DO

1· You only use the edges of your plates. Ask an adult to help you use the tile nippers. Make nips along the edge about ½" to ¾" apart with the tip of the nippers. After you have a pile of pieces, cut them to about ½" wide or as wide as you need them to fit together along the rim of your pot.

2· To glue the cut pieces to the pot, butter the back of one piece with a small amount of tile adhesive, just like you butter toast.

3· Line up the outside edge of each buttered plate piece with the upper edge of the pot and stick it on. Place a second row of pieces under the first row, aligning them with the lower edge of the pot rim. If the pieces don't fit, trim them with the tile nippers, then stick them in place. When both rows are finished, let the pot dry overnight.

4· Squeeze tile grout between the pieces to fill in the spaces. If your grout comes in a can, spread it on with a small rag and push it into the spaces between the shards.

5· Let the grout dry for about 15 minutes, then wipe the surface of the shards clean with a rag. Let the grout dry for about 30 more minutes and wipe the shards clean with a damp rag.

6· Set your pot aside for 2 or 3 days to dry completely. Then you can fill it with soil and plant something in it.

POTATO PRINT SHIRTS

HERE'S A GREAT WAY TO CHANGE AN OLD
STAINED SHIRT INTO A FANCY NEW ONE.
ANYTHING YOU CAN CARVE INTO A POTATO, YOU
CAN PRINT ONTO A SHIRT. ON THE SHIRTS IN
THESE PHOTOS YOU'LL FIND FRUIT, VEGETABLES,
LEAVES, VINES, BIRDS, A SUN...AND MORE. YOU
MIGHT LIKE TO TRY STARS AND MOONS...ANI-
MALS...LETTERS AND NUMBERS...SOCCER
BALLS...OR FLOWERS. OR ALL OF THEM! WHEN
YOU'RE FINISHED WITH THE POTATOES, TOSS
THEM ON YOUR COMPOST PILE (PAGE 311).

WHAT YOU NEED
- A shirt
- Idaho baking potatoes
- Fabric paint
- A pen
- A paintbrush
- Cookie cutters
- A knife
- Some newspaper

WHAT TO DO

1· Cut some potatoes in half lengthwise. Use a cookie cutter to cut out shapes or draw on your design with a pen and then carve around it. Start with simple ones first, like stars, hearts, suns, and moons. Use a round-edged knife, like a butter knife, to cut away the potato around the design. You want your design to stand up from the rest of the potato, so it will print clearly. Practice until you have some that you like.

2· Lay a few sheets of newspaper flat inside the shirt so the paint won't go through to the other side. Paint the design on the potato with fabric paint.

3· Stamp the potato onto your shirt. When you've finished printing, hang the shirt on a hanger with the newspaper still inside. If you want to print both sides of your shirt, wait until one side is completely dry before you print the other side. Read the instructions on the fabric paint to see if you need to do anything to make the paint permanent before you wash the shirt.

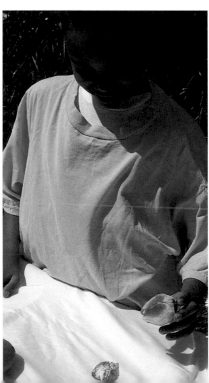

The Great Garbage Mystery

Here's the scene: Your neighbors the Pryors are worried. For the past month, garbage has been disappearing from their kitchen, and it looks like their sweet dog, Pal, must be guilty. They can't find any evidence, like orange peels in his bed, but they think he may have some mysterious disease that makes him hungry for old lettuce, corn husks, and coffee grounds on bread crusts.

Meanwhile, the Pryors have been bragging to you about the healthy new plant their child, Tooperfect, is growing in a big flowerpot on the back porch. But you know Tooperfect pinches Pal when the Pryors aren't around. Yesterday you heard Tooperfect tell Pal, "You're too stupid to understand, but I know where the garbage is going, and I'll never tell. They'll send you away to dog jail. Ha ha ha ha." Then horrible Tooperfect pinched the dog. Hard.

PAL: *Guilty or not guilty?*

With these two clues, you can solve the mystery and save Pal:

1. **Tiny creatures called microorganisms live in soil.**

2. **By breaking food into tiny pieces, microorganisms turn food into fertilizer called compost.**

Who has been stealing the Pryors' garbage? Why? Where has the garbage gone? Why doesn't someone pinch Tooperfect?*

The moral of this story is, even someone who recycles food into compost can't be a hero if they still pinch dogs.

*Tooperfect has been stealing the garbage and turning it into compost in the flowerpot, to get Pal into trouble. Why no one has pinched Tooperfect is still a big mystery.

Cool Tool
Make Your Own Compost

To make your own compost, you need a large flowerpot, enough dirt to fill the pot half full, a large plastic bag, and some food scraps. Save up bread crusts, and vegetable and fruit scraps, like banana peels and leftover broccoli and salad. Don't use meat or dairy products like milk and cheese.

Fill the flowerpot about one-quarter full of dirt. Then add food scraps until the pot is about half full. Then cover the food with a thin layer of dirt to keep it from smelling and to keep bugs away.

Put your pot somewhere outside and cover it with the plastic bag. Add a little water to the pot every few days, just to keep it all damp. When you're adding water, stir the mixture up with a large spoon or a spade. The microorganisms need air and water to do their work.

After three or four weeks, most of the food will turn into soil, and soon the food will be entirely gone. You've made compost—fertilizer! Now you can plant a flower in your pot, or you can spoon your compost into the garden or another potted plant and start over.

If your family has a yard or a garden, you can make an entire compost pile. Good places to find out how to make compost piles are your local garden center or your library.

Save the Manatee

Manatees are gentle, playful mammals who are friendly to humans. They eat mostly sea plants, but if they get hungry enough they will reach up out of the water to eat from overhanging tree branches. Because they are mammals, they have to breathe. Like dolphins, they can stay underwater for many minutes before they come up for air. Their closest modern relative is...the elephant.

- The average manatee weighs about 1,200 pounds and is 10 feet long. Why would something so big and friendly be endangered? Partly because they're so big and friendly.

- They need lots of food. Human beings have filled up many of the coasts manatees used for feeding grounds. Now they have to go farther to find less food. They also sometimes eat trash, which kills them.

- Most manatees in Florida have scars from being run over by boats. They swim slowly near the surface and don't recognize the danger of boats. In 1991, boats killed 53 manatees, which is about 1 out of every 40 that were alive.

What's the Good News?

In 1981, singer Jimmy Buffet and Florida senator Bob Graham started the Save the Manatee Club to help save manatees from becoming extinct. Some of the things the club does are:

- Help rescue and rehabilitate (cure) manatees

- Put up manatee warning signs in Florida waterways

- Help save critical manatee habitat so manatees can live undisturbed and free.

Through the club, anyone who adopts a manatee gets

- An adoption certificate, a photo, and a biography of their manatee

- A membership handbook with information on manatees

- The Save the Manatee Club Newsletter, four times a year.

Some of the Save the Manatee Club's adopted manatees live at Homosassa Springs State Wildlife Park in Florida. The park is for manatees who are recovering from injuries before being released back into the wild.

HANGING AROUND: *Manatees have been on earth for about 60 million years...and one species, the Florida manatee, has nearly disappeared just in the last 20 years. Only about 2,000 are still alive.*

WANT TO KNOW MORE?
Write to:
**Save the Manatee Club
500 N. Maitland Ave.
Maitland, FL 32751, USA**

1-800-432-5646

SKETCH-AND-PRESS NATURE JOURNAL

YOU'LL FIGURE OUT LOADS OF WAYS TO USE THIS NATURE JOURNAL. SKETCH IN IT...WRITE ABOUT PLACES YOU GO AND WHAT YOU SEE...TUCK YOUR FINDS UNDER THE RUBBER BANDS...USE IT AS A TEMPORARY NATURE PRESS (PRESS LEAVES, FERNS, OR FLOWERS INSIDE)...PACK IT IN YOUR BACKPACK ON HIKING AND CAMPING TRIPS. YOU CAN MAKE IT ANY SIZE—WHATEVER WORKS BEST FOR YOU!

WHAT YOU NEED

- Cardboard from used corrugated boxes
- Rubber bands
- White glue
- Packing, duct, or electrical tape
- Cellophane tape
- 4 machine screws (1" or 1½")
- 4 hex or wing nuts
- 8 washers
- Recycled paper
- A hole punch
- An awl
- A ruler
- Scissors
- A craft knife
- A pencil

WHAT TO DO

First, figure out how big you want your journal. The measurements here are for a journal that fits 8½" by 14" paper.

1· Measure a large piece of cardboard into 4 pieces that are each 8½" by 14".

2· Ask an adult to help with cutting and using the awl. Cut the pieces of cardboard with a craft knife or other sharp knife.

3· Glue two of the pieces together with white glue. Fit the pieces together, press them together, and put books on top of them overnight to be sure they stick together well.

4· Cut one of the other pieces in half, so you'll have two pieces that are 8½" by 7" for the covers. Measure and mark a line 1½" in from the side of both cover pieces.

5· Cut along the lines with a craft knife.

6· Tape the cover pieces to the 8½" by 14" back with a small piece of cellophane tape.

7· To make hinges so the front covers will bend, wrap duct or packing tape around each cover and the back in one long piece on each side.

8· Hold the back and front cover pieces together with rubber bands. Mark where you want to put the machine screws. With the awl, make small holes for the machine screws.

9· Put one sheet of paper under the back and mark with a pencil where the holes for the machine screws belong. Use a hole punch to punch holes in as much paper as you want to use.

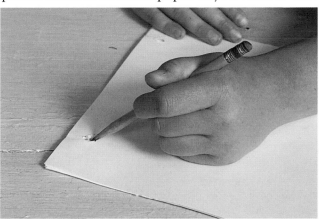

10· To put the book together, thread a washer onto a machine screw and insert the screw from the back. Do this for each hole. Then put on the paper, then the top cover, then another washer and a nut or wing nut.

Ants' ways, beetles' ways, bees' ways, frogs' ways, birds' ways, plants' ways, gave him a new world to explore and when Dickon revealed them all and added foxes' ways, otters' ways, ferrets' ways, squirrels' ways, and trouts' and water-rats' and badgers' ways, there was no end to the things to talk about and think over.

—Frances Hodgson Burnett, *The Secret Garden*

COOL TOOL

Keep a Tree Diary

Many gardeners keep records of their gardens. They write down when they plant, what happens, what kind of weather they had, and so on. Maybe you would like to keep a record of the trees you plant, something like the one here. You could keep it in your nature journal (see page 313) or make a paper bag book for it (see page 324). You could also take photographs of your trees as they grow.

You might write something like this:

My tree is an American dogwood. Its scientific name is C. florida. It could grow to be 40 feet tall with a trunk about 18 inches around.

I planted my dogwood sapling on September 1, 1998. It was 36 inches tall.

Interesting facts about my tree:

1. There are 40 kinds of dogwood. 14 kinds are native to the U.S. and Canada.

2. It is the state flower or tree of North Carolina, Missouri, Virginia, and British Columbia.

3. It is my favorite kind of tree. My grandmother has a pink dogwood in her yard, but mine will have white flowers.

What I will do differently next time:

Plant more than one sapling at the same time, in case something happens to one of them.

My Tree Diary

My tree is a _____ tree.

Its scientific name is _____.

It could grow to be _____ feet tall with a trunk about _____ inches around.

I planted my _____ on _____.
 (DATE)
It was _____ inches tall. (Or I planted my

_____ seeds on _____.
 (DATE)

I first saw my sapling on _____. I plan-
 (DATE)
ted my tree in the earth on_____ when
 (DATE)
it was _____ inches tall.)

Interesting facts about my tree:

What I will do differently next time:

Rockin' Eco-Recycling

ECOLOGY CRAFTS

LIGHT BULB PUPPETS

RECYCLE LIGHT BULBS, NEWSPAPER, FOOD CONTAINERS, AND GROCERY BAGS TO MAKE PUPPETS THAT WILL LIGHT UP ANY STAGE. TRY COUNT DRACULA AND THE RED QUEEN, OR DREAM UP YOUR OWN PUPPET PEOPLE.

WHAT YOU NEED (FOR TWO PUPPETS)

- Two burned-out light bulbs
- A small cottage cheese container
- A small yogurt or sour cream container
- Used brown paper grocery bags
- Used aluminum foil
- Poster paints
- A paintbrush
- A sharp knife
- A pencil
- Scissors
- Tape
- Paper mache mix (see page 321)

WHAT TO DO

Make paper mache mix. For this project, white glue mix works well. Make a pile of pieces of newspaper about ½" by 1".

TO MAKE THE HEADS

1· Cover just the glass part of your light bulbs with aluminum foil. Leave the screw part of the bulb sticking out. Pinch the foil to shape the puppet nose, ears, eyebrows, and chin.

2· Dip the torn newspaper, one piece at a time, into your paper mache mix, and cover all the foil. Let the heads dry.

3· In the back of each head, carefully cut a slit about 3" long that runs up and down, from the top of the head toward the neck. Cut through the paper mache and the foil, but don't break the bulb. Then from the bottom of the bulb, push and twist the light bulb out of the slit. Tape the slit closed. Now add one more layer of paper mache.

4· If you want to have a head that moves, make the neck longer now. Stick your finger into the bottom of the head and wrap foil around the bottom of the head and your finger. Cover the foil with paper mache.

5· When the paper mache is completely dry, paint the head.

TO MAKE THE BODIES

1· Turn the yogurt and cottage cheese containers upside down. When the puppet is finished, your fingers will be the puppet arms. Figure out where you want the center front of the puppet to be. Then cut an armhole on each side of the center for your fingers to fit through. Cut a hole in the top of the container to fit the puppet head in.

2· If your puppet has a head that doesn't move, like the Red Queen, tape the head to the body now.

Why recycle NEWSPAPER ?

Guess what takes up the most space in U.S. landfills (trash dumps). Right—newspapers. By adding water and chemicals, used newspaper gets recycled into pulp to make cereal boxes, egg cartons, construction paper, more newspapers... and many other paper products.

TO MAKE THE RED QUEEN

1· To make the skirt, spread out a brown grocery bag and trace around the bottom of the container. Draw an inner circle about 1" smaller than the first one. Draw an outside circle about 3" to 4" larger than the first one. Cut along the outside and inside circles. This piece is the skirt.

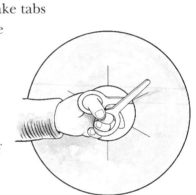

2· To make pleats in the skirt, fold the skirt in half, fold that in half again, fold that in half again until you can't fold anymore. Open it back up. To make tabs to attach the skirt to the body, cut six slits in the waist of the skirt. Make each slit about 1" long and space them evenly around the waist. Tape the tabs to the inside of the body.

3· For the collar, from the grocery bag cut out a circle about 3" across. Draw and cut out a circle about 1" across in the center of the first circle. Cut an opening all the way through the collar. Put the collar around the queen's neck and tape it.

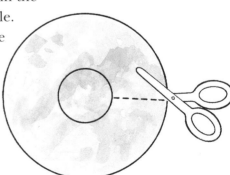

4· Paint the body, the skirt, and the collar.

COOL TOOL

Make Your Own Paper Mache Mix

For some of the projects in this book,
you need to make paper mache.
It's easy...it's kind of gooey or sticky...
so it's fun. Mainly, you tear up old newspaper or brown grocery bags into strips
or little pieces, dip them in
a mix, and stick them on something.
If one kind of paper mache mix works
best for a project, the directions for
that project will say so, but you can use
any of these mixes for any project.

White Glue

In a small bowl or container,
mix 3 parts of white glue and 1 part water.
For instance, 1 cup of glue and
1/3 cup of water.

Wallpaper Paste

Put about a milk gallon jug full of water
in a shallow pan or container—
like a litter box or dishpan.
Sprinkle in about 2 cups
of wallpaper paste mix.
It comes in powder form.
Mix it around with your hands.
It will be lumpy—don't worry.
Add more wallpaper paste mix
or water until the mixture feels
about as thick as runny oatmeal.

Flour

In a small bowl or container,
mix 1 cup of water, 1 cup of flour,
and 1 tablespoon of salt.

TO MAKE THE COUNT

1· For the cape, spread out a brown grocery bag
and cut out a square 6" on each side. On one
side, mark a point 1½" from each corner. From
each of these points, draw a line to the next
closest corner. Cut along the lines. Then make a
curve in the shortest edge of the cape. This is
the neck.

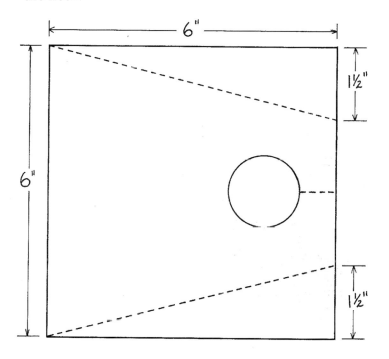

2· Paint the cape and body.

3· Put the puppet head in the top hole of the
body. Then attach the cape around the Count's
neck with a piece of masking tape underneath.
Paint the masking tape to match the cape.

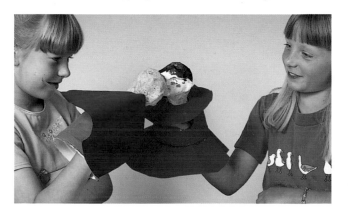

PAPER BAG BOUQUETS

SINCE YOU USE DRIED FLOWERS FOR THESE BOUQUETS, THEY LAST A LONG TIME. IF YOU CAN'T PICK FLOWERS FROM YOUR YARD OR A FRIEND'S GARDEN, YOU CAN FIND DRIED FLOWERS IN A CRAFT DEPARTMENT OR STORE. DRY YOUR OWN FLOWERS BY HANGING THEM UPSIDE DOWN FOR A FEW WEEKS IN A DRY DARK PLACE. SMALL BLOOMS WORK BEST FOR DRYING—AND YOU CAN USE DRIED WEEDS AND GRASSES TOO. INSTEAD OF PAPER BAGS, YOU COULD MAKE SMALL BAGS FROM USED GIFT WRAP, COMIC PAGES, OR CALENDAR PHOTOS.

ECO EXTRA
Nature's Recyclers

Some creatures do nothing but clean up. They're nature's great recyclers, the scavengers. Everything they eat is dead (before you get too disgusted, think about what you eat). For instance, vultures. You've seen them circling high in the sky, riding the air currents, looking for food. They help keep the earth tidy.

WHAT YOU NEED

- Dried flowers
- Small brown paper bags
- Sand, beans, rice, or bird seed for the base
- Scissors or clippers
- Raffia, twine, yarn, ribbon, or string

WHAT TO DO

1· Cut your bag to the size you want. Fill it with sand, beans, rice, or bird seed. This will hold the flower stems and also keep your bag from falling over.

Why recycle PHONE BOOKS?

When new phone books come out every year, most people just throw their old ones in the trash—and you know where the trash goes. Right to the dump. But recycled phone books get turned into ceiling tiles, book covers, and insulation to keep houses warm in winter.

2· Cut the stems of your flowers short enough so they don't fall over when you stick them in the bag.

3· Tie string or raffia around the neck of the bag.

PAPER BAG BOOKS

RECYCLING GROCERY BAGS INTO BOOKS IS A REAL EARTH-SAVER. YOU CAN MAKE THE BOOKS ANY SIZE YOU WANT, WITH AS MANY PAGES AS YOU NEED. USE THEM FOR PHOTO ALBUMS AND DIARIES...FOR WRITING POEMS AND STORIES...AS GIFTS... SKETCH PADS...NATURE JOURNALS. RAID YOUR ART SUPPLIES BOX FOR DECORATIONS (SEE PAGE 386).

WHAT YOU NEED

- Brown paper grocery bags
- Scissors
- White glue, rubber glue, or a glue stick
- Embroidery thread and needle
- An awl
- Decorations—photos, lace, buttons, pebbles, paper, pictures from magazines, wallpaper scraps

WHAT TO DO

1· Cut the bottom off the paper bag. Cut up the side of the bag to make one flat piece. Decide how big you want your book. You can cut this piece in half or in four quarters. Fold the pieces so the writing is on the inside. Glue the insides together to make pages. Use as many bags as you need to make the number of pages you want.

2· Fold the pages in half. Stack the pages, one inside the other. Make holes along the fold with an awl, for your needle to go through.

3· If you're using embroidery thread, use three or four strands. Make a knot at one end of your thread. Sew along the fold, and make a knot at the other end when you're finished.

4· Decorate the cover of your book.

ECO-ENVELOPES

HELP THE EARTH BY MAKING ENVELOPES FROM MAGAZINES AND CALENDARS...AND MAKE SPECIAL ENVELOPES FOR SPECIAL PEOPLE AT THE SAME TIME.

Any fool can destroy trees. They cannot run away.... Through all the wonderful, eventful centuries... God has cared for these trees...but he cannot save them from fools—only Uncle Sam can do that.

—John Muir, *American Forests*

WHAT YOU NEED
- Cardboard or stiff paper
- Magazines, junk mail, catalogues, calendars
- Some envelopes
- A ruler
- Scissors
- White glue, rubber glue, or a glue stick
- Scrap paper

WHAT TO DO

You can make your envelopes any size you want to, but the post office will not deliver mail smaller than 3½" by 5". So be sure any envelope you want to mail is bigger than that.

1· If you want to make standard-sized envelopes, trace different sizes of envelopes on your cardboard. Cut these out.

2· Cut out pictures from old magazines, catalogues, and calendars. Either fold them around the cardboard to make your envelopes, or just fold them to the size you want them.

3· One way to fold them is to fold under about ½" on all four sides. Glue this edge down. Then fold the paper almost in half, but leave about 1" sticking out at the top for your envelope flap. Fold and glue the inside edges.

4· Cut out a label from scrap paper and glue it on.

NATURE'S GARDENS BOTTLES AND JARS

HOW SIMPLE IS THIS? RECYCLED JARS AND BOTTLES PLUS PAINT...AND YOU HAVE A NEAT DECORATION...OR A VASE, OR A CANDY JAR, OR A GIFT. ADD GOOD LAMP OIL AND A WICK FROM A CRAFT STORE (SEE THE PHOTO), AND YOU'VE CREATED AN UNUSUAL "CANDLE." (GET ADULT HELP IF YOU WANT TO MAKE A CANDLE.) ASK FRIENDS TO SAVE BOTTLES AND JARS FOR YOU, BECAUSE ONCE YOU GET STARTED, EVERYONE WILL WANT ONE.

WHAT YOU NEED

- Used bottles and jars
- A used plastic lid or old saucer for paint
- Acrylic paints and small paint brushes or paint pens
- Towels or rags
- Lamp oil and candle wicks if you want to make "candles"

WHAT TO DO

1. Wash your bottles and jars in warm soapy water and let them sit in the water awhile to soak the labels off. You may need to scrub them off with a rough cloth or plastic scrubby.

2. Be sure the outside of a jar or bottle is dry before you start painting. Paint on your design with acrylic paint or with paint pens. Paint pens cost more but are very easy to work with.

Paper or Plastic?

You probably knew that paper bags were made out of trees, but did you know that plastic bags are made from oil? And that making either kind of bag pollutes the environment? Think how many bags we all throw away every week!

What can you do about it? When you buy a candy bar or a pack of notebook paper and the clerk starts to put it in a bag, you can say, "I don't need a bag." You might need a bag if you're buying 10 apples, for instance. But when you don't need a bag, don't take one. Just say no.

You can also save bags and reuse them. Try storing them in a reused plastic bottle (page 337). Projects in this book show you how to make hats, bouquets, and books out of paper grocery bags. You can also reuse plastic and paper bags by taking them shopping and using them instead of new bags. Or you can reuse them to carry things, like books you're taking back to the library.

Paper or plastic? What if you answered, "Neither one"? You can, every time you remember to bring your backpack or your own bag with you. You might not want to say to the clerk, "Hey, I care about the earth. I'm protecting the environment." But you could think it.

Recycling Kids, Inc.

How can a baby food jar help save a humpback whale? When you decorate it, fill it with candy, and sell it...then use the money to adopt a whale. That's the kind of project third graders do at Twin Lakes School in El Monte, California.

They run a business called Recycling Kids, Inc. Every year, students in June Burton's class take over the business from last year's students.

- First, they collect trash from school and at home—milk caps, detergent lids, film capsules, tissue boxes, all kinds of throw-aways...
- Then they paint them, or glue on ribbons and decorations and stickers, and turn them into...
- Bird feeders, candle holders, candy jars, pencil boxes, desk sets—50 items altogether—and...

  Sell them on holidays to other students and in the community, so they can...
- Adopt endangered species and endangered habitats.

So far Recycling Kids, Inc., has adopted
five MANATEES,
five HUMPBACK WHALES,
four acres of RAINFOREST,
and two species of DOLPHINS.

WANT TO KNOW MORE?

Write to:
Recycling Kids, Inc.
3900 Gilman Road, Room 3
El Monte, CA 91732

TURNING TRASH INTO TREASURES: *Third graders in Recycling Kids, Inc., make magnets and wind chimes from juice lids... Happy Earth pins from milk caps.*

TOTALY RECYCLED ALBUMS

ALL REUSED MATERIALS...QUICK AND EASY TO MAKE...PERFECT GIFTS FOR FRIENDS... JUST WHAT YOU NEED FOR THE PHOTOS FROM YOUR VACATION OR THE JOURNAL OF YOUR FIRST CRAZY YEAR IN MIDDLE SCHOOL. (WHO KNEW IT WOULD BE SO MUCH FUN?)

WHAT YOU NEED

- 10 to 12 sheets of recycled office copy paper
- String, scrap cross-current wire, or other fine wire
- Bubble wrap or polyethylene foam wrap (white or green packing material)
- White craft .glue
- A needle big enough for your string or wire
- An awl or ice pick
- Scissors
- A flattened out cardboard box to work on

WHAT TO DO

1· Ask someone you know who works in an office for some recycled copy paper. You need paper that has only been used on one side. Cut the pages to the size you want. Cut packing foam or bubble wrap to fit your pages. Cut 2 covers for each book. Stack your pages between the covers.

2· Spread the cardboard on your work surface. Ask an adult to help you make 5 holes on the right-hand edge of your book with the awl or ice pick, ½" from the edge, an equal distance apart.

3· Thread your needle with string or wire. Sew your book together using one of the methods here or one you make up yourself. Then decorate your book as you like. (For photo albums, bubble-wrap and other transparent covers don't really need any decoration—the photos show through.)

Sewing Method #1

1· Push the needle up through the center hole, letting the tail end of the thread hang loose. Sew around the spine and back up through the same hole.

2· Going toward the bottom of the book, sew down into the next 2 holes in the same way. Wrap the thread around the spine as before.

3· Bring your thread around the lower edge of the spine and sew back up through the spine. When you get to the fourth and fifth hole, sew as before. Then sew back down the spine to finish where you began. Tie off your thread tightly.

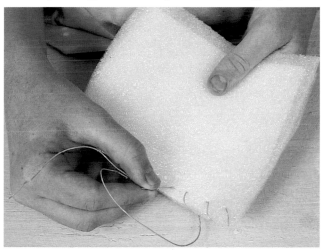

Sewing Method #2

Whipstitch the edge with a single strand of wire. At the top and bottom of the spine, simply wrap the wire off at the end and cut it close to the book.

CALENDAR BOXES

WHAT A GREAT WAY TO SAVE TREES! (EVERY TIME YOU
REUSE PAPER, THINK OF IT AS SAVING PART OF A TREE.)
DEPENDING ON HOW THICK YOUR CALENDAR PAGES ARE,
YOU CAN MAKE TERRIFIC GIFT BOXES, JEWELRY BOXES, OR
JUST NEAT-LOOKING BOXES FOR THE FUN OF IT. IT'S REALLY
EASY—BET YOU CAN'T MAKE JUST ONE! (YOU DON'T NEED
GLUE, BUT TO MAKE THE BOX LAST LONGER, YOU MIGHT
WANT TO USE A FEW DABS FROM A GLUE STICK.)

WHAT YOU NEED
• Old calendars or other paper
• Scissors

WHAT TO DO

1· Pick out a calendar picture you like. Fold your picture in half and measure the short side. Then cut the longer side to the same length. Now cut the picture in half, so you have two squares. You will use one square to make the top of your box and one to make the bottom.

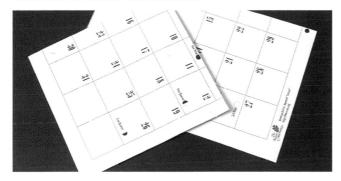

Why recycle ALUMINUM CANS?

Every three months in the United States we throw away enough aluminum to rebuild all the planes in all U.S. airlines. In recycling, aluminum cans get melted, pressed into sheets, and shaped into new cans or other things made of aluminum.

2· Fold one square in half diagonally—matching opposite corners.

3· Open the square. With a corner pointed toward you, fold the right-hand corner into the center of the square.

4· Fold the right-hand side to the center line. Refold these same folds two or three times.

5· Open the square. Do the same folds and refolds on the left-hand side. When you open the square you will have seven fold lines going up and down, evenly spaced.

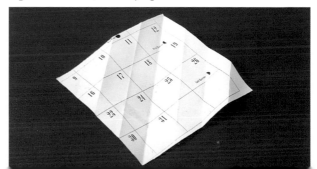

6· Turn the square so the fold lines go across. Fold in half diagonally again and repeat the folds with the new right-hand and left-hand corners.

7· When you open the square you will have fold lines running across and down, forming squares. With one corner pointed toward you, cut along the two lines on either side of the center line, cutting two squares up from the bottom point. Now make these same cuts from the opposite point.

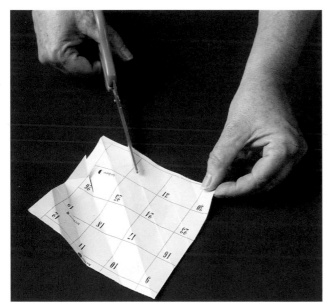

8· Make the sides of the box by folding in the long, uncut corners to the center, then fold in the cut corners—all four points meet in the center.

9· Stand up the four sides of the box.

10· Turn in the points of the long flaps and fold the ends under, then slip the ends under the short (cut) flap on one side, then on the other side. Here's your box bottom. Repeat these steps for the top, and you've made your first box.

Hurray for the Tree Musketeers!

The Earth might not get saved by adults with big ideas. It might get saved by kids starting out with little ones.

In 1987, a Brownie troop in El Segundo, California, used paper plates on a camping trip. They decided to pay the earth back for the plates by planting a sapling—they called it Marcie the Marvelous Tree. They were eight years old.

Some of the Brownies decided they wanted to plant more trees in their community, enough to make a pollution barrier around their town. They called themselves the Tree Musketeers. To get more people interested, they put on TV quiz shows called "Tree Stumpers." Kids ran the cameras, wrote the shows, and produced them. The Tree Musketeers founders were ten years old.

The Musketeers Branch Out

When the founders were eleven, Tree Musketeers opened their town's first recycling center. The next year they led the committee that wrote their town's waste management plan. They helped plan a national urban forest conference.

In 1993, Tree Musketeers held the National Youth Environmental Summit, the first national environmental conference organized by kids. The founders were fourteen. When they were sixteen, they held a second conference, the Second National Partners for the Planet Youth Summit—600 young people came from environmental groups all over the country.

Today Marcie the Marvelous Tree is 50 feet tall, and the founders of Tree Musketeers are college age.

- *Tree Musketeers has planted more than 700 trees in their hometown.*
- *The group sends out* **Grassroots Youth Magazine** *every two months to more than 50,000 readers.*
- *The Partners for the Planet network supports kids' environmental activities all over the country.*

TO START YOUR OWN CLUB
or hook up with Partners for the Planet, write to:
**Tree Musketeers
136 Main Street, Dept. P
El Segundo, CA 90245**

TREE MUSKETEERS *founder Tara Church made a speech to the El Segundo, California, City Council when she was nine. She invited the community to the 1988 Arbor Day celebration.*

GROWN UP: *Tara Church at seventeen spoke at the capitol building in Salt Lake City, Utah. Tree Musketeers, founded by a Brownie troop in 1987, was sponsoring a national meeting for kids, called the 1995 Partners for the Planet Youth Summit.*

THAT CAN'T BE PAPER! BEADS

YOU WON'T BELIEVE HOW REALISTIC PAPER BEADS CAN LOOK UNTIL YOU'VE TRIED THIS. THIS MAKES A GREAT ACTIVITY FOR A PARTY, TOO...AND EVERYONE HAS A NECKLACE OR BRACELET TO WEAR HOME. IT'S SO EASY, YOU CAN INVITE LITTLE BROTHERS AND SISTERS TO JOIN IN—YOU CAN CUT THE PAPER UP FOR THEM.

WHAT YOU NEED

- Bright-colored paper from magazines, gift wrap, catalogues, etc.
- White glue or a glue stick
- Scissors
- String, yarn, fishing line, plastic-coated wire, etc.

WHAT TO DO

1· Cut long, skinny triangles of paper, about 1" wide and 4" long.

2· For each bead, smear glue on half of one triangle, toward the tip.

3· As you roll each triangle up, leave a hole through the middle for your string to go through.

4· When the glue has dried, string the beads into necklaces and bracelets.

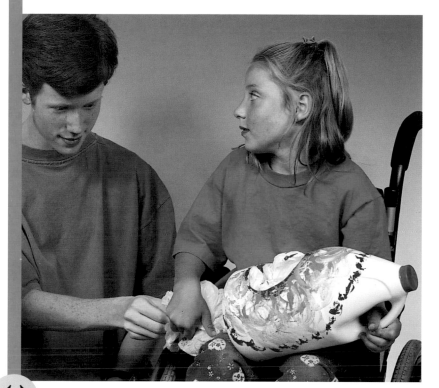

ℰasy RECYCLE BIN

WHAT YOU NEED
- A large heavy-plastic bottle, washed out with soapy water
- Strong scissors or a knife
- Acrylic paints and a paintbrush

WHAT TO DO

Cut or carve out a hole in the side of the bottle, then paint the bottle in bright colors. Or you can glue on pictures cut from magazines and comic strips...or any other paper.

Y OU'LL BE AMAZED AT HOW MANY PLASTIC BAGS YOU CAN STORE IN THIS EASY-TO-MAKE STORAGE BIN. IT'S A GREAT WAY TO RECYCLE PLASTIC BAGS AND TO REUSE PLASTIC BOTTLES. YOU CAN MAKE RECYCLING EVEN EASIER FOR YOUR FAMILY BY GIVING A BIN TO EACH PERSON, DECORATED JUST FOR THEM.

Why recycle PLASTIC?

Every hour, people in the United States throw out 2.5 million plastic bottles and jugs—that's enough to wrap around the earth 4 times in a year. Picture that for a minute. Recycled plastic milk jugs and soda bottles get shredded, melted, and made into vests, carpet, t-shirts, and teddy bears.

Is That a SODA BOTTLE You're Wearing?

Okay, so what happens to all those newspapers and plastic bottles and glass and cans you put in the recycle bins?

Imagine pajamas and t-shirts made out of soda bottles...bikes made from old refrigerators and milk jugs...sandals with soles made of tires. Sound like science fiction? Nope. It's here and it's now and it's good for the planet.

Sometimes, the stuff you recycle gets turned back into what it was—that's what happens to most glass, aluminum cans, and paper.

But...used plastic bottles get shredded and melted and turned into...carpets... t-shirts...hats, gloves, and jackets. Your new bike or wagon might have steel parts made from steel cans, old cars, and appliances like washing machines. The soles of those sandals in your closet might once have been tires.

Only certain companies make things from recycled materials. This is a good reason to read labels and tags before you buy something. If you see the recycling symbol on a label, either the product itself or the package is made of recycled materials. Sometimes instead the package will say "Made of recycled materials."

You be the recycling detective—check out paper towels, baseball bats, cans, skateboards, writing paper, greeting cards, cereal boxes. Whenever you choose something recycled instead of something made of all new materials, you're helping the planet stay healthy.

RECYCLED FASHION SHOW: *Students at Erwin High School in Asheville, North Carolina, gave a fashion show to promote recycling at a Career Expo Day. These cherry-red long johns are made of recycled plastic soda bottles and reclaimed cotton. The teddy bear fabric comes entirely from plastic soda bottles, and the wagon wheels and steel are from recycled materials.*

RE(BI)CYCLED? *Sports equipment like this bike and golf club can be made from recycled materials—steel from old cars and appliances, plastic parts from milk jugs, grips and pedals from recycled rubber... and a bike pack from plastic soda bottles.*

PICTURE-PERFECT POSTCARDS

WHAT YOU NEED

- Light-colored, thin cardboard from old boxes (cereal boxes, for instance). You can also use poster board.
- Scissors
- A ruler
- White glue, rubber glue, or a glue stick
- Photographs or pictures from magazines

WHAT TO DO

1· If you're using photographs, trace around your photograph onto the cardboard. If you're using other pictures, draw a rectangle on the cardboard about 6" by 4". Cut it out.

2· On the side you will write on (the blank side on cereal-box cardboard), draw a line across the card to divide it for the message and the address. Glue your photo or pictures on the other side. Be sure to glue it on tight. If it comes off, your friends will wonder why you're writing to them on a cereal box.

WHAT MAKES THESE POSTCARDS PERFECT IS THAT YOU TAKE THE PICTURES, OR CHOOSE THEM, AND YOU MAKE THE POSTCARDS. SEND A POSTCARD OF YOUR DOG TO YOUR COUSIN WHO THINKS HER DOG IS SO GREAT...A POSTCARD OF A COLORFUL AUTUMN TREE TO YOUR FRIEND IN MIAMI WHO NEVER GETS TO SEE FALL COLORS... A POSTCARD OF YOURSELF TO EVERYONE!

Why recycle CORRUGATED CARDBOARD?

Making new corrugated boxes out of recycled cardboard uses up much less energy and creates much less pollution than making them from trees. Brown paper bags are made of the same paper as cardboard— you can find out from your recycler if you can recycle them with corrugated cardboard.

339

COOL CUT-AND-PASTE BOTTLES AND JARS

AS EASY AS CUTTING AND PASTING...AND A PLANET-SAVING WAY TO REUSE GLASS OR PLASTIC. THE FANCY NAME FOR THIS CUT-AND-PASTE METHOD IS DECOUPAGE. YOU CAN DECOUPAGE JUST ABOUT ANYTHING—FURNITURE, BOXES, TRAYS, YOUR LITTLE BROTHER.

WHAT YOU NEED
- Used bottles and jars
- Vases from garage sales or secondhand stores
- Old magazines, photos, drawings, fabric scraps
- Decoupage glue from a craft department
- A glue brush
- Sandpaper
- For the Ocean of Fish bottle: sand and food color

WHAT TO DO

1· Wash your bottles and jars in warm soapy water. Let them sit in the water to soak the labels off. You may need to scrub them off with a rough cloth or plastic scrubby.

2· Look at magazine pictures, junk mail, old clothes, wallpaper samples, ticket stubs, play programs, or any paper or fabric at all to choose what you want to glue on your bottle.

3· Brush decoupage glue on a piece of your paper or fabric and stick it on your bottle or jar. You might want to glue on just a few things...

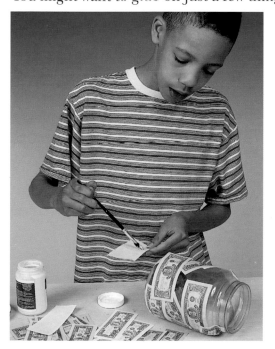

4· Or you might want to cover your whole bottle.

5· After you've glued everything on, brush a coat of decoupage glue over the whole design. Let the glue dry. You can add more coats of glue to seal your design better.

6· You can sand between each coat or sand after all your coats of glue. See which effect you like. You can use a clean rag to wipe off the sanded glue so your bottle is smooth.

TO MAKE AN OCEAN OF FISH BOTTLE

1. Glue on fish from fabric or pictures of fish. Brush layers of glue over them and sand them smooth.

2. Put some sand in the bottom of your bottle or jar.

3. Pour in water and add a little blue or green food color.

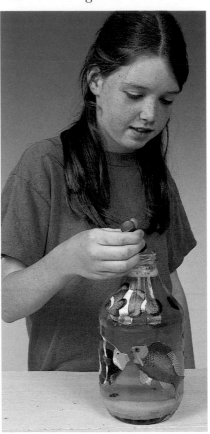

Why recycle GLASS?

Making glass out of recycled materials cuts air pollution by up to 20 percent. Used glass bottles and jars are recycled by crushing and melting them, then making them into new glass products.

Terrific Eco-TRASH

ECOLOGY CRAFTS

FANTASTIC FLOWER POTS

EVERY GARDENER HAS STACKS OF MUDDY, MOSS-COVERED TERRA-COTTA (CLAY) FLOWERPOTS LYING AROUND THAT YOU CAN TURN INTO TRULY TERRIFIC POTS WITH JUST A LITTLE PAINT...AND A LOT OF FUN. HAVE A POT-PAINTING PARTY! YOU CAN FILL YOUR WINDOWSILLS WITH THESE POTS, AND PEOPLE ALSO LOVE TO GET THEM AS GIFTS.

WHAT YOU NEED

- A terra cotta pot and saucer, scrubbed clean with water and dried. If you can't find a terra cotta saucer, use any saucer or plastic lid.
- Acrylic paints
- Small paintbrushes
- Urethane sealer
- A larger paintbrush for the urethane
- Paint thinner for cleaning the brush
- Rags
- A jar of water

1· To prepare your pot and saucer, paint them with a very thin coat of urethane sealer. This is so your paint will stay on the surface of the pot, instead of being absorbed by the clay. Clean your brush with paint thinner and a rag. Let the pot and saucer dry completely. This takes at least 12 hours.

2· Decide on your design. If you want to, you can draw your design in pencil before you paint. After you paint on one color, let that color dry. Swish your brush in the water to clean it, and wipe it with a rag before you go on to the next color.

3· When all the paint is dry, seal the pot and saucer with another thin coat of urethane. Keep brushing the urethane on lightly, and try not to let it drip or run down the side of the pot. Clean your brush with paint thinner and a rag, and wait at least 12 hours for your pot and saucer to dry...then add potting soil and a plant!

345

DOG BISCUIT PHOTO FRAME

WHAT YOU NEED
- Old picture frame
- Dog biscuits
- Gold paint (or any color you like)
- Craft glue

WHAT TO DO

1· Glue the dog biscuits to the frame. (Or you might think it's easier to paint the frame first, let it dry, then glue on the biscuits, then paint the biscuits.)

RECYCLE AN OLD PICTURE FRAME INTO THE PERFECT FRAME FOR YOUR DOG'S PICTURE. OR GIVE THIS FUNNY FRAME TO A FRIEND WHO LOVES THEIR DOG.

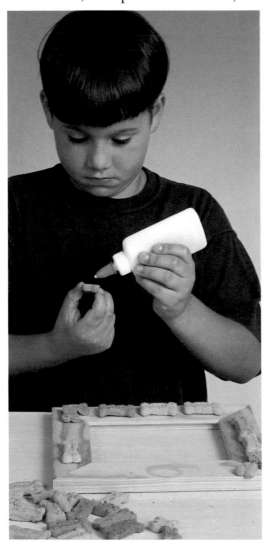

2· Paint the biscuits and the frame.

EGGSHELL MOSAIC

WHAT YOU NEED

- Eggshells
- Food coloring
- Water
- Small paintbrushes
- A piece of corrugated cardboard
- White glue
- A pencil
- 4 or 5 cups or bowls (1 for each color)
- Vinegar
- Newspaper

THE HARDEST THING ABOUT MAKING THESE PICTURES IS WAITING UNTIL YOU HAVE SAVED UP ENOUGH EGGSHELLS. YOU NEED SHELLS FROM ABOUT 12 EGGS—JUST RINSE THEM AND STORE THEM IN THE REFRIGERATOR UNTIL YOU'RE READY TO USE THEM. THE MOSAIC IN THE PHOTO SHOWS HOT-AIR BALLOONS RISING OVER MOUNTAINS.

WHAT TO DO

You can color your eggshells ahead of time, or you can paint them after you glue them on the cardboard, or you can do some shells each way.

1· If you're coloring your eggshells before you glue them, mix one color of food coloring in each cup or bowl to the shade you want. Add a teaspoon of vinegar to each color. Then put some eggshells in each color and leave them there overnight. In the morning, lay them on newspaper to dry.

2· Sketch your design on the cardboard, if you want to. Then spread glue on the cardboard and glue on the eggshells according to your design. You can break the shells into smaller pieces to fit them to the space, if you need to.

3· If you glue on white eggshells, paint them with a brush to make your design. You can add trims of beads, ribbon, string, or other items for decoration. You can also glue a frame on your picture made from ribbon, rope, or whatever you like.

Mosaic—An Earth-Friendly Art

Most artists care very deeply about saving the earth and its beauty. Mosaic artists often re-use materials like colored glass and tile to make their beautiful pictures and designs. They also use natural materials like stones and pebbles. Terry Taylor made this bird feeder and garden stepping stone from broken plates.

Artists have made mosaics for more than 2,000 years—at least. Buildings all around the world have whole ceilings, walls, and floors decorated with mosaics hundreds of years old. Near Mexico City, mosaics cover the outside of an entire 10-story library built not long ago. Today people have mosaics on their garden walls, patios, and walks. Or hanging on their walls, like this dog mosaic by George Fishman.

Keep your eyes open— you can probably spot mosaics in the town where you live.

LICENSE PLATE BIRD FEEDER

EXCEPT FOR THE SCREWS, THIS BIRD FEEDER IS ENTIRELY RECYCLED—FROM OLD LICENSE PLATES, WOOD SCRAPS, AND BRANCHES FROM FALLEN TREES. BE SURE TO HANG IT NEAR SOME BUSHES OR TREES, SO THE BIRDS HAVE A SAFE PLACE TO FLY TO NEARBY. YOUR BIRD VISITORS WILL LIKE YOUR RESTAURANT EVEN BETTER IF YOU OFFER THEM SOME WATER ALONG WITH THE BIRDSEED. YOU CAN RECYCLE AN ALUMINUM PAN FROM A FROZEN DINNER FOR A BIRDBATH...OR USE A LARGE TERRA COTTA SAUCER FROM A FLOWERPOT.

WHAT YOU NEED

- 2 license plates
- 4 thick sticks for the uprights, 5½" long
- 4 thick sticks for floor sides, 2 about 12" long and 2 about 8½" long
- Plywood scrap for floor, about 8½" by 9¼"
- Wood scraps for roof ends, to make 2 triangles about 10½" long by 3" at the point
- 8 #10 tapping screws, 5/8" long
- 8 #6 galvanized dry-wall screws, 1 5/8" long
- 10 #6 galvanized dry-wall screws, 1¼" long
- A screwdriver
- A handsaw
- A pencil
- A ruler
- A hammer and a nail
- Twine or wire

WHAT TO DO

1· With your ruler and a pencil, on your wood scraps measure 2 triangles for the roof ends. The base should be about 10½". Then measure 3" up from the middle of the base, and draw lines from that point to each end of the base to make a triangle. On the plywood scrap, measure a rectangle for your floor, about 8½" by 10¼". Unless you have had a lot of practice with a handsaw, ask an adult to help you saw these pieces out.

2· Make a few holes in the floor piece so rain water can drain out of your feeder. You can make these with a hammer and nail or with screws and the screwdriver.

3· Saw the 4 sticks that fit around your floor to the right lengths. Screw these to the edges of the floor with the 1¼" dry-wall screws. First screw in the 2 sticks that fit along the short sides of the floor. Then attach the long sticks. They will stick out about an inch on each end.

4· Saw the 4 sticks to hold up your roof—called uprights—to the same length. Screw 2 uprights to each roof end, using 4 dry-wall screws 1⅝" long. Follow the picture.

5· Holding a roof end parallel to the short side of the floor, screw the bottom of the uprights to the corners of the floor, using 1 dry-wall screw 1⅝" long for each upright. A helper comes in handy for this step.

6. Screw the license plates to the roof ends to finish your roof, using the tapping screws. Run twine or wire through the roof to hang your feeder.

ECO EXTRA
Finding Feathers

If you find a bird feather with the shaft running straight down the middle, it's a tail feather. Wing and body feathers have shafts a little off-center. The small, fluffy feathers are down feathers, soft underfeathers from under the bird's wings and on the belly.

You're Invited!

To What?
A WILDLIFE PARTY

Where?
YOUR BACKYARD, DECK, OR PATIO

When?
AS SOON AS YOU CAN GET ORGANIZED

You don't have any wild animals in your yard? What about those squirrels on your patio? And those ferocious butterflies? And that man-eating chickadee?

You probably have some other wild animals around that you don't even know about. If you keep a bird feeder full of seed, you can be pretty sure that flying squirrels visit it at night. Chipmunks and raccoons like to party around houses. So do mice. Toads. Moles. Rabbits. Possums. Bats. When you think about it, your backyard looks a lot like a jungle. It's pretty wild out there already!

If you want to help protect some of these wild creatures, you and your family can:

- *Offer them a drink. Water will bring you more wild guests than anything else you can offer. Make a backyard wetland (page 292). Or a birdbath. Butterflies need damp earth to drink from— they can't drink from a birdbath.*
- *Plant trees and bushes for food and shelter. Ask your local garden center what will be best.*
- *Plant bright flowers for butterflies.*
- *Plant sweet-smelling white flowers for moths and bats.*
- *Plant red flowers for hummingbirds or put up a hummingbird feeder.*
- *Start a pile of branches for small animals to hide in.*
- *Hang bird feeders in safe places, and keep them filled with mixed birdseed and sunflower seed.*
- *Put up birdhouses. Find out from a bird book what kinds are best and how to hang them.*
- *If you have a cat, put a bell on its collar to warn birds and small animals.*

351

CORNY SUNFLOWERS

NO ONE WILL GUESS WHAT YOUR SUNFLOWERS ARE MADE OF! YOU CAN DRY YOUR OWN CORNHUSKS FOR THIS PROJECT. SEE PAGE 354. FOR MORE CORN HUSK FLOWERS, SEE PAGE 221.

WHAT YOU NEED

- Dried cornhusks. If you never eat corn on the cob, you can get these at a craft store.
- A seed pod or small pinecone for the center. Or you can make a center out of cornhusk, or draw one and color it brown.
- Sticks, wire, coat hanger, chopstick, pick-up stick, or pipe cleaner for stems
- White craft glue, or a low-temperature glue gun with glue
- Yellow and green markers or food coloring or cloth dye
- Scissors

WHAT TO DO

1· Color the cornhusks. You can dye them in food coloring mixed with water or in cloth dye—you can get both from the grocery store. Just follow the directions. Or you can color the husks with yellow and green markers. When the husks are dry, cut out petals and leaves. The flowers in the picture each have about 18 or 20 petals and 2 leaves.

2· Glue the stem to the sunflower center with white glue or a glue gun. If it's a sharp stick, stick it through the center, then glue it. One petal at a time, glue half the petals to the center, making a complete circle of petals. If you use a glue gun, ask an adult for help.

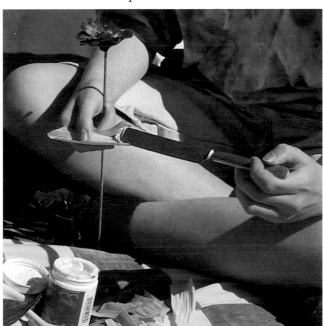

3· If you use white glue, let the first layer of petals dry before you start the second layer. Glue more petals under the first layer, making another complete circle of petals. These petals should show in between the petals of the first layer. If you have petals left, after your glue has dried, add a third layer of petals.

4· Glue the leaves under the petals.

COOL TOOL

Dry Your Own CORNHUSKS

Native American Indians used cornhusks to weave clothing or wrap food for cooking. Tamales, a Mexican food, are made by mixing ground meat and seasonings, rolling the mixture in cornmeal dough, and wrapping the little pies in cornhusks to steam them. To eat a tamale, you unwrap the cornhusks, like opening a package.

Besides the angels and sunflowers in this book, you'll probably discover lots of other cornhusk projects you would like to make. So it's a good idea to know how to dry your own husks. It's easy, it's cheap, and you get to eat the corn on the cob.

All you do is this:

- Save the husks after you peel them off the corn and let them dry in the air for two or three days— in the sun, if you can.

- You could lay them out on newspaper to dry or hang them on a line with clothespins. If you put them on newspaper, turn them over every day so they don't mildew.

- Then store them in a box until you're ready to use them.

You can leave husks their natural color, like the angels in this book, or you can paint or dye them, like the sunflowers.

TOO STIFF? To make dry cornhusks easier to work with, soak them in hot water for a few minutes right before you use them. Then lay them on a towel, ready to be turned into angels, sunflowers, dolls, baskets, hats, or whatever you dream up.

CORNHUSK ANGELS

ANGELS ARE HANDY TO HAVE AROUND ANY TIME, NOT
JUST AT CHRISTMAS. MAYBE SOMEONE YOU KNOW NEEDS
A GUARDIAN ANGEL RIGHT NOW. YOU CAN DRY YOUR OWN
CORNHUSKS FOR THESE ANGELS OR GET THEM AT A
CRAFT STORE. (TO DRY YOUR OWN, SEE PAGE 354.)

WHAT YOU NEED (FOR ONE ANGEL)
- About 8 dried cornhusks
- For the head, a little clay, play dough, or putty (anything you can stick wire through)
- Some thin wire, string, or raffia
- A 3" piece of heavy wire
- Scissors
- White glue or craft glue
- Bits of cloth, lace, and ribbon, tinsel or aluminum foil scraps
- Corn silk or yarn for hair, if you want it

WHAT TO DO
Soak the cornhusks in hot water for about fifteen minutes to soften them.

TO MAKE THE HEAD
1· For the head, make a ball of clay about as big as an acorn.

2· Make a fishhook in one end of your heavy wire. Now make a piece of husk about 2½" wide and 5" long. Pinch it in the middle and put the wire hook around the pinched middle.

3· Stick the other end of the wire into the top of the clay head and push it all the way through until just the end of the hook with the cornhusk in it shows at the top.

4· To finish the head, wrap the two ends of the husk over the ball to cover it. Twist a piece of thin wire (or string or raffia) around the neck to hold the husk tight. Cut the ends of the wire short.

TO MAKE THE BODY AND ROBE

1· Spread out a bigger piece of husk, about 8" or 9" long. Lay the head in one end of the husk and tie the end around the neck with another piece of thin wire, string, or raffia.

2· Now pull the long end of the husk over the wire and the short end so they don't show.

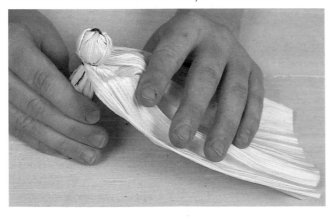

TO MAKE THE WINGS

1· For each wing, you need a strip of husk about 8" long. Hold the ends together.

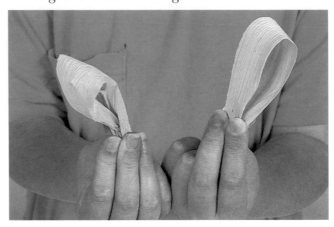

2· Having a helper for this step makes it easier. Hold the ends of the wings at the back of the angel's waist. Tie string, raffia, or thin wire around the waist and the wings to hold them on. You might want to wrap it around a few times.

TO FINISH YOUR ANGEL

Decorate your angel any way you want to—it's your angel. You could make a sash out of any fabric or ribbon and tie it on. You might glue on hair made from corn silk or yarn. For a halo, you can make a loop of gold or silver ribbon, tinsel, or aluminum foil and glue it on.

BEACH GLASS JEWELRY

WHEN BOTTLES END UP IN THE OCEAN, THEY BREAK INTO SMALL PIECES. STIRRED AROUND AND AROUND BY THE WAVES AND SAND, THE PIECES OF GLASS END UP ON THE BEACH, SMOOTH AS BEACH PEBBLES. YOU'LL HAVE AS MUCH FUN COLLECTING BEACH GLASS AS YOU WILL MAKING GREAT PENDANTS, PINS, OR EARRINGS WITH IT. BETTER COME HOME WITH PLENTY OF EXTRA GLASS TO MAKE JEWELRY FOR FRIENDS!

WHAT YOU NEED
- Beach glass
- Jewelry bails (tiny clamps)
- Pin and earring backs
- Cord (whatever you like)
- Jewelry cement or silicon glue
- Scissors

WHAT TO DO

1· Pick out pieces of glass you like. Use the flattest pieces for pins. Any shape works for pendants or earrings.

357

2. To make a pin or pendant, glue two or three pieces together if you want to. When the glue is dry, glue a pin-back on the pin and allow to dry. For a pendant, glue a jewelry bail to one edge. Leave enough space at the top to thread your cord through.

3. To make earrings, glue a jewelry bail to one edge of each piece of glass you've chosen. They don't have to match, of course. (Remember not to make the earrings too heavy, unless you want your earlobes dangling around your ankles.) Attach whatever kind of earring fastener you want— you can get them in craft departments.

You Don't Need a Garage for a Garage Sale

Have your own garage sale!

The miracle about garage sales is, other people want stuff you don't want anymore, and they actually pay you for it! Everyone wins. You're helping the planet because other people will reuse your things...they can buy things they want at good prices...and you're making money.

You can hold your sale in your yard, your carport, your driveway...or on the sidewalk...or actually in your garage.

- Figure out what you and your family want to sell. If you don't have enough for a good sale, ask friends or neighbors to join you.

- Gather everything you're going to sell and put price tags on everything.

- Put up posters and notices to advertise the day and time of your sale. Put an ad in the paper about it. Leave yourself plenty of time before the sale begins to put your stuff out.

- On the day of your sale, put your items out so people can see them easily and so they look good. Smile...here comes your first customer!

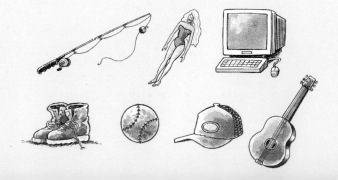

GARAGE SALE TODAY!
BOOKS 50¢
GAMES 75¢
GOOD SOCCER STUFF
25¢-$2

KISSY FISH PIÑATA

WHAT YOU NEED

- A 12" balloon
- Some newspaper
- Brown paper bags or a big piece of plain newsprint
- Paper mache mix (see page 321). White glue paper mache mix works well for the piñata.
- A bowl
- A 2" square of cardboard
- Masking tape
- 2 paper plates (recycled are fine)
- A sharp knife
- Scissors
- Poster paints and brushes
- Strong string for hanging

PIÑATAS FILLED WITH CANDIES, SMALL GIFTS, AND FRUIT ARE A TRADITION AT BIRTHDAYS AND CHRISTMAS IN LATIN AMERICA. KIDS TAKE TURNS TRYING TO BREAK THE PIÑATA WITH A LONG STICK. SOUNDS EASY—UNTIL YOU FIND OUT THE PERSON WITH THE STICK IS BLINDFOLDED. YOU CAN MAKE PIÑATAS ANY SHAPE YOU WANT. THIS PAPER MACHE KISSING FISH IS MADE MOSTLY FROM NEWSPAPER—BUT DON'T FORGET THE CANDY! (IF YOU DON'T WANT ANYONE TO BREAK YOUR PIÑATA, YOU CAN JUST HANG IT UP FOR DECORATION AND GIVE YOUR GUESTS THE CANDY.)

WHAT TO DO

1· Mix about a pint of paper mache mix in a bowl. Blow up the balloon. Tear a pile of newspaper strips about 5" long and 2" wide. Dip the newspaper strips into the paper mache mix—get them good and wet. Run the strips in different directions, and cover the whole balloon with strips.

2· Brush off the extra mix with a clean brush. Set the balloon in a bowl to drip dry. When that layer is dry, put on another layer of strips. (You can make the layers dry faster by putting the balloon in front of a fan.)

3· When the second layer is dry, with a sharp knife cut a door 3" square in one side of the balloon. Only cut three sides of the door. The balloon will break, but that is okay. Pull the balloon out through the door.

4· Reach through the door to the other side of the piñata and make a small hole for your string to go through. Tie a fat knot on one end of your string. Pull the string through a hole in the 2" square of cardboard. Stick the unknotted end of the string through the door in the piñata, then out the hole on the other side.

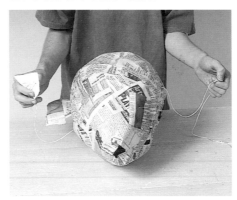

5· Fill the piñata with wrapped candies and any other small gifts you want to. Then tape the door shut with masking tape.

6· Cut fins, eyelids, and tail from the edges of paper plates. Make lips from rolled pieces of newspaper taped with masking tape. Tape all these parts to the body with masking tape.

7· Add one more layer of paper mache. Use brown paper bags or plain newsprint if you can, because printed newspaper will show through the paint. Cover all the fish except the fins and eyelids.

8· Paint the fish with poster paints. Let one color dry before you put on the next color.

You're ready for...the party!

Trees, Please

Planting a tree is one of the best things you can do to save the Earth.

Right now, for every tree we plant, 30 are getting cut down or burned down.
We have a lot of work to do. Luckily, growing trees is fun.

Don't Plant Palm Trees in Alaska

If you decide to plant a tree, you can buy a young tree from a nursery or you can start with a seed. Even though trees—like us—grow by themselves, you will be like a parent to this tree. You can make sure your tree will be healthy by thinking about a few things before you plant it.

- *What kinds of trees grow well where you live? You can be pretty sure a lemon tree won't grow outdoors in Michigan, and you'll probably be disappointed if you plant a blue spruce in Florida.*

- *Will your tree have plenty of room to grow... up and out? To be sure, find out how tall and how wide your tree will be when it's full grown.*

- *Who will take care of the tree? Just like any other baby, it will need water, food, and love. In the first year, for instance, it needs water every week.*

- *Is the soil okay—will your tree get enough to eat? Will it get enough sun?*

If you think you can make a good home for a tree, you can buy a young tree, called a sapling, from a nursery, or you can plant a seed.

THE MIRACLE OF TREES *begins with seeds. These are honey locust, Douglas fir, and pond pine seeds from Trees for Life. More than 700,000 kids in the United States have planted their own trees through Trees for Life projects.*

DIG IT! *To plant a seedling tree, you start with a hole as deep and twice as wide as your pot.*

Planting a Sapling

Ask at the nursery for any special instructions for planting and caring for your new sapling. Here's what to do for most trees:

- *Dig a hole as high as the pot your sapling is in and two times as wide.*

- *Make sure the soil around your hole is loose, and get rid of any rocks you find.*

- *Take the pot off. If the roots are growing around and around, straighten them out or cut them. If a lot of roots are sticking out of the soil, cut the root ball vertically with your shovel three or four times.*

- *Put the tree in the hole. Make sure when you fill in the hole that the soil comes to the same height on the tree as the soil in the pot did. Pack the soil down by stamping on it to make sure no air pockets are left.*

- *Make a dam around the hole with soil to hold in the water. Water the tree well.*

MULCH IT! *Volunteers spread mulch around a new tree along a highway in North Carolina. Mulch keeps weeds out and water in. You can mulch your new tree with 4" to 6" of wood chips, pine needles, straw, sawdust, or tea grounds. Just don't let the mulch touch the trunk—the bark might rot from not getting enough air.*

Taking Care of Your New Tree

If your tree can't stand up by itself, you need to hold it up with stakes. (Not steaks that you eat, of course.) You can get stakes at a garden center. Tie the tree loosely to the stakes with strips of cloth or other soft material.

For the first year, water your tree with two to three gallons of water every week. Then water it every other week in the summer and once a month in winter.

Rock-a-Bye, Baby

You can plant tree seeds in small pots or half an old milk carton filled with potting soil from a garden center. A few kinds of seeds are ready to grow right away, like Douglas fir and Ponderosa pine. Other seeds that are easy to grow are loblolly pine, bald cypress, date palm, and cabbage palm.

Some seeds need to be prepared first, like honey locust seeds. They must soak in hot water for several days. In fact, most tree seeds are so hard to grow that it's easier to get a sapling from a nursery. Find out if your seeds need special preparation before you plant them. A good place to find out about growing trees from seeds is: Trees for Life, 1103 Jefferson, Wichita, Kansas 67203.

Besides Trees for Life, other groups especially interested in trees are the National Arbor Day Foundation, Trees Corps, and Tree Musketeers. You can find out more about these groups at the library and on the Internet. The U.S. Forest Service also has excellent information on trees.

TREES FOR LIFE: *These kids are transplanting their Trees for Life seedlings from cartons to outdoor homes. Trees for Life started with an eighth-grade class at Wilbur Junior High School in Wichita, Kansas. They held a car wash and earned enough money to plant 103 fruit trees in India. Now Trees for Life has planted more than 30 million fruit trees in many countries...to protect the environment and feed hungry people. One fruit tree can provide more than 10,000 pounds of fruit!*

GOURD WITCH

BESIDES WITCHES, YOU CAN PAINT ALL KINDS OF FACES ON GOURDS. ANIMAL FACES
LIKE PIGS AND SHARKS AND RACCOONS...CARTOON FACES...DRACULA OR BATMAN
OR EVEN SOMEONE YOU KNOW. FOR WITCH HAIR, INSTEAD OF SPANISH MOSS
YOU CAN USE SCRAPS OF YARN OR FABRIC, WEEDS OR STRAW...OR PACKING
MATERIAL...OR YOU CAN PAINT HAIR. YOU MIGHT WANT TO PAINT A MUCH
SCARIER WITCH THAN THE FRIENDLY ONE IN THIS PICTURE.

WHAT YOU NEED

- A gourd, scrubbed clean with a stiff brush
- A sponge
- A black felt-tip marker
- A pencil
- White glue or paste
- Acrylic paints (for this witch—orange, red, black, and white)
- Small paintbrushes
- An old saucer or plastic lid for paint
- Spanish moss or other pretend hair
- String

WHAT TO DO

1· Tie a string around the stem so you can hang the gourd up to dry. With your marker, draw a line around the top part of the gourd for the hat. Paint the hat black. Hang the gourd to dry.

2· Squeeze or pour some orange paint into your saucer. Dip in your sponge and pat orange paint all over the gourd, except the hat. Hang it to dry. If you need to, sponge on a second coat of orange paint.

3· When the orange paint is completely dry, draw the eyes, nose, and mouth with a pencil. Paint in the white oval eyes and the red nose. Let the paint dry. With your black marker, outline the eyes and nose and draw over the mouth. Draw in the round eye pupil with your pencil, then ink it in with your pen. Dab in the white eye highlights with either end of your paint brush.

4· Draw a line of thick white glue around the bottom of the hat. Press on Spanish moss or some other hair.

ECO EXTRA

The oldest living things on earth are trees.

The oldest tree is 4,600 years old. It is a bristlecone pine in California.

Eco-Party

The next time you have a party,
you can make it a special celebration
of the Earth too. Lots of the
Earth-friendly projects in this book
are perfect for parties...
maybe you've thought of that already.

What You Can Make

- Party invitations and envelopes (page 326). On the back of each invitation, you can write, "Made of 100% reused materials."

- Gifts! Everyone loves to get handmade gifts, and this book is full of ideas for them.

- Gift wrap and gift boxes...Wrap presents and prizes in gift wrap you print yourself (page 280)...or in the Sunday comics...or in wrapping paper and ribbon saved from other gifts. Put small gifts in pretty boxes you've made from calendars (page 332).

- A tablecloth or place mats...You can print these yourself too, just like the gift wrap.

- A kissy fish piñata (page 359) full of wrapped candy and little gifts...or just for decoration.

- Sand candles and cornhusk sunflowers for decoration (page 192 and 352)

- Grocery bag party hats (page 283). You can make these ahead of time for your guests, and let them decorate them however they want to at the party.

What Else You Can Do

Use reusable cups and plates instead of paper plates. Usually after paper plates are used, they can't be recycled. If you can't use breakable dishes, use reusable plastic ones.

If you use plastic forks and spoons, wash and save them instead of throwing them away.

Make a special Party Box to store gift wrap and other supplies for your next party!

·5· Happenin' Eco-HITS

ECOLOGY CRAFTS

WANT TO BE A HOUSEPAINTER? AND HAVE LOADS OF FUN? ONCE YOU'VE PAINTED ONE OF THESE LITTLE ROCK HOUSES, YOU'LL PROBABLY WANT TO CREATE A WHOLE TOWN. THIS IS ALSO GREAT FUN TO DO WITH FRIENDS...BUILD A CITY...A METROPOLIS...A KINGDOM!

WHAT YOU NEED
• Rocks that look like houses
• A cleaning brush
• A pencil
• Acrylic paints
• Small paintbrushes
• Felt-tip markers

WHAT TO DO
1· Collect rocks that look like houses to you. The bottom of the house needs to be fairly flat, so the house will stand up. Rocks with smooth sides are easier to paint than rough rocks. Scrub your rocks clean with a stiff brush.

368

2. Look at the rock for awhile, so it can tell you what kind of house it should be. You can also look at pictures of different kinds of houses for ideas. Draw in the general design with a pencil. Draw in the windows, door, roofline, chimney, and other features with a felt-tip pen.

3. Think about colors. Use smaller brushes for little details like shutters. Do one color at a time, and let the paint dry before you do the next color. Try some shading, if you want to—use a little darker shade of a color to show depth. For the tiniest details like shingles or bricks, use a felt-tip pen. If the house has bushes or vines, add them last. Use your pen to draw vines.

PAPER MACHE BIRD

YOU MIGHT WANT TO MODEL SOME OF THE BIRDS YOU SEE NEAR YOUR HOUSE, OR YOU MIGHT RATHER HAVE SOMETHING MORE UNUSUAL SITTING ON A SHELF IN YOUR ROOM, LIKE A PENGUIN OR A YELLOW-BELLIED SAPSUCKER. YOU CAN FIND HUNDREDS OF BIRD PICTURES AT THE LIBRARY AND IN NATURE MAGAZINES, AND MAKE A WHOLE TREE FULL OF BIRDS.

WHAT YOU NEED

- A picture of a bird
- Wire that you can bend
- Used aluminum foil
- Paper mache mix in a small bowl or pan (see page 321)
- Newspaper
- White latex paint or gesso from a craft store
- Acrylic paints
- Small paintbrushes
- Twig, basket, napkin ring, or other mount

WHAT TO DO

1· Shape your bird from wire—don't forget the feet! Then cover all but the feet with aluminum foil, and shape the bird's body, head, and beak more exactly.

2· Tear newspaper into strips about ¼" wide. Dip them in the paper mache mix and crisscross them all over your bird, except the feet, until the bird is covered. Allow the bird to dry completely. You can dry it faster in front of a fan, or with a hair dryer, or in an oven set at 150 degrees. If you use an oven, ask an adult for help.

3· Paint the whole bird with white latex paint or gesso. Allow it to dry.

4· Paint the bird with acrylic paints, matching the colors in your picture. Once it has dried, you can display your bird on a branch…in a small basket of pebbles or marbles…on a napkin ring…in a little nest of sticks…or whatever you can imagine.

A Wonderful Wild Man:
JOHN MUIR

More than a hundred years ago, before anyone had ever heard of the word *ecology*, John Muir saw it, believed in it, and wrote about it. He believed every tree and pebble and person and mountain was connected to everything else, all part of the web of life.

> *"When I was a boy in Scotland, I was fond of everything that was wild, and all my life I've been growing fonder and fonder of wild places and wild creatures."*
>
> —John Muir, *The Story of My Boyhood and Youth*

So what's so great about that? Lots of people believe that. But back when John Muir was young, most people *didn't* believe that. Back then the United States was busy wrecking the environment, cutting down all the trees, and stripping coal off the mountains. No land was protected. There were no national parks, no national monuments, and no national forests.

John Muir wrote about the beauty of the mountains and glaciers, and about how precious every creature was. He convinced presidents and Congress of his ideas, and by the time he died, people in the United States had begun to think differently. The government decided that it was important to take care of the land and all the country's natural resources…to use them wisely…to conserve them, to save them for everyone's children and their grandchildren.

IN DUNBAR, SCOTLAND, the house where John Muir was born is now a memorial museum. Nearby lies John Muir Country Park, eight miles of wild seacoast set aside and protected. When I visited the park this year, in just a few hours I saw goldfinches, chaffinches, and bramblings in the pine woods, and on the seashore Eurasian wigeons, flocks of oyster-catchers, sandpipers, gulls—and seven human beings.

Three U.S. presidents especially paid attention to John Muir—Theodore Roosevelt, Woodrow Wilson, and William Howard Taft. While they held office, the United States set aside land for more than 50 national parks, 200 national monuments, and 140 million acres of national forest.

> John Muir was "what few nature lovers are—a man able to influence contemporary thought and action on the subjects to which he had devoted his life...so as to secure the preservation of great natural phenomena—wonderful canyons, giant trees, slopes of flower-spangled hillsides."
>
> —President Theodore Roosevelt, January 1915

Have you heard of Yosemite National Park? Or even visited it? Or the Petrified Forest or the Grand Canyon? Or Mt. Rainier in Washington State, or Sequoia National Park? John Muir personally helped create all those national parks. No wonder he's often called the Father of the U.S. National Park System. And he wasn't even born in the United States!

John Muir was born in Dunbar, Scotland on April 21, 1838. (Congress made April 21, 1988—150 years later—John Muir Day.) When he was eleven, his family moved to the United States. It took their ship six weeks to cross the stormy North Atlantic Ocean.

In Wisconsin, John worked with his brothers from dawn to dark on their father's farm. Their father beat them often. Even when John got mumps and pneumonia, his father made him keep working and refused to call a doctor. John went to college for three years, then he quit to ramble around North America. He worked in sawmills, on farms, in a broom factory, in a carriage factory, and as a sheepherder. When he was twenty-nine, an accident changed his life.

A tool slipped, and a metal spike pierced his right eye. He became totally blind. If he ever could see again, he decided, he would turn his eyes to the fields and woods. In a month, his sight returned, and he set off to walk from Indianapolis to the Gulf of Mexico, 1,000 miles. When he traveled, this time and the many times afterward, he traveled alone, wearing hob-nailed boots. He carried only an old blanket, a hand lens, a pencil and notebook, and for food a bag of hard bread and tea leaves. He never carried a gun.

On this long trip John Muir began to see all of nature as connected. He saw that every rock and plant and human being had its own part to play in the universe, and he began studying the interconnections. After his 1,000-mile walk, he sailed to Cuba, then to Panama, then to San Francisco. He made his home in California for the rest of his life.

> "Around my native town of Dunbar, by the stormy North Sea, there was no lack of wildness.... With red-blooded playmates, wild as myself, I loved to wander in the fields, to hear the birds sing, and along the seashore to gaze and wonder at the shells and seaweeds, eels and crabs in the pools among the rocks when the tide was low."
>
> —John Muir, *The Story of My Boyhood and Youth*

John Muir loved climbing in California's Sierra Nevada mountains. He pioneered what is called "clean climbing" in the United States. He didn't take much equipment when he climbed—no ropes, spikes, or harnesses. He urged everyone to "climb the mountains and get their good tidings." When he helped found a group to guard the environment, he called it the Sierra Club. He hoped the club would "do something for wildness and make the mountains glad."

John Muir taught himself geology and botany. He became an expert on glaciers, an explorer, mountain climber, and teacher. He wrote ten books and hundreds of articles for magazines. More than two hundred sites in the United States have been named in his honor, including the Muir Glacier and Mt. Muir in Alaska and the John Muir Wilderness and the John Muir Trail in the High Sierra.

The Sierra Club Today

The Sierra Club is a nonprofit group that works to save the natural environment. It proposes to:

- Explore, enjoy, and protect the wild places of the earth,
- Use the earth's ecosystems and resources responsibly and encourage others to do that, and
- Teach people to protect and restore the quality of the natural and human environment.

Teenagers high school age and older can join the Sierra Student Coalition. The members explore the planet...work for clean air and water, safe homes, schools, and work places...and work to get good environmental laws passed. Their motto is: *The world is in your hands. Don't drop it.*

THE SIERRA CLUB *helps protect the planet's wild places, so endangered species like this golden eagle can survive.*

BOTTLE GARDENS

SIMPLE BOTTLE GARDEN

THIS TINY ECOSYSTEM YOU CAN MAKE FOR YOUR ROOM STARTS WITH A RECYCLED JAR. RESTAURANTS OFTEN USE VERY LARGE JARS—THEY WILL PROBABLY GIVE YOU ONE IF YOU ASK. IT'S EASIEST IF YOU CAN FIT YOUR HAND IN THE JAR. IF YOU CAN'T, USE STICKS TO PLACE THE PARTS OF YOUR GARDEN WHERE YOU WANT THEM. ONCE YOU'VE CREATED A NEW ECOSYSTEM, IT'S YOUR JOB TO MAKE SURE IT STAYS HEALTHY—YOU'LL NEED TO BE THE RAINMAKER BY WATERING IT WITH A SPRAY BOTTLE WHEN IT LOOKS DRY.

WHAT YOU NEED

- A large jar with a wide neck
- Clean pebbles and small stones
- Bark from the ground with moss, ivy, or ferns on it
- A spray bottle and water
- If you can't fit your hand in the jar, 2 sticks

WHAT TO DO

1· Collect stones and pebbles from a creek. You can also buy these.

2· Look for interesting bark lying on the ground. If you find bark with moss or small ferns growing on it, soak it in cold water.

3· Be sure your jar is squeaky clean. First put in the pebbles, for drainage. Then place the bark. Take your time deciding how to arrange your ecosystem. If you have moss or ferns growing on your bark, you will soon see drops of moisture on the inside of the glass. Plants give off water, and in this enclosed ecosystem, they can reuse the same water. They still need you to spray them every few days when they get dry.

GREEN BOTTLE GARDEN

FOR THIS ECOSYSTEM, YOU'LL ADD MORE PLANTS, SO YOU'LL SEE MORE THINGS GOING ON IN YOUR GARDEN. YOU'LL ALSO NEED TO WATCH IT CAREFULLY TO MAKE SURE THE PLANTS DON'T DRY OUT.

WHAT YOU NEED

- A large jar with a wide neck and a lid, or an old saucer for a top
- Pebbles
- Potting soil from a garden store. You can try dirt from your yard, but potting soil is usually healthier for the plants.
- Small plants and moss from your yard or a garden store—ferns and ivy do well
- Bark and stones if you want them
- A spray bottle and water
- A large spoon
- If you can't fit your hand in the jar, 2 sticks

WHAT TO DO

1· Start with a squeaky clean jar. Cover the bottom with pebbles for drainage. Spoon in the soil. Take your time deciding where you want to put your plants, stones, and bark. Remember that the plants need space to grow.

2· Start at the edges of the jar and make a little hole for each plant. Put the plants in carefully, one at a time. Then place the stones and bark, if you want them in your garden. When you're finished, give the garden a good spray. Cover the top of the jar with a lid or a saucer to keep the water inside. Spray it when it looks dry, at least once a week.

376

DESERT IN A JAR

FOR CAN CREATE A DESERT ECOSYSTEM AT HOME—NOT WITH COYOTES OR SIDEWINDERS, BUT WITH CACTUS, SAND, AND PEBBLES. LIKE ANY OTHER GROWING THINGS, CACTUSES NEED WATER, SO SPRINKLE A LITTLE ON THE ROCKS WHEN YOU CANNOT SEE ANY DROPS OF WATER ON THE INSIDE OF THE JAR. YOU CAN OFTEN GET SAND FROM A CONSTRUCTION SITE, IF YOU ASK.

WHAT YOU NEED

- A large jar with a lid
- Cactuses from a garden store
- Sand from a garden store or toy store, or ask at a construction site
- Pebbles or small rocks
- A hammer and nail

WHAT TO DO

Follow the directions for the Green Bottle Garden, only add sand instead of soil. After you plant your cactuses, sprinkle in a little water to wet the sand. Make small holes in the lid of the jar with your hammer and nail. Then screw on the lid. Remember to sprinkle in water when there are no water drops on the sides of the jar.

ECO EXTRA

Some desert plants can sprout, flower, and bear seeds in only two weeks. They have to. It may rain in the desert just once a year. The habitats with the greatest variety of wildlife are tropical rain forests, where it rains every day.

How Is a RAIN FOREST Like Your Bathroom?

In a rain forest, guess what happens almost every day? That's right. It rains. So rain forests are very wet and humid. And since the sun shines for 12 hours a day there, they are also very warm. Standing in a rain forest feels a lot like standing in your bathroom after you take a bath. Except you probably don't have orchids and monkeys in your bathroom. All rain forests lie near the equator—in Hawaii, Australia, Asia, Africa, and South America. The largest is in Brazil.

What's Going On?

Rain forests used to cover 20 percent of the earth. Today they cover only 6 percent. Where have the trees gone? People have burned them down so they could plant crops instead, and cut them so they could sell the wood. This is happening very fast. People are burning off more than 4,000 acres of rain forest every hour.

Who Lives in Rain Forests?

Almost as many people live in the rain forests as live in the United States. Besides all the people, half of all the different kinds of plants, animals, birds, and insects in the world live in rain forests—400,000 species. And we think there are at least 9 million species there that we don't know about yet. Some we do know about are:

- Jaguars, ocelots, and deer
- Many kinds of monkeys
- Teak, mahogany, and rosewood trees
- Toucans, parrots, and macaws
- Many varieties of orchids

Why Should You Care?

Since you probably don't live in a rain forest, you might think you don't need to worry about them. But think about this:

- Every day in the rain forest a species becomes extinct. Without help, we will lose one rain forest species every hour.

- One of every four medicines comes from rain forest plants. Scientists believe somewhere among rain forest plants lies the cure for cancer and other diseases. If we destroy the rain forest, we destroy the cures.

- Destroying the rain forests may change the weather all over the world. The earth may become too hot.

What Can You Do?

- Reduce, reuse, and recycle. (You already knew that, right?)

- Talk to people about how important saving the rain forests is.

- Adopt a piece of rain forest through a group like the Nature Conservancy or the National Arbor Day Foundation. (Find out how at the library or on the Internet.)

LEUKEMIA FIGHTER: The rosy periwinkle produces a substance that helps fight leukemia in children.

 # PAPER QUILTS

THESE QUILTS MAY NOT KEEP YOU TOASTY WARM ON SNOWY NIGHTS, BUT THEY'RE LOTS OF FUN TO MAKE...AND A GREAT WAY TO REUSE PAPER AND SAVE TREES. TRY ANY INTERESTING PAPER—OLD SHEET MUSIC...MAGAZINES AND CATALOGUES...ENDS OF GIFT WRAP AND WALLPAPER. YOU COULD ALSO MAKE SMALL QUILTS FOR SPECIAL GREETING CARDS OR TO DECORATE ALBUMS OR NOTEBOOKS.

WHAT YOU NEED

- Bright paper scraps (You can get books full of wallpaper samples free from wallpaper stores.)
- Poster board or cardboard
- Scissors
- Stick glue
- A ruler
- A pencil and pen
- A homemade marking tool

WHAT TO DO

1· To speed up measuring your quilt pieces, make a marking tool from a scrap of poster board or an old cereal box. Cut a strip about 12" long and exactly ¹⁄₁₆" narrower than you want your quilt squares to be. The 1" squares in the quilts in these photos were made with a marking tool ¹⁵⁄₁₆" wide. If you want 2" squares, make your marking tool 1¹⁵⁄₁₆" wide.

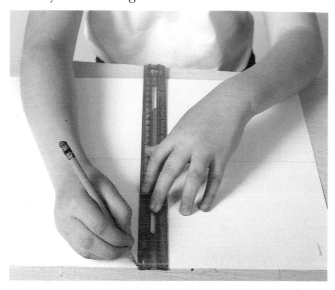

2· Gather all the papers you plan to use, along with pages cut from wallpaper books, magazines, and so on. You can plan your quilt design now if you want to, and pick out colors for that design. Or you can just pick colors you like and plan your design later.

3· Use your marking tool to measure off strips of each paper you want to use. Draw your lines on the back of the paper. The strips need to be right next to each other, so lay your marking tool along one edge of the paper and mark a line along the tool's other side. Now lay the marking tool on the new line and mark a line along the other side. Keep going until you have as many strips as you need.

4· For most quilts, you now turn the paper sideways and repeat drawing strips with your marking tool, so you end up with squares marked out on the back of your paper. For some quilts, like the Notation Quilt in the picture, you use strips that are two or three squares long. Read the directions for the quilt you want to make before you cut. Once you know what shapes you need, cut along the lines. Then organize the squares and strips for each color into piles—an easy way to keep them separate is to put the piles in a muffin tin.

5· If you're not making one of the quilts here, decide what size poster board you want to use and cut it out. Now you can lay out your squares on the poster board and try different patterns to see what you like best. Before you start gluing, mark the center of your poster board. First mark the center of each side, then draw lines connecting the marks on opposite sides—you make a big cross on the poster board, and the center of the cross is the center of the paper. Your quilt will probably turn out straighter if you draw quite a few lines down and across your paper to serve as guidelines. Your poster board will end up looking like a big piece of graph paper.

6· When you glue, it is easier to spread your glue on a section of poster board than on each square. Don't try to glue down more than two or three squares at a time. It's a good idea to start at one corner or in the middle of the paper. To finish your quilt, trim the edges. Attach a string across the back, if you want to hang it up. Or frame it any way you like and then attach a string or wire for hanging.

TO MAKE THE TRIP AROUND THE WORLD QUILT:

This is a traditional quilt pattern. The quilt in the picture uses eight different papers cut in 1" squares and glued on a piece of poster board 11" by 14".

1· Mark the center of your poster board and draw your guidelines. Glue the center of the first square over the center of your poster board, with each corner of the square on a guideline. Work out from the center.

2· At the edges of the poster board, finish with a row of triangles that you make by cutting squares diagonally, from corner to corner.

TO MAKE THE RAINBOW PATH QUILT:

Making quilts by laying patches in diagonal lines is traditional, but copying a rainbow makes this quilt special. The quilt in the picture uses 1" squares in the rainbow's seven colors—red, orange, yellow, green, blue, indigo (blue), and violet. The poster board is 11" by 14". Sometimes two or three shades of a color are laid beside each other before starting the next color.

Mark the center of your poster board and draw your guidelines. Start gluing from the lower left corner and work one row at a time, laying squares diagonally toward the upper right corner.

TO MAKE THE NOTATION QUILT:

Modern quilts often have pieces laid in a pattern that makes a familiar picture, like cats or flowers or—as in this quilt—musical notes. You could make a quilt just like this one or design yours with a different picture.

1· Besides cutting squares, make some strips 2 squares long and some 3 squares long. Mark the center of your poster board and draw your guidelines.

2· Plan how you will lay the squares out. Then shape the tops and bottoms of the notes by taking out parts of the notes—diagonally cut half-squares. Replace them with diagonally cut half-squares of your background design. (If you look at the picture, you can see how to do this.) To make the stems of the notes, cut squares in half.

3· Before you start gluing, mark where you want the border to go along the left side of the poster board and along the bottom. Glue the border squares on last.

4· Begin gluing at the bottom of the quilt, inside the border. Start at the left side and work toward the right. Then glue on the border. Last add the staff lines and flowers.

BEAUTIFUL EARTH NATURAL COSMETICS

NATURAL WONDERS: LIP GLOSS, AFTER-BATH POWDER, AND BATH SALTS YOU CAN MAKE FROM NATURE'S MATERIALS... NOTHING ARTIFICIAL, AND EARTH FRIENDLY.

OCEAN WAVES BATH SALTS

Just what you need after a hard day at school, or on the soccer field, or cleaning your room. Drop a handful of your Ocean Waves Bath Salts into a hot tub and relax...or give them to someone else who needs to relax more than you do.

WHAT YOU NEED

- A mixing bowl
- A spoon for mixing
- Measuring spoons
- A whisk or fork
- Blue or green food coloring (unless you want red, for Shell Pink Bath Salts, or yellow, for Sunny Days Bath Salts)
- 1/4 teaspoon of essential oil or perfume oil for fragrance. You can find all kinds of scents at the health food store. (You can add this or not.)
- A jar with a top, washed and dried
- 1 cup of Epsom salts from the grocery store
- 1 cup of sea salt from the grocery store
- 3 tablespoons of dehydrated milk

WHAT TO DO

1· Mix the salts in the mixing bowl.

2· Add eight drops of food coloring and mix it in with the whisk or a fork. If you want it a darker color, add a few more drops of food coloring until you have the color you like.

3· Add the dehydrated milk and mix it in well.

4· If you want your bath salts to have fragrance, mix in the essential oil or perfume now.

5· Be sure your jar is totally dry before you spoon your bath salts into it. Decorate the jar however you like...add a bow...add a label...name it yourself.

LAVENDER AND ROSES POWDER

Make this sweet-smelling gift for a friend...or dust on your own brand of body powder yourself after a bath or shower. It's easy to make...and all the ingredients are natural. You can get lavender and rose petals at craft stores and health food stores.

WHAT YOU NEED
- A stainless steel, glass, or plastic bowl or other container for mixing
- Measuring cup and spoons
- A whisk or fork
- A recycled glass jar with a tight-fitting lid for storing
- A coffee filter
- A bit of string
- An electric blender or a mortar and pestle
- 1½ cups of corn starch
- ½ cup of baking soda
- 3 tablespoons of lavender flowers
- 2 tablespoons of rose petals
- 1 teaspoon of cloves
- 1 teaspoon of ground cinnamon or a cinnamon stick
- 1 teaspoon of dried lemon or orange peel

WHAT TO DO

1· Mix the cornstarch and baking soda together in the bowl with your whisk or fork.

2· Grind the lavender and rose petals in the blender or by hand with the mortar and pestle, until they are powder.

3· Add the flower powder to the bowl. Mix again.

4· Make a fragrance packet. Put the cloves, cinnamon, and orange or lemon peel in the center of the coffee filter. Tie with a string to make a pouch.

5· Put the pouch in the bottom of your jar. Carefully scoop the mixture from your bowl on top of it. Put the lid on the jar and put the jar in a brown bag for at least two weeks.

6· After two or three weeks, open the jar and remove the pouch. Your powder is ready to use. You can decorate the jar and add a pretty powder puff... or put the powder in a recycled shaker...or punch holes in the jar lid to make it into a shaker...or come up with your own idea for packaging.

7· You may want to add a ribbon or make a label with the name of your special powder on it.

EMONADE LIP GLOSS

You can go pretty wild with this all-natural lip gloss recipe. Pick the color, pick the flavor, decorate the label...and name it yourself. Cocolicious Coconut? Bananafana? Aren't Ya Orange? Gorilla Vanilla? Well, maybe not.

WHAT YOU NEED
- A small pan and a glass measuring cup or a double boiler
- Measuring spoons
- Reused lip balm tube or small pot
- 3 tablespoons of almond or olive oil
- 1 tablespoon of beeswax from a health food store
- ¼ teaspoon of flavoring, such as lemon, orange, vanilla, strawberry...
- Food coloring
- For labels—gift wrap or fabric scraps, paper, glue, colored pens

WHAT TO DO

Before you start, wash your old lip balm tube or little pot with warm soapy water. You may want to soak these overnight to remove labels.

1· Put two or three cups of water in the bottom of your double boiler or in your small pan. Measure the almond or olive oil and the beeswax into the top of the double boiler, or in your glass measuring cup.

2· Ask an adult to help you heat the pan over medium heat until the beeswax melts, and to take the pan off the stove.

3· Let the wax cool for a minute or two. Then add the flavoring and two or three drops of food coloring.

4· Carefully pour the liquid into the glass measuring cup or any container with a pouring lip. Then pour from the measuring cup into the empty tube or little pot. Don't move the tube or pot for at least fifteen minutes, until the lip gloss is cool.

5· Make your label and decorate with gift wrap or fabric, or colored pens...whatever works for you!

COOL TOOL
Make an Earth-Friendly Art Box

You know from experience that you can make really neat things with ordinary stuff from around your house—like collages and puppets and costumes. And you've probably noticed that you can make most of the projects in this book from ordinary stuff, too. Mostly from things you reuse, like cans and magazines. You can make even more interesting projects if you start collecting and saving all kinds of materials. Tin cans, for instance. And buttons. And calendars.

When you start a project, wouldn't it be great to have all the supplies on hand? And in one place? How about making a big art box, maybe from a cardboard box, to store all your art supplies in? You could decorate it, or you could just write "**ART BOX**" on it in big letters, so no one will use it for anything else.

Some things to collect just for the projects in this book (of course you'll wash them first, if they need it—otherwise you'll find yourself with an interesting collection of bugs and blue mossy gunk and nose-pinching smells):

- *cereal boxes*
- *tin cans*
- *yogurt, cottage cheese, and milk cartons*
- *buttons, fabric scraps, ribbon, yarn*
- *old plates, broken pots*
- *beads, screws, nails*
- *jars, bottles, jar tops*
- *brown grocery bags*
- *newspaper, magazines, calendars, catalogues*
- *parts of old board games*
- *egg cartons, frozen dinner trays*

You get the idea. The next time you can't think of anything to do, take a look at your Art Box for inspiration. And remind yourself what an awesome earth-saver you are.

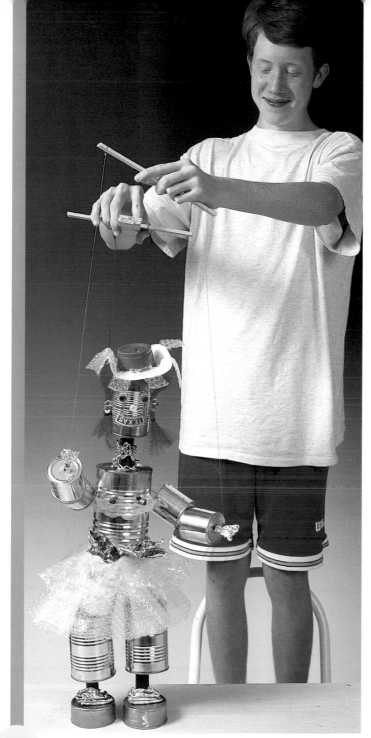

TIN CAN MARIONETTE

WHAT YOU NEED

- Tin cans! With their top and bottom lids still on. The marionette in the picture uses these sizes: 1 soup can for head, 1 large juice can for body, 6 evaporated milk cans for arms and thighs, 2 dog food cans for legs, 2 cat food cans for feet
- Bubble wrap
- A mesh orange or grapefruit bag for hair
- Old hardware—screws, nuts, bolts, chain
- A roll of strong wire
- Pop tops
- Scraps of gold gift wrap and ribbon, buttons
- A paper plate
- A plastic cup
- 1 piece of plastic pipe or paper towel roll, about 3"
- 2 pieces of plastic pipe or paper towel roll, about 8" each
- A hot glue gun
- A hammer and nail
- An old wooden yardstick or scraps of wood for the controls
- Fishing line
- A Sharp knife
- Aluminum foil

WHAT TO DO

1· If they're not already empty, drain your cans by punching their tops with a punch-type can opener or with a hammer and nail. Take one end off the dog food cans.

WHEN FORESTS COVERED THE WORLD, MARIONETTES WERE MADE OF WOOD. TODAY, A GREAT WAY YOU CAN CONSERVE WOOD AND RECYCLE AT THE SAME TIME IS TO MAKE MARIONETTES OUT OF...TIN CANS! AND POP TOPS, SCRAPS OF BUBBLE WRAP AND ALUMINUM FOIL... A MESH ORANGE BAG...ALL KINDS OF ODDS AND ENDS.

2. To put your marionette together, you're going to thread wire through holes in the cans. Look at the drawing to see where to punch holes with a hammer and nail to thread the wire through.

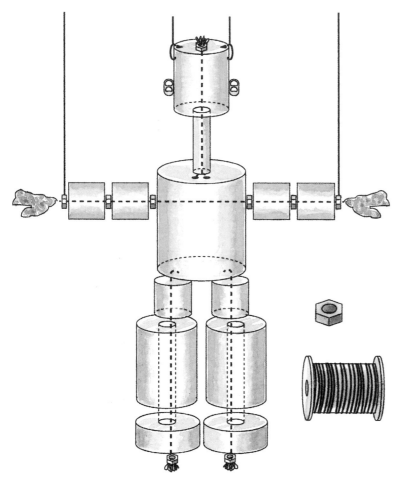

- For the soup can head, a hole in the center of the top and bottom. Two holes on each side at the top to attach the control wires.

- For each milk can, holes in the center of the top and bottom.

- For the large juice can body: Four holes in the bottom—two at the top of each leg. Two holes in the top for the neck. One hole toward the top of each side for the arm wires.

- For each dog food can leg, a hole in the top.

- For each cat food can foot, a hole toward the back of the top.

3. Lay your cans and pieces of pipe out on a table in the shape of the marionette. Look at the drawing to be sure of what goes where.

4. Starting at the top, thread your wire through the soup can, then through the 3" pipe neck. Hook the end through the two holes in the top of the juice can body, and cut the wire off. On top of the head, cut the other end of your wire, leaving about 14". Make that 14" into a coil or bunch and secure it by screwing a nut in the hole at the top of the head.

5. To attach the arms, thread fishing line straight through two milk cans, then through the juice can, then through the other two milk cans. Leave enough line at each end to attach hands. Shape the hands from wire and wrap aluminum foil around them.

6. To attach the legs and feet, start at the feet. Leave enough wire at the bottom to wrap around a nut, to keep the wire from pulling through the hole. Run your wire through one foot, one long piece of pipe, and one milk can. Hook the end through one set of holes in the bottom of the juice can body, and cut the wire off. Do the same thing for the other leg.

7. Ask an adult to help you hot glue the neck pipe to the head and the body, and hot glue the milk cans and feet to the leg pipes.

8. Now add all the special decoration you want to. The marionette in the picture has an orange mesh bag glued on for hair, bubble wrap for a skirt, buttons for eyes and nose, and a chain necklace. Her hat is a part of a plastic cup and bubble wrap glued on a paper plate. Her ears are pop tops.

TO MAKE THE CONTROLS

Look at the drawing of the controls as you follow these directions. You need two pieces of yardstick or scrap wood each about 9½" long, and one piece about 14" long. In the drawing, the short pieces are 2 and 3. The long piece is 1.

1. Glue one short piece to the middle of the long piece. This is marked X in the drawing.

2. With a sharp knife, make notches in this short piece on either side of the long piece. These notches are marked A and B in the drawing. Make notches toward each end of the other short piece. These are marked C and D. These notches are where you will wrap the control wires.

3. You need four control wires, or lines. Look at the drawing to see how to wrap them. When you wrap the wire on the controls and hook the ends through the head, you need to have about 12" of wire between the head and your controls. You need about 30" of wire between each wrist and your controls.

4. To make your marionette wave, walk, dance, and sit down, you hold stick 3 in one hand and the cross (sticks 1 and 2) in the other hand.

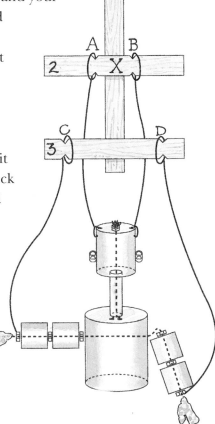

Adopt a Piece of THE PLANET

Somewhere nearby lies a bit of the Earth that needs your help. Maybe it's a place you pass on your way to school. Or in your neighborhood. Or in your own yard. Maybe your school would let you and some friends adopt a part of your schoolyard.

What can you do when you find a bit of land to adopt?

- *Pick up litter.*
- *Plant some grass, seeds, or seedling plants to make the soil healthy again.*
- *Plant some flowers.*
- *Plant some bushes or trees to make a habitat for squirrels and birds.*
- *Hang up a bird feeder, a birdhouse, or a birdbath.*

Another way to adopt a piece of the planet is to write to a group that is protecting endangered ecosystems. That way you help save special lands and the animals, birds, and plants that live there. For instance, you can adopt a piece of rain forest through the Nature Conservancy, the National Arbor Day Foundation, and other groups (page 377). You can find their addresses on the Internet and at the library.

BISON *are an endangered species, and so is their home, the tallgrass prairie. You can adopt an acre of tallgrass prairie through the Nature Conservancy.*

BEAN AND PASTA MOSAIC

Y OU CAN MAKE MOSAICS FROM JUST ABOUT ANYTHING YOU CAN GLUE DOWN—BITS OF PAPER, PEBBLES, BEACH GLASS, OR BEANS AND PASTA LIKE THE ONE HERE. USE ANY KIND OF BEANS AND ANY KIND OF PASTA. DEPENDING ON WHAT YOU CHOOSE FOR YOUR BASE, YOU CAN ALSO MAKE MOSAIC JEWELRY OR DECORATE OLD BOXES OR COOKIE TINS.

WHAT YOU NEED

- Beans and pasta
- White glue or glue stick
- Corrugated cardboard, a jar lid, a box, or whatever you want for a base
- A pencil and paper
- Paint and a paintbrush if you need them

WHAT TO DO

1· Paint your base, if you want to.

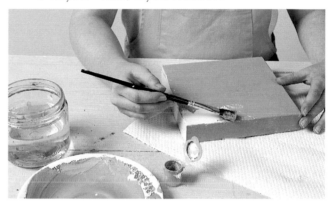

2· You can draw your design on a piece of paper. Or you can draw it right on your base. Or you can design your mosaic as you go along. Or you can lay out your beans and pasta on a piece of paper and transfer the design a little at a time to your base. You may find the easiest way to plan your design is to start at the center.

3· Glue on your beans and pasta in the design you have planned.

It Is Always Sunrise Somewhere

When we contemplate the globe as one great dewdrop,
    striped and dotted with continents and islands,
     flying through space with all the other stars,
    all singing and shining together as one,
      the whole universe appears as an infinite storm of beauty.

This grand show is eternal.
        It is always sunrise somewhere.
            The dew is never all dried at once.
                A shower is forever falling, vapor forever rising.

Eternal sunrise, eternal sunset,
        eternal dawn and gloaming,
    on seas and continents and islands,
    each in its turn, as the round earth rolls.

—John Muir, *My First Summer in the Sierra*

Project Designers

EVANS CARTER (twig frame, paper beads, seed mosaic) creates art and order in Asheville, North Carolina, at home and at Lark Books.

MAYA CONTENTO (potato print t-shirts, print gift wrap, calendar boxes, paper bag books) styles food, cooks gourmet meals, and designs shirts in Asheville, North Carolina.

KATHY COOPER (collecting bag) is the author of *The Complete Book of Floorclothes* (Lark Books). She and her daughter **SUNNY**, 7½, who drew the design for the bag in this book, live and play in King, North Carolina.

JAN COPE (collection box, log cabin planter, wetland, gardens in a jar, painted flowerpots) loves creative projects, and frequently redesigns her garden, her house, and her life.

CINDY CRANDALL-FRAZIER (paper quilts) wrote *Sock Doll Workshop* (Lark Books) and taught herself art and design. She has a big paper quilt on her dining room wall in Williamsburg, Virginia.

Mural artist **ROLF HOLMQUIST** (bat house, bird feeder, dog biscuit frame) is building a house full of beautiful old wood in Micaville, North Carolina.

JUDY HORN (cornhusk angels, sunflowers, bag bouquets) owns the Cornhusk Shoppe in Weaverville, North Carolina, where she creates wonderful wreaths and other items from... cornhusks.

LIZ HUGHEY (sand candles, nature's garden bottles, decoupage bottles) draws beautiful flowers and colorful designs on everything in Gainesville, Florida, except her latest major creation, a baby boy.

A book designer at Lark Books, **DANA IRWIN** (marionette, chair, bird) has been a creative artist since birth, and probably before.

ELAINE KNOLL (gourd birdhouse and witch) transforms gourds into all kinds of art in Leicester, North Carolina.

Swannanoa, North Carolina, artist **NANCY MCGAHA** (eggshell mosaic) beads elegant vests and smocks natural clothing...and of course eats lots of eggs.

DEBBIE MIDKIFF (powder, lip balm, bath salts) owns the Weed Patch in Barboursville, West Virginia, where she concocts all kinds of natural products for people and animals.

In Coon Rapids, Minnesota, **JULIE PETERSON** (birch bark canoe, basket) designs kits and finished products from birch bark and other natural materials. For a list, send a self-addressed legal size envelope to Minnesota Naturals, 10291 Mississippi Blvd., Coon Rapids, MN 55433.

When he isn't creating beautiful mosaics and paper art from objects he uncovers at flea markets and antique stores, **TERRY TAYLOR** (achy breaky pots, recycled albums, beach glass jewelry, nature journal) wanders the world seeking books and art for the Lark Books catalog.

An accomplished potter and visual artist, **PAMELLA WILSON** (clay pots, kiln, piñata, bag bonnets, puppets, rock houses) also shines at the art of friendship in Asheville, North Carolina.

Metric Conversion Table

LENGTH

- To convert inches to centimeters, multiply the number of inches by 2.5.

- To convert feet to meters, divide the number of feet by 3.25.

INCHES	CM	INCHES	CM
1/8	.5	12	31
1/4	1	13	33.5
3/8	1.25	14	36
1/2	1.5	15	38.5
5/8	1.75	16	41
3/4	2	17	44
7/8	2.25	18	46
1	2.5	19	49
1 1/4	3.5	20	51
1 1/2	4	21	54
1 3/4	4.5	22	56.5
2	5	23	59
2 1/2	6.5	24	62
3	8	25	64
3 1/2	9	26	67
4	10	27	69
4 1/2	11.5	28	72
5	13	29	74.5
5 1/2	14	30	77
6	15	31	79.5
7	18	32	82
8	21	33	85
9	23	34	87
10	26	35	90
11	28	36	92.5

"Winter will pass, the days will lengthen, the ice will melt in the pasture pond. The song sparrow will return and sing, the frogs will awake, the warm wind will blow again. All these sights and sounds and smells will be yours to enjoy, Wilbur—this lovely world, these precious days...."

—E. B. White, *Charlotte's Web*

VOLUME

1 fluid ounce		29.6 ml
1 pint		473 ml
1 quart		946 ml
1 gallon		3.785 l

Acknowledgements

Special Thanks to:

Bonnie Greene, Erik Diehn, David Diehn, and Michael Diehn for help with projects in this book. Thanks also to all the terrific kids who participated in this book by letting us take photographs of them as they made the projects; to friends who contributed projects; to the organizations and friends who let us take photographs in their backyards; and to the people who contributed additional photography.

Additional Photography

Albin P. Dearing/The Davey Tree Expert Co., Kent, OH
Bill Lea, Franklin, NC
Merlin D. Tuttle, Bat Conservation International, Austin, TX
The French Government Tourist Office, New York, NY
Tim Barnwell, Asheville, NC
Evan Bracken
Stephanie Akers
Center for Marine Conservation,
Bill Duyck
Tim Black, Lake City, TN
Cornell Laboratory of Ornithology, Ithica, NY
Kids F.A.C.E. (Kids for a Clean Environment),
Deborah Morgenthal
National Wildflower Research Center
bobbe needham
Quality Forward
Recycling Kids, Inc.
Tree Musketeers, Inc.
Trees for Life
Merlin D. Tuttle, Bat Conservation International
U.S. Fish and Wildlife Service,

Ronald L. Bell
Ashton Graham
Robin Hunter
Sue Mathews
Tom S. Smylie
Bob Stevens
Pamella Wilson

Location Photography

University of North Carolina BotanicalGardens in Asheville, North Carolina;

Warren Wilson College Garden in Swannanoa, North Carolina; and

John and Rebecca Casey's garden, Warren Wilson College.

Enthusiastic Kids

Keltie Buchholz (recycle bin, eco-party)
Lacey Buchholz (eco-party)
James, Samuel, and **Thadeaus Caldwell** (bottle gardens, potato print shirts, painted pots, eco-hits)
Leigh and Natalie Cowart (bat house, sand candles, paper bag bouquets, nature's gardens bottles, eco-adventures)
Mary Cowart, mom (sand candles)
Nathan Cox (piñata, recycle bin, marionette, chair, eco-party)
Steven Day (pinch pots)
Dana Detwiler (eco-hits)
Worth Frady, friend (bat house)
Beulah Freeman, mom (log cabin planter)
Sarah Freeman (log cabin planter, collecting bag, beach glass jewelry, eco-adventures)
Kathy Holmes, mom (nature journal)
Chris Martin, great grocery guy
Amy Mathena, mom (collections box, paper bag books)
Ivan Mathena (collections box, paper bag books, paper quilts, eco-recycling)

Maggie Mathena (paper bag books, paper quilts, bean and pasta mosaic, eco-recycling)
Amanda McGrayne (bath salts, paper beads, vegetable paper, hands paper)
Ian McGrayne (dog biscuit frame, vegetable paper, hands paper)
Amanda McKinney (birdhouse, eggshell mosaic, gourd witch, eco-adventures)
Ashley McKinney (birdhouse, gourd witch, beach glass jewelry, eco-adventures)
Llael Moffitt (birch basket, pinch pots, paper bag bouquets, lip gloss, sunflowers, nature's gardens bottles, eco-extravaganzas)
Josh Noles (bird feeder, achy breaky pots, nature's gardens bottles, decoupage bottles, rock houses, eco-extravaganzas)
Mary Noles, mom (bird feeder)
Jonathan Roberts (pinch pots, canoe)
French Sconyers-Snow (achy breaky pots, rock houses, eco-extravaganzas)
Faye Stevens (bird, bag bonnets, eco-envelopes, puppets, eco-party)
Anthony Thomas, dad (canoe)
Cece Thomas (powder, paper quilts, eco-recycling)
Trenton Thomas (twig frame, nature's gardens bottles, rock houses, decoupage bottles, eco-extravaganzas)
Jessamyn Weis (backyard wetland, nature journal, paper beads)
Karla Weis (paper beads)
Grace Williams (fish bottle, albums, cabbage rose paper, vegetable paper, hands paper, cornhusk angels)
Whitney Young (postcards, bag bonnets, puppets, eco-party)
Rachel Zitin (decoupage bottles, albums, cabbage rose paper, hands paper, cornhusk angels)

iNDEX

Accordion-fold book, 33

Acorns, 106

Air, 149

Air pressure, 149

Animal tracks, 227, 229-30

Ant house, 189

Apple crisp, 109

Apple monsters, 219-20

Art box, 386

Bandanna, 217-18

Bark, 249-50

Bark rubbing, 249-50

Barometer, 148-49

Basketry, collecting materials, 83; vine basket 86

Bat house, 303-06

Bath bags, 186

Bath salts, 382-83

Bats, 56; big brown, 306; facts about, 306; Indiana, 305; little brown, 303

Beach basket, 199-202

Beads, 336

Bear, grizzly, 289

Bentley, Wilson, 236

Bigfoot, 230

Birch bark basket, 273

Birch bark canoe, 297-99

Bird, Bird feeder, papier mâché, 369-70

Birdhouse, 20; gourd, 285-86;

cleaning, 287; hanging, 287

Birds, 156, 159; calls, 27; cement bath, 143-44; drinking fountain, 22, feeders, 138, 239-41; 349-51; food, 241-42; migration,141; nesting shelf, 156-57; wing structure, 26

Birds' tree, 238

Bison, 390

Bluebird, 288

Bookmarks, 163-64

Books, journals, and albums, 313-15, 324-25, 330-31

Bottle gardens, 374-76

Bottles, in projects, 327-29, 340-42, 374; recycling, 338

Brown, Tom, Jr., 228

Bug box, 191

Cactus, 376; hedgehog, 288

Calendar boxes, 332-34

Cans, aluminum and tin, in projects, 387; recycling, 333

Cardboard, in projects, 271, 295, 313, 330, 339, 347, 391; recycling, 339

Cassiopeia, 243-44

Casts of animal tracks, 225-26

Caves, 131

Cement birdbath, 142-44

Center for Marine Conservation, 294

Chair, 277

Chili peppers, 103

Church, Tara, 335

Clay, finding and cleaning, 268; pinch pots and animals, 266-67

Clouds, 146, 147

Collecting bag, 272

Collections box, 295-96

Compost, 311

Constellation viewers, 248

Cornhusk angels, 355-56

Conhusk, sunflowers, 352; drying, 354; flowers, 221-22;

Cosmetics, natural, 382-85

Crane, whooping, 290

Daylily leaf hat, 70

Drying flowers, 59-60

Dyes, blackberry, onion skin, 68

Eagle, bald, 288

Earth Day, 275, 300

Earth flag, 275

Ecology, defined, 261

Eggs, 156, 158, 159; dyed with onion skins, 160-61; with leaves and flowers, 158

Envelopes, 326

Evergreen, garland, 208; trees, 153, 207; wrapping paper, 116

Fern picture frame, 37

Fish, kites, 154-55; print, 195; print T-shirt, 63; stripes, 65

Fleas, 187

Flower, color and shape, 62; lamp shade, 28; note cards, 73; pots, 307-308, 344-45

Frost, 89

Garage sales, organizing, 358

Garden, edge bricks, 42; markers, 57; trellis, 53

Garland, 125

Geese, Canada, 300

Gift, tags, 163-64; wrap, 280-82

Glass, recycling, 342

Gourds, dipper, 90; drum, 92; in projects, 97, 363-64, 285-86; shakeree 94; witch, 363-64

Grass mat, 16

Hatchery, 29

Hats, 283-84

Herbal vinegars, 49

Herbs, 185-86

Herb dolls, 185

Homemade paper, 209-12

Hummingbirds, 52

Ice, 118

Icicles, 119

Jars, in projects, 327-29, 340

Jewelry, beach glass, 357

Kaleidoscope, 177-79

Kids F.A.C.E., 275-76

Kiln, making, 269

Kite, 24

Leaf, collection box, 205; print, 175-76; stained glass, 203

Leaves, 176, 180, 204, 206, 207

Lip gloss, 385

Litter, 290, 294

Lotus book, 76

Manatee, 289, 312

Marine Mammal Care Center, 276

Marionette, 387-89

Metric conversion, 394

Mint leaf candy, 48

Mosaic, as an art, 348; bean and pasta, 391; eggshell, 347

Moths, 31

Muir, John, 371-72, 392

Mushroom spore prints, 181-82

National Arbor Day Foundation, 377, 390

Natural paints, 129

Nature Conservancy, 377, 390

Nature, sketching, 132; observing, 135; journal, 33

Newspaper, in projects, 318, 359, 369; recycling, 320, 331

Nocturne night dial, 243-46

North Star, 244

Note cards, 163-64

Ocean, 147, 153, 194, 197

Pan pipes, 183-84

Paper bag bouquets, 322-23

Paper bags, in projects, 283-84, 322, 324

Papier mâché, making, 321

Party, ecology-conscious, 365-66

Pelican, brown, 288

Pennyroyal, 187-88

Periwinkle, rosy, 377

Pet collars, 187-88

Picture frame, dog biscuit, 346; twig, 271

Piñata, 359-60

Pitfall trap, 47

Plant perfumes, 186

Planter, 301-02

Plaster of Paris, 225-26

Plastic, recycling, 337-38

Pocket sundial, 173-74

Poe, Melissa, 275-76

Pomander, 255

Pond, 292-93

Pooter, 190

Postcards, 339

Potato paper, 120; print shirts, 309-10

Potpourri, 59

Powder, body, 384

Pressed flowers, 73

Puppets, 318-20

Quilts, paper, 378-81

Rain, 145, 147, 197; forest, 377

Recycling Kids, Inc., 329

Recycling, 264, 320, 323, 328, 329, 337; bin, 337

Reducing, 263

Reusing, 263, 327-28, 386

Rock houses, 368-69

Roots and vegetables, 100

Roots, 101

Rose petal jam, 50

Rutabaga lantern, 99

Sand, 197; candles, 192-93;
    painting, 197-98

Save the Manatee Club, 312

Sawdust kiln, 269

Seashells, 36; candles, 117;
    wind chime, 35

Seeds, 108; drying frame, 104;
    packets,107; mosaics, 213-
    214;necklace, 98; that travel,
    242

Sierra Club, 373

Sketchbook, 136

Snow, 124, 145, 147, 231-32;
    candles, 231-32; sculpture,
    233-34

Soap, 256-57

Species, endangered, 288-90, 312,
    377, 390

Star trail, 247-48

Steenburg, Tom, 230

Stepping stones, 45

Sun, clock, 171-72; flowers,
    352-53; prints, 169-70

Terrarium, 126

Trees, 81-82, branch hideaway, 79;
    Christmas, 382; 307-308;
    diary, 316; 307-308; facts,
    279, 364; Musketeers, 335; for
    Life, 361, 362; planting, 361-
    62

Turnip lanterns, 223-24

Twig, and cone wreath, 215-16;
    shelf, 112; weaving, 251-52;

wreath, 66

Violets, candied, 165-66

Wasps' and hornets' nests, 75

Water cycle, 19

Wetlands, 292-94; 300

Whimmy diddle, 253-54

Whistle, 38

Wild vegetables, 58

Wildflowers, candles, 162;
    in winter, 128

Wildlife, backyard, 351

Wind, 152-53; power, 152;
    mills, 152; names, 151, 155;
    vanes, 150-51

Wood gathering, 110

Wormery, 167-68

Worms, 167-68